Parents Speak Out
Then and Now

SECOND EDITION

Parents Speak Out
Then and Now

H. Rutherford Turnbull III
Ann P. Turnbull

The University of Kansas

Charles E. Merrill Publishing Company
A Bell & Howell Company
Columbus   Toronto   London   Sydney

Published by
Charles E. Merrill Publishing Company
A Bell & Howell Company
Columbus, Ohio 43216

This book was set in Italia.
Cover design: Thomas Owen Miller
Production coordination: Martha Morss

Library of Congress Catalog Card Number: 84-061748
International Standard Book Number: 0-675-20404-6

Printed in the United States of America
          4   5   6   7—91   90   89   88   87

To Our Children

Contents

Preface

Parents Speak Out is a collection of powerful stories that describe how those who sought help for persons with disabilities and their families, and those who tried to provide it, met with a mixture of success and failure. *Parents Speak Out* is unique among books about disabilities because most of the contributors not only are parents, or relatives, of someone with a disability but they also work directly or indirectly in organizations and professions that serve disabled citizens. The authors' lives are diverse. They live in large cities, in suburbs, in small towns. Some are married, some are remarried, and some are single parents. Some are relatively young and have young children; others are well into middle age or older and their children are adults. The disabilities of their children range from the mild to the severe. Some live with their children; others have found homes for them outside their natural or original homes; and still others have brought their children back home.

Below the varied terrains of these lives, however, is a common bedrock. All of the writers know the difficulty of living normally while relating to and caring for a person who is disabled, of being heard as an advocate for and recognized as a case manager of their child, of finding the right assessment of their child's condition and the right services for their child's needs.

While the personal essays in this collection document—with candor, eloquence, and detail—the tension, strain, and frustration of living with and seeking help for a person with a disability, they also testify to the rich quality of life experienced by these parents. The chronic nature of mental retardation and other handicaps unleashes anger, confusion, and despair. Even the most competent, caring, and well-balanced parent can feel overwhelmed. And yet in the years of hard struggle these parents have discovered moments of exquisite joy. Along with the special loneliness they feel come special lessons and revelations, a special understanding of human limitations and possibilities. There is at the core of these lives a kind of poetry. These are stories about learning and prevailing, and collectively they disspell the notion, common among many professionals and lay persons, that a child with a disability is invariably a burden and a cause of family distress.

We hope that *Parents Speak Out* will hearten and embolden parents and relatives, instruct professionals, and enlighten the public. In the decade since this book was first published, the national commitment to the education of all children with disabilities and their integration into the mainstream of society has been reaffirmed many times over. More recently, however, the decision of whether parents and professionals may make the decision not to sustain the life of newborns with disabilities has been publicly debated. We fervently hope that this book will strengthen the commitment to enhancing the lives of people with disabilities and insuring the treatment of newborns with disabilities. Each of the stories presented here, we believe, refutes the idea that some lives are not worth living.

This is the second edition of *Parents Speak Out*. Readers familiar with the first edition will find important differences between this edition and the earlier book, published in 1978. This edition is divided into three sections. The first contains essays written for the first edition and follow-up essays written in 1983; this section gives a picture of life then and now. The second section is comprised of essays from the earlier book without updates, by authors who wished to make no additional statement at this time. The last section presents the stories of three new contributors, who bring important and varied perspectives to the book. Each essay is followed by questions designed to help the reader analyze the writer's point of view and think about how people have lived and, more to the point, how they might live.

We hope that *Parents Speak Out* will be a long-term contribution to parents, families, and professionals who work with people with disabilities. Our plan is to revise this volume every five to six years, adding updates (thus giving a picture of the life cycle of several families) as well as new essays. Each new edition will offer new windows into the lives of some very ordinary, yet very heroic, people.

H.R.T.
A.P.T.

Acknowledgements

We are deeply grateful to Marilyn Fischer, Dorothy Johanning, Mary Beth Johnston, Jean Roberts, Lori Llewellyn, Thelma Dillon, and Jon Gaines for their professional and personal support in preparing this evaluation in the manuscript preparation process. We extend our special thanks to Marilyn Fischer for her careful and helpful editorial contributions.

In the completion of the second edition, we continue to be mindful of Don Stedman, our former colleague at the University of North Carolina at Chapel Hill, whose ideas and guidance led to the original conception of the book.

As always, Vicki Knight, the special education editor at Charles E. Merrill Publishing Company, has served as a tremendous source of assistance, support, and friendship.

In conclusion, we join with all the other authors in acknowledging our children, whose profound influence on our values and thinking has prodded us both individually and collectively to continue to speak out both then and now. And likely for always.

HRT
APT

Part One

Jane B. Schulz was an associate professor and coordinator of the mental retardation program in the Department of Special Education at Western Carolina University when she first contributed to *Parents Speak Out* in 1978. After serving on the university's faculty for five years, she took a year off to serve as a resource teacher in the local public schools. In addition, for several summers she coordinated a one-month camping and educational program for severely retarded children.

She has served as a member of the Human Rights Committee at a residential institution for mentally retarded persons in North Carolina and was the president of the North Carolina Federation of the Council for Exceptional Children.

She coauthored *Mainstreaming Handicapped Students: A Guide for Classroom Teachers* and has produced several slide/tape programs on integrating disabled children into regular education programs. She has expressed her interest in child-parent-teacher communication, mainstreaming, and

Jane and Billy Schulz

teacher education in numerous articles. She is a sought-after speaker for professional and parent groups.

In 1978 her son Billy graduated from high school and was employed at minimum wage as a worker in a lumber yard. He continued to live at home with Jane and her husband and other children. Later Billy moved into an apartment and then into a trailer. He is living independently, with assistance from a local adult-services program for disabled persons. He has left his job at the lumber yard and is working at the Western Carolina University library. He is now twenty-five years old and single.

The Parent-
Professional
Conflict

Jane B. Schulz

Articles, books, and lectures dealing with the education of handicapped children seem to agree wholeheartedly on one point: the team approach is indicated. While the composition of the team may vary with the disability, the discipline, or the situation, usually the classroom teacher and the parents are prominent members. This is certainly appropriate, for who spends more time and energy with the handicapped child than the teacher and the parents? Who is more involved, more concerned, more knowledgeable?

When I was teaching kindergarten, a young mother approached me at registration and said, "I want Angie to be in your class because she needs help and I understand you have a handicapped child." This and similar experiences have indicated to me the strength of the combined parent-teacher perspective. Couldn't the parent-teacher team function in the same way?

While there are probably many parents and teachers who work well together toward the best education for the child, traditionally there is a conflict. In describing the growth and functions of parent groups, Cain (1976) recently noted that parents, through negative experiences with educators, have lacked confidence in professionals. He stated that while attitudes are now more positive, the professional usually acts in an advisory capacity.

The parent of a hearing-impaired child has described the efforts required to establish and maintain a cooperative working relationship with a school. She finds that it is not easy to ask for additional services, conferences, or evaluations. She feels that it is essential to ask and to continue to ask if you care about your child's education (Kean 1975).

My own experience supports these statements. As a parent I am critical of the educational system which, I feel, has not served the needs of my child. As an educator I am responsible, in part, for the inefficiency of the system and therefore the object of my own dissatisfaction.

3

Why is such a logical, essential relationship literally inoperable? One of the factors cited by professionals most frequently is the attitude of parents. As a parent I am sensitive to this allegation; as a teacher I know it is true. Parents appear to fall into two categories: the overprotective and the uncaring. As a kindergarten teacher I was the observer when the children were separated from their parents. The children sometimes cried; this seemed to please the parents who were still reluctant to relinquish the dependency of their child. The same attitudes present in parents of normal children appear to be exaggerated in parents of handicapped children. In an interview with the foster mother of a mentally retarded child, I asked the woman why she took a handicapped child. Her reply, "Because I was lonely." Because she needs this child, she bucks the system at every turn, thriving on the child's dependence. In this situation the teacher is furnished inaccurate information and insufficient feedback, and the child is truant. While this case is extreme, it is not unusual. Unfortunately, overprotection devalues the child and denies educational needs.

Another block to a good parent-teacher relationship is the parent who has little interest in his child. Early in my career in special education I had a bitter lesson in this area. As the instigator of a summer recreational program for handicapped children in a good-sized city, I had engaged the cooperation of the entire community. We obtained buildings, materials, and volunteers; planned detailed programs; and sent out notices to parents of all the handicapped children on the superintendent's roster. On the opening day, we were ready for seventy-five children. Three came. That night we hastily set up a transportation system, and I determined that in the future this would be the first step. In asking why some parents do not seem to care, several answers have become apparent to me through the years. Some parents may not understand the value of educational programs; others may not agree with the philosophies of a particular program nor feel it is worthwhile (as educators, we find this difficult to accept!). In some cases one has to say, "This is part of the child's problem—her parents don't care."

In addition to the overprotective parent and the uncaring parent, there are many parents who have skills to contribute to their child's education. There are parents who have skills that would be valuable assets to the teachers and to many children. There are parents who could assist professional educators in reaching and teaching less able parents.

There has been a reluctance on the part of schools to admit that they need help. This concept is certainly changing. With the admission of all children, administrators and other personnel are having to assume tremendous tasks; they are ready to accept any help available. The inflexibility of schedules, personnel, and facilities *must* become a thing of the past. Certainly administrators are becoming more aware of the needs of exceptional children. I was delighted with the attitude of a principal who was approached about admitting a severely handicapped child to his school. His

Jane B. Schulz

immediate response was "We want to serve all school-aged children in the county. Will you help us plan for him?"

A final factor that is detrimental to the parent-teacher relationship is the reluctance on the part of the teacher to accept the abilities of the parents. Since I was a parent before I was a teacher, I readily relate to this problem. There have been so many times I wanted to say, "I have a son who is retarded. I taught him to walk, to use the bathroom, to feed himself, to say his first words, to interact with the family. I know my son; I can help you to know him and to teach him."

My suggestions were never welcomed. I was enthusiastically encouraged to help with the field trip to the airport and to make popcorn balls for the Christmas party. And yet, during periodic visits to the classroom, I saw teen-agers wasting valuable time taking naps, obese children constantly snacking, my son learning things he had known five years before. As a teacher I know these practices were educationally unsound. Perhaps the threat to the teacher is that a lack of good educational programming will be discovered.

In examining the problem and contemplating solutions, there appear to be two factors crucial to effective parent-professional interaction: communication and respect. While these elements are essential to any good relationship, they seem to be missing in many of our parent-teacher confrontations.

No school program can be maximally effective without carry-over in the home. This requires constant contact and communication between the two settings. Several years ago I was asked to talk with a parent group at a nearby private school for retarded children. My function was to provide a setting for interaction between the teachers and the parents. During the ensuing information exchange, one of the teachers described the effectiveness of the toilet-training program. A vocal parent exclaimed that she wished her child could be toilet trained. The amazed teacher declared, "But your child *is* toilet trained!" Following the meeting, the teacher and the mother got together and outlined a strategy for continuing the school program in the home. They also planned future conferences to discuss further developments in the child's education.

In an early experience as a special education teacher, I was led to an understanding of the importance of communicating with the child, of including him in child-related discussions. We had assembled a child psychiatrist, the school principal, the mother of the child, and me to try to resolve Mike's severe emotional problems. The psychiatrist immediately asked why Mike was not present. I was amazed at the suggestion and said so. The doctor replied, "Doesn't he know we're talking about him? If you were in that position, wouldn't you rather be on this side of the door?"

Communication which includes the teacher, the parents, and the child is a rewarding experience. The focus of our summer camp program was to help prepare severely handicapped children for school. In assessing the needs of a charming, verbal child with severe physical handicaps, we found him to be overbearing and sometimes abusive in making demands on other people. We could see this behavior as his chief handicap in the school setting. The parent conference included him, his teacher, both parents, his brother, and his sister. We related our observations, backed up with a video-tape record of offensive behavior. The parents readily saw the problem, as did the child. As a team, we worked out a strategy to help him improve his own behavior. Such planning avoids confusion and misunderstanding; it fosters good communication.

Communication can be facilitated; respect has to grow. Parents of handicapped children are subjected to constant humiliation; it is incredible that much of it comes from persons engaged in the "helping" professions. One learns to deal with the impudent stares of strangers ("You seem interested in my son; would you like to meet him?") One expects more understanding from persons claiming to be experts in areas of exceptionality.

My good friend and I attended a conference concerned with educating severely handicapped children. Both of us were there as college professors in special education and as parents of retarded children. As we listened intently to one of the major speakers, we heard him say, "This book would be valuable to parents of retarded children, since it is written on an eighth-grade reading level."

The current concept of *parent training* is extremely insulting. Some colleagues told me of an encounter with a young mother and her two boys, aged seven and twelve, both mentally retarded and blind. My associate suggested that parent training was indicated. I wondered at the time who we knew that could tell this mother anything. In fact, I immediately wanted to meet and learn from a woman who had raised children with such complicated problems. Since that time I have had the distinct pleasure of working with her and her children. We pooled our resources; we learned from each other. Parent training? This mother and father were good parents long before I came along.

Part of the block to understanding and respecting parents may come from the age-old, hopefully changing idea that the professional knows everything. We have particularly elevated the physician and the college professor into positions of unerring wisdom.

I returned to college after my children were in school. Although older than my fellow students, I was in awe of my teachers. One morning after I dropped off my son, who has Down's syndrome, at his class and visited with the boys and girls there, I drove to the university to attend a class in speech and hearing. The professor, in discussing speech development of the retarded child, made the profound statement: "There are no mongoloid girls." Somewhat later, in a course related to curriculum for the retarded child, the professor, who had had years of experience teaching retarded youngsters, declared: "Retarded children have no imagination." I returned home that afternoon to find my retarded son riding a "horse" he had constructed from a chair, some blankets, and a rope.

6

The thought began to develop that I knew more about some things than the professionals did. I began to gain confidence in the knowledge I had gained as a parent. Years later, I am still convinced that I have learned more from my own children than from any other resource.

Members of the medical profession seem to be particularly deified. My first disillusion came when we learned what the distinct features of our child implied, eighteen months and five physicians after his birth. It is now inconceivable to me that such ignorance (or cowardice) could have prevailed. Fortunately, the sensitivity of the pediatrician who did reveal the facts to us almost obliterated our negative feelings.

Years later, as an educator, I had an experience which further revealed to me the fact that physicians are human and do not, cannot, know everything. I had been asked to evaluate David for probable placement in a special class. He had been having difficulty for the four years that he had been in school. Consultation and a battery of tests revealed that his measured intelligence was below normal and that he would probably profit from special education. Convincing his mother was another thing. It was finally accomplished and David was placed in a special class, where he began to blossom under individualized instruction. David's mother then took him in for a routine physical examination and, after a ten-minute examination, was informed, "This child is not retarded." David was taken from the special class.

Recently a friend who is a nurse and I took a youngster to a physician for some advice. We asked a particular question, to which the physician replied, "I don't know." The nurse looked at me and whispered, "Didn't that sound beautiful?"

Nonetheless, while I have been offended as a parent, I have also been rebuffed as a teacher. I have found that many parents think that no one else knows their problems, no one else has experienced their heartaches, no one else understands. In conferences the parents of my students would frequently say, "But you don't know what we go through." While I could empathize on one level as a parent, I also was angered as a teacher because in many cases the teacher spends more time with the child than the parent does. To say the teacher does not understand is insulting. Moreover, the teacher sometimes spends hours outlining remedial or developmental procedures which should be continued at home. In many cases, it is obvious that the procedures have not been followed.

Parents need to demonstrate their respect for the teacher and the school. One teacher asked me, "May I spank your son if I think it's necessary?" I was taken aback for a moment, then quickly realized that if I was leaving my child in this teacher's hands, she needed complete authority. I answered yes, and although I don't believe she ever spanked him, she knew that I respected her judgment.

Respect for the child is, of course, the essential bond between the parent and the professional. When I was in graduate school, I happened to be sitting in the coffee shop with a friend when a young woman stopped by our table. She was a friend of my companion, and had just graduated in special education. When asked what she would be doing in the fall, she replied, "Oh, I'll be teaching a bunch of nuts over at Fifth Avenue School." My son was one of those nuts. It was not a good year for him. His teacher had no respect for him; she expected very little from her students and got exactly that. How could I respect her?

By contrast, my son had one teacher who expected him to learn. She was hard on him. He had homework, he had to learn parts for class plays, he had responsibilities in the classroom. He also had an entry in the community science fair, won a state-wide art contest, and discovered that he could read. This teacher, in one year, accomplished more with my son than had been accomplished in all these other years put together. She valued him as a person who was capable of learning and of accepting responsibility. She valued me as a parent but let me know that she had everything under control in the classroom.

Is there any way to resolve the conflict existing between parents and professionals working with handicapped children? There has to be. Most of the negative incidences I have related occurred through ignorance or thoughtlessness. The parents and the teachers simply do not seem to be aware of the lack of communication and respect that sometimes exists. Awareness, therefore, seems to be the starting point.

During my first experience of working with severely handicapped children, other than my own, one incident indicated some potential for creating empathy between parents and teachers. For ten days, teachers and children lived together, ate together, slept together, and learned together. At the end of that time, one young man (a psychologist) said that he had gained tremendous respect for teachers and for parents. Living with children with overwhelming problems had made him very sympathetic to people who would be dealing with them on a daily basis. He further revealed that he had seen in the teachers patience and kindness that he had not known existed. At the same time, the teachers expressed a tremendous empathy with the parents. As an example, we had observed marks across one child's back on the first day and speculated that he had been whipped. We were aghast. At the end of the ten days, after discovering how very difficult and obnoxious this child could be, we wondered if we would not also beat him if provoked. Sleeping in the same room with a child who gets up repeatedly or eating with a child who throws her food gives one a very deep sense of compassion for the families who do it every day. Interestingly, when the parents came for conferences, they were delighted with the gains the children had made; plans were formulated to continue the work at home. Parents, teachers, and children were concerned for each other; they were working together.

There are many programs being instituted for the preschool and severely handicapped child. These programs rely heavily on parent-professional

Jane B. Schulz

cooperation. Perhaps this reliance can be generalized to other areas of exceptionality. As we grow in our understanding of the needs of the child, hopefully we will realize that the handicapped child is dependent on the cooperation of concerned parents and professionals. Awareness of our individual problems, our unique abilities, and our strength as a team will facilitate that cooperation.

REFERENCES

Cain, L. F. Parent groups: Their role in a better life for the handicapped. *Exceptional Children,* May 1976, 432–437.

Kean, J. Successful integration: The parents' role. *The Exceptional Parent,* October 1975, *5,* 35–40

QUESTIONS TO CONSIDER

1. What are Jane's views on the fundamental ingredients of a supportive parent-professional relationship?

2. Jane describes a positive experience she and Billy had with a teacher. What were the characteristics of the teacher? What can you infer about Jane's values? How do you predict Jane's values will influence her relationships with professionals in the future?

3. When this essay was written, Billy had recently graduated from high school and was earning minimum wage in a lumber yard. His successful vocational placement represents an important milestone. Now that Billy is competitively employed, do you predict Jane's involvement with professionals will decrease, stay the same, or increase?

4. What are the positive contributions that Billy has made to Jane? How do you think these contributions have been helpful to Jane? What will be Billy's future contributions to his family?

UPDATE:
Growing Up Together

Jane B. Schulz

Earlier this year, my son Billy and I were guest speakers at a meeting attended by over a hundred parents and teachers of handicapped children. After my presentation I sat and watched as Billy showed slides and told the audience about his work, his family, and his trailer. It was an awesome moment for me. I thought back to over twenty-five years ago, when Billy was banging his head on the floor, a time when I never dreamed that he would achieve the life-style he was now describing. But then I realized that twenty-five years ago my speaking to such an audience was also a remote possibility.

Billy and I have grown together. One question that he continues to pursue is also one that I am attempting to answer: what does *growing up* mean? As he left his teens, graduated from high school, got a job, moved away from home, and ultimately established his own household, Billy continued to ask, "Mom, am I a man now? Have I grown up?"

In responding to Billy's questions, I am defining my own growth and, I hope, describing the process that parents of handicapped children and adults can expect. Growing up, for Billy and for me, has involved awareness, anguish, and acceptance.

Awareness

After a great deal of thought and time, I tried to tell Billy what *growing up* means: being ready to be an adult, understanding your rights and responsibilities, learning to make decisions, learning to live with prejudice, recognizing opportunities, and thinking of others. Awareness of this process has helped me to evaluate, in retrospect, my own growth as well as his.

Readiness. As with any child, giving up childhood pleasures and attachments has been difficult for Billy. An example occurred at Christmas time,

11

when we decided to draw names rather than giving gifts to everyone. After the drawing Billy said to me, "I want Santa to bring me a toaster for my kitchen." I responded, "But Billy, I didn't draw your name." Indignantly he declared, "I not talking 'bout names; I talking 'bout Santa Claus!"

With the same naiveté we, his parents, expected him to enter the working world whether he was ready or not. Following his high school graduation, Billy worked successfully at a local lumber yard. All of us were very proud of him and expected his life to progress smoothly. Problems began to occur. The foreman worked with Billy and consulted with us. One day Billy refused to go to work. Nothing we said or did, in kindness or in anger, made him budge. Months later he confided to a friend that one of his co-workers had threatened to push him off a high place and to beat him up if he told anyone. Careful consideration told us that Billy was not ready for competitive employment and that we needed to reexamine our goals for him.

Subsequent evaluation at a local sheltered workshop indicated that Billy "lacked the initiative to work an eight-hour day, found it difficult to communicate with his supervisors as well as other co-workers, and had not been given the opportunity to fully develop in the area of decision making." Based on the recommendations of workshop personnel and vocational rehabilitation counselors, we agreed to move our son to a group home and enter him in a sheltered workshop. At that time there was neither a workshop nor a group home in our immediate community, so Billy moved away. His becoming ready to grow up was difficult for us all.

Rights and Responsibilities. We as parents of handicapped children have fought for the rights of our school-aged children. We have not fought as hard for the rights of handicapped adults. In meeting with group-home workers, I found myself again in an intimidating position. I reacted as I had reacted to domineering school officials in the past: I retreated.

During our weekend visits I watched Billy revolt against the forced companionship of an unchosen roommate, the rage of an ill-tempered house parent, and the confusion of group living; but I held back. Finally, I intervened. As a team the staff and I discussed the alternatives and moved Billy into a supervised individual setting.

I realized then that the group-home directors were concerned with his welfare. I also began to realize that their constraints were unacceptable to me. Their apartment options were limited to the downtown tenement-house type, their supervision, though performed by caring people, was spasmodic. Billy's apartment was broken into and food was stolen. He was afraid. Another move placed him in a former motel where other handicapped people lived under group-home supervision. The environment was considered ideal by the group-home directors. I did not consider it ideal but questioned my judgment. Again I retreated.

I watched Billy regress for two years before I reexamined the situation

Jane B. Schulz

and my own behavior. I could no longer relinquish my parental rights, my professional judgment, and my ultimate responsibility for my son's welfare. In an impassioned effort to remedy the situation, I wrote a letter to Billy's landlord. I referred to the exorbitant rent, the substandard housing, the lack of adequate utilities. I stated that I had tried to stay out of the situation because there were agencies working with Billy, but that I could no longer live with it. I asked for satisfaction and an immediate reply.

I sent copies of the letter to the agencies involved. One agency member called to express his indignation at my writing such a letter and to ask if I would meet to discuss the situation. I responded that I would welcome a meeting. No meeting was called. No action was taken. We brought Billy home and helped him move into a trailer.

Billy has the right to equal treatment and choice of life style. Living in his trailer, he is learning that he also has responsibilities. He must pay his bills, keep his trailer clean, and follow the conditions of his lease.

I have the right to evaluate Billy's situation, disagree with agency officials, and expect appropriate action. I have responsibility not only for my son but to him. I have also come to believe that I am responsible to all handicapped adults who have no advocates.

Decisions. The ability to make decisions comes with practice. Such practice has been limited in school and at home for many retarded children. Merely selecting clothes, choosing games, and deciding which movies to see cannot prepare children to make sound decisions on larger issues.

During Billy's early rebellion against the group home and the sheltered workshop, we brought him home one weekend to make some decisions. I was angry and frustrated: I knew that he had no alternatives to the workshop and thus to the group-home. He was unhappy and confused. As we talked, I realized that he was cornered; that he had no options. In desperation I resorted to a technique that had worked for us in many situations before—a contract. We discussed the terms. I went to my typewriter and drew up a document, which Billy and I signed and took to the group-home directors.

Contract

1. I will work hard at the workshop—no goofing off—until Christmas time.
2. I will do my work at the group home.
3. I will come home one weekend each month:
   September 15 (John and Barbara are coming)
   October 13 (Dad's birthday)
   November 23 (Thanksgiving)
4. At Christmas time if I don't want to return to the group home, I will stay home and work.

Billy accepted the terms of the contract and stayed at the workshop and group home for two years.

Billy has improved in his decision-making ability. He decided to join Weight Watchers but frequently decides not to follow the diet. After he acquired his present part-time job, he decided to discontinue his affiliation with the new sheltered workshop in our community. Sometimes his decisions are unwise, and sometimes they're better than mine.

My major decision (a good one) has been to become Billy's "case manager." His father and I have identified benefits available to him, have decided how much help he needs, and have decided that we are the best supervisors he could have.

Prejudice. Billy's experience at the lumber yard taught me that he needs to deal with ridicule and prejudice in their many subtle forms. Recently at the grocery store I had completed my shopping and was standing by to help Billy write his check. He had done a good job of shopping and proudly unloaded his cart at the check-out counter. The cashier rang up his items and, coming to the bag of coffee beans, turned around completely to ask *me*, "How does he want it ground?" I responded, "Why don't you ask him?" Billy answered, "Percolator, please."

Less subtle instances have to be dealt with more directly. Several months ago Billy told us he had subscribed to a magazine. We discovered that an unscrupulous salesman had entered his home and maneuvered him into ordering, of all things, a business magazine. After we stopped payment of the check, we set up some rules about writing checks and about asking for advice. It was also necessary to acknowledge the existence of people who are not to be trusted.

I am learning, with Billy's help, to ignore the subtle insults. Although he is sensitive to stares and ridicule, he is more forgiving than I am. I am working on tolerance for people who do not have my background in understanding and accepting differences.

Opportunities. A grown-up needs to recognize good opportunities and react to them. Luck helps, too. As I was working in my office one day, our university librarian came in to say he was developing a position that a handicapped person could fill. He wondered if we knew anyone who would qualify. A year later, in the midst of the decision about Billy's apartment, the job became available. Billy came home to apply for it, and he did so confidently. As he headed for the personnel office, a friend said, "I hope you get the job." Billy replied, "I will." And he did.

The library job has been a wonderful opportunity for Billy. It has enabled him to develop skills, to live and work near his family, to earn a decent wage, and to gain respect.

Other opportunities continue to be available for Billy and for me. Sometimes I feel that I have almost exploited him in my professional development. He has enabled me to relate to parents, students, and teachers. He has helped me recognize opportunities to grow and to facilitate growth in others.

Jane B. Schulz

Thinking of Others. Normal child development proceeds from concern for self to concern for others. In no area has Billy advanced more than in his thoughtfulness. Sometimes it is pretty unsophisticated, as illustrated by a phone call home when he was living away:

"Mom, why don't you and Dad come for dinner tomorrow night?"
"We'd love to! What are you having?"
"Beef stroganoff."
"Wow! Do you know how to make it?"
"No, but you can show me."
"Well, okay. Do you have all the stuff?"
"I've got the noodles."

Earlier that year he had expressed his genuine concern for us during a severe drought. He phoned to ask, "Mom, are you all right?" "Yes, why?" "I did see on TV you have no water, and I so worried about you."

Sometimes Billy's love and his unique ways of expressing it are overwhelming. Recently as I entered our church, I saw listed in the bulletin a favorite anthem of mine. Under the title was the dedication: "To Dr. Jane Schulz at the request of her son Billy."

Concern for other handicapped people is the final stage of growth for parents. Certainly our first efforts must be spent in integrating our handicapped children into our own families. Further energy is spent in asking questions, finding answers, and acquiring knowledge. But the skills we gain in assisting our children must go beyond their development.

Anguish

Billy and I have experienced severe growing pains in both our separate and joint development. Parents in general share the anguish of watching their children experience disappointment and rejection, make mistakes and unwise decisions, and leave home. The difference for parents of handicapped children is that the precedents are unclear and the alternatives are limited.

Handicapped children themselves, in addition to normal developmental changes, have many difficult problems to deal with. They must come to terms with their handicap, endure social ostracism in school and the community, face early and permanent separation from their families, and plan for a future that may be uncertain and dismal.

Facing Retardation. When Billy was small, we had no problem accepting his retardation; neither did he. He was happy, healthy, and confident of his place in the family. As he grew older and more integrated in school and social activities, his differences naturally became more apparent to us, to him, and to other people. We have always used the term *retarded* freely; and Billy himself, in helping me arrange my office, has said, "Reading books go here, 'tarded books go here," or "Come watch TV, Mom; it's 'tarded children." As an adult, however, he does not use the term often and frequently attempts to deny his own retardation. The problem, and the anguish, are more often expressed in specific situations.

Seeing his siblings marry has been traumatic for Billy. When his brother Tom married, we had a long talk about the possibility of Billy's marrying and the reasons it probably would not happen. It would have been easy to say, "You can't afford it," or "You don't have a house to live in." I finally had to say, "Because you're retarded." It's not a good reason, but it's *the* reason.

My outlook has changed as Billy has grown. Several things have become apparent to me that I could not anticipate as the parent of a young child. There is an obvious difference between us and our friends of comparable age. As young parents we shared responsibilities, problems, and anxieties. As middle-aged parents our concerns are quite different.

Another source of pain is the need to explain Billy's retardation to our extended family. Our children's spouses lack the background that our children have; understanding Billy's problem is difficult for them and their families. One of the saddest moments that I recall was seeing our oldest grandson ask Billy, whom he adored, to read him a story and then realize that his eighteen-year-old uncle couldn't read yet.

Social Ostracism. Following his graduation from high school, Billy was working at a lumber yard. During this successful period I met a co-worker in the hall one day who stopped to tell me what he thought was a wonderful story. His son Clarence, who had graduated with Billy, and a group of friends at a party were discussing the activities of their fellow graduates. They concluded that Billy was more successful than anyone else and was making more money. My co-worker asked, "Isn't that marvelous?" I agreed but, in retrospect, wondered, Why wasn't Billy invited to the party?

A similar situation occurred when a friend of mine had a Christmas party. Everyone in the family was invited except Billy. I thought it must be an oversight, but the friend later explained apologetically, "I thought Billy's presence might make the other guests uncomfortable." This kind of attitude is difficult to accept, particularly when he had been included very successfully in a similar party. I find myself crying at the unfairness.

Separation. Is anything comparable to the anguish parents feel when their children leave home? When our oldest son, John, went to college, I went into his room, picked up his guitar, and thought I couldn't bear it. It was difficult, even though I knew what to expect from his departure: it was an approved, accepted part of his development, a part of his plan for advancement.

Separation from handicapped children is not the same. Handicapped children and their parents don't know what to expect from separation. It may be exploratory, temporary, or permanent. It can be filled with uncertainty and guilt.

Jane B. Schulz

My definition of anguish is seeing Billy, suitcase in hand, climb the steps of the group home and then receiving his phone call:

"Mom, I had a dream about you last night and I cried a lot."
"I'm sorry, Billy. What's wrong?"
"A little bit homesick. Have to stay here. Fred said."
"Oh . . ."
"I love you, Mom."
"I love you too, Billy."

Although I look upon the two years' separation with all its problems and uncertainties as the most painful experience of my life, I now see it as a vital part of Billy's growth and of mine.

The Future. The greatest anxiety for parents of handicapped children is uncertainty of the future. The services established for our handicapped population have only been stopgaps. With the exception of rare, lifelong institutional placements, we don't have plans for the future.

We had thought for years that living in a group home and working in a supervised setting was the answer for Billy's future. That combination didn't work for him, and the alternatives are severely limited. As parents and advocates we must exert our energy and resources to build viable solutions for the future.

Acceptance

Ultimate growth results in learning to change the things that can be changed and to accept the things that cannot be changed, a wise thought borrowed from a popular prayer. Acceptance has been the most difficult task for me. I have come to accept, however, several factors that Billy and I must live with: his loneliness, our need for support and for realistic goals, the lifelong nature of my commitment, his need for independence, and our evolving contributions.

Loneliness. Because we live in a rural area, there are few social activities designed for handicapped people. Billy does make friends with the people he works with and with his neighbors in the trailer park, and the friendships are genuine. Unfortunately, they are usually restricted to the particular environments in which they have developed. As a result, Billy has learned to enjoy his own company and the solitude of his home. Our gregarious son-in-law is alarmed that Billy enjoys spending so much time alone. I think that aptitude is his lifesaver.

At one time I had hoped that Billy could find a girl to marry and avoid loneliness. Now when I see his romantic illusions, I wonder if we have helped him create an impossible dream. Marriage is difficult for many normal people; perhaps he doesn't need it. And I certainly don't need someone else to supervise! Alone, he is happier than most other people I know. I hope that's enough.

Need for Support. I remember a story about a young retarded man who worked in a restaurant. One day he was sent to get a can of peaches and was found sometime later opening cans in the pantry in hopes of finding peaches. The story suggests that retarded people need to know when to ask for help. So do their parents.

Even as we acknowledge that we can't rely entirely on public agencies, we also realize that we need support in many areas. Family support is essential: Billy's siblings support him and me in unique ways, as do other family members. Beyond the family unit Billy has sought weekly help and support this year from a counselor. And the people he works with are his staunch allies and trainers.

In addition, we have acknowledged Billy's need for financial assistance. We have overcome, in part, our middle class aversion to housing and living supplements, although we do not recommend food stamps. (Our reluctance is based partly on the notion that Billy's weight problem calls for a ceiling on his food allowance.)

Even though I am a professional in special education, I have acknowledged my need for advice, suggestions, and help from other people. I also need to acknowledge the contributions of those other people to Billy's well-being.

Realistic Goals. The ability to set realistic goals is a major development in itself. I have always expected too much from Billy, from myself, and from others. I now realize that Billy's total independence is not realistic and that his semi-independence is admirable. He works twenty hours a week at the university library, he recently got a raise, he attends Sunday school and church regularly, he does his own cooking, and he maintains his own living quarters. He has accomplished much.

Lifelong Commitment. All parents continue to be concerned about their children, even in their adulthood. Parents of handicapped children, in addition, are responsible for their adult children. After accepting this fact, we can settle into comfortable situations in keeping with our own status and our children's characteristics. It is also important to consider our own convenience.

Independence. As a group parents of handicapped children have been labeled overprotective. Accepting semi-independence and working toward full independence are compatible but difficult tasks. When we suggested putting a trailer for Billy on the lot behind our house, he decided that would be "too close." We settled for one in a trailer park not too far away. We are trying now to honor and encourage his moves toward independence. We continue to have power struggles over such matters as clean clothes, as I

18   *Jane B. Schulz*

try to decide whether my values or his welfare are at stake. He is a powerful adversary.

I am also developing my own independence as an individual with things to do and places to go that do not include Billy. I am developing personal confidence as I realize my own potential.

Contributions. I did not choose to have a retarded child, nor do I feel glorified because of the experience. Our family simply accepted Billy, along with his retardation, and did the best we could. However, the things we have learned in the process have helped other people.

Parents and siblings of handicapped children frequently contact me for advice and solace. In addition, my professional status is enhanced by my experiences as a parent of a handicapped child. And in student evaluations I am told that the sharing of these experiences adds greatly to my teaching effectiveness.

Billy's contribution is more subtle. The group of parents who heard him speak with me earlier this year were impressed with his accomplishments and became hopeful for their own children. Further, as the only handicapped employee at the university library, he is visible to many people and probably has an influence we are not aware of. One fellow employee recognized his contribution and paid tribute in a library publication:

He presents a beautiful rose to Brenda to adorn her desk . . . those who lunch beneath the dogwood in front of the library expect his black lunch box and lively company . . . he is known to sing while he works and a portable radio is one of his many friends . . . he displays with pride a new WCU T-shirt and is apt to hug you and tell you how much he likes you . . . his name is Billy Schulz.

Billy was hired last September to do a tedious book processing job for three days a week. It's the kind of job very few of us could do, repetitive work, confining, and offering little variation in daily routine. This Billy Schulz, however, does the job well and takes pride in his work. He looks forward to coming to work and he sees in his work features to be envied by many people, happiness and fulfillment. In short, Billy is an asset to Hunter Library.

A university is an appropriate place to learn something and we have learned something through our experience with Billy. As a candidate for the job as a trainee last fall, we knew Billy as being mentally retarded and thought about all the things he could not do. Now, we have learned that he is Billy Schulz and we know the things he can do. The roses, the T-shirts, the lunch box and radio, and those smiles and hugs of friendship, they are now a part of the library because Billy works here. (Sanders, 1981, p. 1)

Billy has come a long way. When overbearing people attempt to tell him what to do in his own domain, he is likely to protest, "I'm a grown man!" Both of us continue to make mistakes and to learn, but I think we can say with confidence that we have grown up.

REFERENCES

Sanders, J. Billy works here. *Hunter's Clarion,* 1981, *3*(4), 1.

QUESTIONS TO CONSIDER

1. Review the questions on page 9. How accurate were your predictions?

2. What are the issues in Billy's adult life with which he has needed assistance? What inferences can you draw about how the family life cycle influences the nature and intensity of the parent-professional relationship?

3. What are Jane's views of her role as a case manager? Do you think these views will stay the same or change over the next six years?

Mary S. Akerley, a former teacher, has been active in local, state, and national affairs of the National Society for Autistic Children: she has served as its president and a member of its board of directors. She has been a member of the Maryland Developmental Disabilities Council, the National Association for Mental Health, and a consortium concerned with the developmentally disabled, as well as other groups. She has also served as the assistant director for services at the Center for the Handicapped in Silver Springs, Maryland.

When NSAC—now called the National Society for Children and Adults with Autism—opened a Washington, D.C., office in 1978, Mary joined the staff as director of national affairs. In 1980 she became program specialist and interdepartmental liaison for the Office of Independent Living for the Disabled in the United States Department of Housing and Urban Development. In August 1980 she left that position to enroll as a full-time student at the University of Maryland School of Law, from which she was graduated with honors in May 1983.

Ed and Mary Akerley

In 1978 her son, Edward Michael, was twelve years old. In the five years since then he has been busy. He changed his nickname from Eddie to Ed, and he successfully completed a semimainstreamed junior high program in which he led the school's aluminum recycling drive for two consecutive years. In 1984 he was a twelfth-grade student in his local public high school and was enrolled in only two special classes. His favorite subject was French, in which he received straight As much to the surprise of the educators who had done their best to convince him that he should not even enroll in it. He also testified before Congress several times on special education issues, the last time in 1980 as an invited witness. That testimony, in his own handwriting, was entered in full and without change in the record of the Select Committee on Education, House Committee on Education and Labor, United States Congress.

False Gods and Angry Prophets

Mary S. Akerley

It's hot and sunny, a magnificent day. We're on our way south on I-95, heading for the National Society for Autistic Children conference in Orlando. It's a perfect setting for thinking back because if it weren't for Eddie, none of us would be here enjoying this particular drive, in this particular place, on our way to a delightful vacation.

The four kids are, of course, all wearing T-shirts expressing their individual allegiances to some cause, place, or rock group. But so are Mom and Dad, and I think that's significant because I doubt very much that we could have brought ourselves to do something so "undignified" without Eddie's help. John is an engineer, I'm a former English teacher, and Eddie is our youngest child—he has autism. Autism is a very traumatic but effective cure for caring too much about what other people think of you. It is perhaps the ultimate liberator.

My T-shirt has two very nasty-looking vultures on it; one is saying to the other, "Patience my ass . . . I'm going to kill something!" The shirt was a gift from an NSAC friend, another member of the battered parent club. Most of us, like the hungry vulture, have run out of patience and have struck out for ourselves . . . and for our children.

We don't begin in anger. We start out the way all parents of all children do: with respect—reverence really—for the professional and his skills. The pediatrician, the teacher, the writer of books and articles on child development they are the sources of wisdom from which we must draw in order to be good parents. We believe, we consult, we do as we are told, and all goes well unless . . . one of our kids has a handicap.

We parents are almost always the first to notice that something is amiss, and one of our early consolations is often our pediatrician's assurance that "it's nothing—he'll outgrow it." That, of course, is exactly what we want to hear because it corresponds perfectly to the dwindling hope in our hearts, so we defer to the expert and our child loses another year. Finally,

23

the time does come when not even the most conservative professional can deny the existence of a problem. The difficulty now is to define it and plan accordingly. With luck our pediatrician refers us to an appropriate specialist, and we are (or should be) on our way.

We transfer our trust to the new god and wait expectantly for the oracle to speak. Instead of the strong, authoritative voice of wisdom, we more often hear an evasive stammer "Can't give you a definite diagnosis . . . uh [*mumble, mumble*] . . . virtually untestable. . . . Let us see him . . . [*cough, cough*] . . . again in a year." Ironically, when the oracle is loud and clear, it is often wrong. "Seriously emotionally disturbed it's a severe withdrawal reaction to maternal ambivalance." We have just been treated to our first dose of professional puffery, and it is very bitter medicine—all the more so for being almost totally ineffective.

One potentially redeeming feature may be realized here if the parents react with sufficient anger to take charge, to assert their right to be their child's "case manager." Unfortunately, this is not likely to happen at such an early stage; it takes more than one false god to make us give up religion entirely. And when—or if—we do manage to assert ourselves, our behavior is viewed by the professionals as the final stage in our own pathology; any of us who may still be practicing religion are immediately excommunicated.

This is not empty theory; we have lived it. When Eddie was still an infant, we suspected all was not right. By the time he was a year old, we were sure. These were not the feelings of our pediatrician, who clearly viewed us as overanxious parents. All he saw was an unusually beautiful child in perfect physical health who was perhaps "just a little slow." Our difficulties in managing the child were not regarded as significant, even when the setting for one such scene was the doctor's office. "I have lots of children in my practice who act like that." Then God help you, doctor, and the children, too!

It took a sit-in on the occasion of Eddie's three-year checkup to convince the man to do something. I had warned the office nurse when I made the appointment that I would not leave the consulting room until I got help, and I held my ground. It was my first act of parental assertion; had it not been successful, my son would probably still be wordless, friendless, essentially lifeless.

We were referred to a pediatric neurologist. Considering what I know now, it was an unusually enlightened choice. For most parents of children like Eddie, the first referral is to a child psychiatrist, who considers them— not their child—the primary patients. The neurologist and her colleague, a psychologist, completed the best evaluation they could with a subject who was at best uncooperative, at worst totally unresponsive.

The results, however, were singularly unhelpful. "We can't give you a diagnosis; his symptoms don't fit any known syndrome. We've never seen a child like this." John and I didn't know whether to weep or take a bow. I remember trying to pry something more specific from them. "Is he retarded?

Mary S. Akerley

Autistic [I had learned the word about two weeks earlier]? Disturbed?" Perhaps all of the above although none of the above seemed more like it. At least none of the familiar labels appeared to hit the mark precisely enough for the pros to be comfortable with it; and in their desire to be precise, they overlooked the need to be supportive. We felt totally abandoned. If they didn't know what was wrong, who would? And if no one knew what was wrong, then who would know what to do? Eddie was trapped in his misery, and we were trapped right in there with him.

Perhaps I am being unfair. Autism is a toughie to diagnose: the early signs are subtle, and Eddie had partially lost one of the primary symptoms— an inability to relate to people. In response to my stumbling efforts he had become very attached to me—overly so, in fact. Nevertheless, I find it hard to excuse either specialist. Both should have known that autism must be diagnosed retrospectively because most of the children do progress at least a little, and the behaviors Eddie exhibited were not unusual signs of development in an autistic child. Within a year I had learned all that; why hadn't they?

They did recommend that we get help from a child therapist and gave us three names. I picked the person most convenient to our home and called her. She was not taking any new patients, but she did encourage me to talk. Something in my tale of woe must have moved her because she took us on. What is more, she helped. Her approach was purely practical: examine a piece of distressing behavior and explore ways of eliminating or changing it. It was a soft form of behavior modification, and it worked. On the other hand, she did not shy away from the theoretical. She actually suggested books for me to read and, when pressed, ventured a diagnosis and a rather classy one at that—symbiotic psychosis with autistic defenses. Many years later, when Eddie entered public school and John and I reviewed the mountain of records that followed him there, the only good words about us as parents were hers.

Ironically, it was this genuinely helpful therapist who introduced us to the parent-eating variety. Our helpful therapist was a consultant for a special school and managed to get Eddie enrolled there. She continued as his therapist for that school year with the understanding that we would switch to a staff psychiatrist when the new school year began. In this case "staff psychiatrist" equalled a very green resident, fresh out of Freudian U. and, as we later discovered, utterly powerless to deviate from established practice even when his own common sense suggested it.

So much has been written about traditional psychiatrists abusing the parents of autistic children that even one more word seems superfluous, yet the abuse continues and so must the protests. We worked with two doctors—sequentially—at that school, neither of whom ever came right out and said, "You caused the problem," even though both based everything they said on that premise. Our involvement with a parent organization was viewed as a way of avoiding our emotional duty to our child despite the fact that he was improving dramatically, in no small part because of what we had learned through that involvement. Our failure to need their kind of help was "blocking"; our by-now angry fighting back, "resistance." The real mind-blower for Doctor Number One was my refusal to admit that I hated and resented Eddie because I had had to turn down a graduate fellowship when full-time study would have kept me away from him too much. Doctor Number Two picked up the theme and kept working with me (*on* me was more like it) to admit my anger. Finally I blew. "You bet I'm angry, Dr. B., and I know what I'm angry at—you!"

Again, perhaps I'm being too harsh. Both of these doctors had had many years of school; neither had ever had a child. Obviously they still had a great deal to learn about the priorities of love. Yet even now I cannot write these words without feeling a rage that makes my pen tremble. I am still angry.

The worst professional damage—not to us but to Eddie— occurred during this time. We took him back to the neurologist for a reevaluation, as she had suggested we do as soon as we felt he could endure all the testing involved. When we advised Doctor Number One of our plans, she came close to losing her professional cool. "You didn't ask my permission! You're going to put him through all that for nothing; you're clutching at straws just to prove it's not your fault! If you go through with this, he can't stay here."

Her diatribe produced a fury in me that was quelled only by her last sentence. Fear took over. There is not exactly a wealth of choices when it comes to schools for autistic children, and this one was doing a good job. We didn't want Eddie to lose this help that he needed so badly, but we didn't want him deprived of any helpful medical intervention either. It was a cruel choice, especially since it was so unnecessary and artificial. Thank God we again had the guts to take over and be proper parents. Eddie and I moved into Children's Hospital for three days for the most complete neurological evaluation possible. We had, in effect, called the school's bluff. They didn't want to give up what they had termed, in our presence, "an interesting case" (us or Eddie?)—especially one which looked more and more like a success story. Doctor Number One even visited Eddie in the hospital.

The testing was an ordeal for Eddie, as it would be for any five year old, but hardly the trauma our expert had predicted. And it was well worth the effort. The testing revealed that Eddie was what is now called a *purine* autistic; that is, his uric acid level was significantly high—two to three times the normal level for a child his age.

To reverse this situation, there was an experimental treatment regime similar to that used for gout patients. Naturally, we were eager to begin it just as, naturally, the school was not. They reintroduced the "heads we win, tails you lose" decision-making process by again threatening to expel Eddie if we insisted on allowing the neurologist to treat him. There was no way to circumvent the situation: the neurologist refused to jeopardize a successful school placement for an unproven medical methodology, and

Mary S. Akerley

the dietary restrictions alone made secrecy impossible. In addition, cooperation was essential: school personnel, psychiatric and educational, were to serve as evaluators of behavioral change.

Our discouragement was relieved slightly by the news that Doctor Number One was leaving and, come fall, we would have a new therapist. The neurologist suggested we wait and hope for a more cooperative, open doctor. As soon as Doctor Number Two arrived, she contacted him to discuss her proposed neurological management. Immediately afterwards, she called us, elated. "Good news, Mrs. Akerley. It looks as though you got a winner this time. I've just talked to Dr. B., and he's very interested and willing to cooperate."

For some as yet unexplained reason, Dr. B. was too busy to begin seeing us until school had been in session for six weeks. Perhaps it took that long for the school's supervising psychiatrist to indoctrinate him into the proper ways of treating autistic children and their parents. When we encountered one another at last, there was no support for any neurological intervention—only the hostility we had come to know so well. I wondered then how many times human hope can be crushed before it refuses to rise again. Fortunately, I have yet to find out.

By then I had lost all vestiges of a cooperative patient and of a tactful human being. The one benefit I had derived from years of enforced therapy was a mouth unrestrained by the graceful social manners my poor mother had worked so hard to instill. Besides, therapy was my hour, not his, so I delivered my reaction to his rejection in "plainspeak." "I don't believe what I'm hearing. You told our neurologist that you were very interested in her work and very willing to participate in her treatment plan for Eddie. She couldn't believe we had finally gotten a cooperative shrink. Now you're giving us an unqualified, unexplained no. I don't believe it's your decision. You're still in training, and you're just doing what you've been told, following the institution line. Is this the way you're going to handle treatment all year? Will you have to get permission for everything you want to do? When do they let you make up your own mind? When do we get to work with a fully qualified therapist? I'm tired of being someone's lab assignment!"

Needless to say, he defended the decision as his own; in fact, he brought it up frequently in the months that followed, but I never bought it. Nor was he too professional to parry with the charge that the only reason we were eager to resume therapy that fall was to get started on the new neurological treatment. I never tried to deny it. John and I had long since given up any hope of real help from therapy and had come to regard our fifty-minute hour as an unavoidable part of the school's tuition. We had found other, more valid sources of help for ourselves, and we had found them all on our own. No professional had ever suggested we join a parent's organization; in fact, they all appeared threatened by such groups and by the growing competence and self-assurance we derived from our participation.

Eddie's therapy (two thirty-minute sessions per week) was a different matter. While he was now speaking, it was typical autistic speech, not useful enough for talk therapy. So he played with toys from the doctor's collection (carefully selected for psychoanalytic potential), and the therapist interpreted his play. Anyone familiar with the play of an autistic child might be tempted to feel considerable sympathy for the psychiatrist and hope his boredom threshold was very high. Let me remind anyone so inclined that autistic play is replete with opportunities for the properly trained observer to see fixation, withdrawal, hostility, sexual repression, and a host of other Freudian goodies. And see them he did.

John and I, in our hour, heard some of these interpretations; two come to mind as excellent examples. Eddie was fascinated by telephone poles; ergo, he had phallic anxieties. The second, I thought, was considerably more imaginative. One of Eddie's favorite playthings was a set of wooden dowels that were part of a construction-type toy. His way of enjoying them was to stand them on end, lie down, and move his head back and forth behind them. (He played similar eye games in front of store windows in which basically vertical items were displayed, not a typical behavior for an autistic child.) I chose to see his little game, after trying it myself, as an independent discovery of the theory of relativity. Not so. The learned doctor, who patiently explained to me that I had clearly kept Eddie in his crib and playpen too much because he was now reliving the behind-bars trauma! My response was really more innocent than sarcastic, although it was not perceived that way. "If it was so awful, why is he reliving it with such obvious pleasure?" No answer came.

If all this psychoanalytic nonsense had been shared only with us, I probably would have been more amused than frightened. But I had seen this type of therapy when visiting other similar programs and had every reason to believe that Eddie's behavior was being interpreted to him as well. For example: "Oh, I see you've dropped the mother doll. I guess you would like to reject your mommy the way she has rejected you." I knew his receptive language was up to following this kind of talk, and the possibility of his ever hearing it frightened me.

If those child therapists really wanted to help Eddie, I believe they should have tried to make themselves psychologically invisible. They should have done all in their power to enhance the normal relationships in his life. Instead, motivated by Technicolor rescue fantasies, they charged between a child and the people who loved him most in an egocentric effort to make themselves paramount.

I remember when Eddie learned to kiss. We had taught him the mechanics and had been getting back a lifeless touching of his lips to our cheeks. Then one night at bedtime it happened—a real kiss. I could hardly wait to report this exciting mark of progress to Doctor Number Two. At our regular session a few days later, he preempted me (he had seen Eddie the day before).

"Eddie kissed me," he announced smugly with the most self-satisfied look I have ever seen on a human face.

"Me, too" was all I could say.

"When?" There was actually fear in his voice, and when he heard the answer, he was visibly upset. "That means he kissed you before he kissed me!"

Right, Doctor, and that is as it should be.

The entire situation had taken on a terrible irony. Eddie was being denied a treatment which was based on objective, scientific evidence while being forced to undergo a therapy based on subjective, introspective fantasy. Fortunately, thanks to several gifted teachers and a truly creative speech therapist, he had progressed to the point where a change of schools seemed called for. This gave us the courage to contact the neurologist and suggest that treatment begin. Meanwhile, we began looking into possible schools.

Sound medical practice is basically conservative, so the doctor first tried to bring Eddie's uric acid level down by diet alone: no meat, no fish, no nuts, no whole grains, no chocolate, no cola—most of his favorite foods (and a lot of things he refused to eat!) were eliminated. I gave him a simple but honest explanation of why he could no longer have them, which he seemed to understand and accept. Eventually he got to be better than I at watching his diet. I sent him off to school with jelly or catsup sandwiches, fruit, plain cookies, and skim milk; I even included food for snack time. I felt excited, hopeful, and—with the expulsion threat defused—invulnerable. I had underestimated Doctor Number Two's resourcefulness. Unable to wait for my next scheduled appointment, he called me at home with a brand-new threat: the diet was going to give Eddie an oral fixation! My response is not printable; and since I do not believe in superstitions Eddie stayed on the diet, and I retained my lovely feeling of freedom. Our child was ours again, and we would make the decisions that we would have to live with.

The diet by itself was not effective; so allopurinol, a drug which inhibits the body's production of uric acid, was introduced. Within a week we had a different child. He began to play with toys in normal, creative ways; his language skills took a quantum leap forward; and his behavior calmed down. His teachers, who did not know about the medication, could not believe the difference. We could, because we had always believed that within Eddie lay a great deal of potential that the right treatment would bring out.

That was all a long time ago; the worst, thank God, is behind us. Eddie's new school was a replay of the first but with a more normal academic program, from which he benefited enormously. We did not suffer this time because all our reverence for false gods was gone, and we no longer doubted our own competence. One day I kept Eddie out for an appointment with the neurologist; the next day I caught hell because I had not asked permission. Would they have felt the same way if it had been a dental appointment? Oh yes, indeed. Perhaps then it was time to get something straight: did they, by chance, consider themselves the primary case managers? Of course. Well, we did not—that responsibility was ours alone. They were providing a service which we had determined we wished to purchase for our child; we were the customers, and we would call the shots. I did not ask permission from my other children's schools to make professional appointments, and I had no intention of mothering Eddie any differently.

So that our poor therapist would not feel entirely useless, we made up interesting problems for him to work on. We specialized in religious crises, taking our cue from an early session which he filled with his own life story. He was an ex-priest married to an ex-nun, and they had not waited for Rome to dispense them from their vows before beginning their life together. I'm still not sure of the reason for this astonishing confession—perhaps to set us at ease, perhaps to challenge us to play Can You Top This? We tried. Since we were not allowed to talk about Eddie, we spent a lot of time on the therapist's children—two boys aged three and five, whom their daddy seemed to have a great deal of difficulty managing.

One day he advised us that the entire staff had observed that we acted like strangers in the waiting room before our appointment (it was 8:00 A.M., for God's sake!), whereupon we graciously offered to make love the very next week if the school would provide a comfortable couch. They didn't, but we were finally excused from therapy with the inspiring words, "Well, you've won! You don't have to come in any more!" Cured, were we? Not really, just vocal. I had been on a fairly well publicized TV talk show the week before (I was then president of the state chapter of NSAC) and had used the opportunity to blast the inflated costs of private special schools, citing enforced, useless psychotherapy as a prime factor.

Eddie is now in our public school's SLD (specific learning disabilities) program. To be sure, he is still very much on the periphery of life, and that is hard for all of us . . . so near and yet so far. But there has been more progress than any of the many people who have worked with him over the years ever dared hope for. We are elated and grateful; but I, at least, have not forgiven those who, instead of helping, added to our pain. I believe there can be no greater sin.

True, we survived; and we are stronger, richer people for the experience. But we are exceptions. Average parents do not get a chance to speak out in books or on television; they have to sit still and take it. We cannot even always find them to offer help; the chances are 60–40 that they've already gone under.

The people whose words you read here have survived in spite of the professionals, not because of them. There are many lessons for would-be helpers to learn from their stories: respect for parental competence, humility in the face of one's own ignorance, acceptance of the contributions of other professional disciplines. But they all stem from the eloquently simple tenet of the physician's code: Do no harm.

Mary S. Akerley

QUESTIONS TO CONSIDER

1. Mary describes positive and negative encounters with professionals. What were the characteristics of the professionals with whom she had positive and negative relationships? What can you infer about her values? What types of relationships do you predict for Mary's future?

2. What was the impact on Mary of being blamed for Eddie's problems? How do you think this blame influenced her relationships with Eddie, her husband, and professionals?

3. Through her experiences with Eddie, Mary became a very active member of parent organizations. What are your predictions about her future contributions to these organizations?

4. How has Eddie influenced Mary's personal growth? How do you expect her personal growth to influence her future priorities?

UPDATE:

The Loneliness of the Long-Distance Swimmer

Mary S. Akerley

This is, (dare I say, "I promise"?) my last word on autism. It is time now for me to turn around—perhaps even turn away—at least a little. I no longer have the duty or the right to aggressively manage my son's life. He turned eighteen this month, he is on the honor roll in public high school, and he has had his first date. He has even attended his first stag party (his brother-in-law-to-be's bachelor party) and has endured his first hangover.

Does all this mean that autistic Eddie is now Norman-Rockwell-normal Ed? No. Does it mean that I was wrong six years ago when I wrote in "False Gods and Angry Prophets" that parents should react to professional arrogance and incompetence "with sufficient anger to take charge, to assert their right to be their child's 'case manager'?" No. It's just that Ed isn't a "case" anymore, and I am no longer qualified to fill a professional role in his life.

Let me illustrate: One night when Ed was still very young— about eight, I think—he interrupted his bedtime story (an important ritual for him) by putting his hands, palms down, on the pages of the open book. Naturally, I turned my attention from the book to him. He looked directly at me and said, "Mommy, I'm broken. Fix me." If we had ever been even slightly tempted to conceal from him the nature or severity of his handicap (and I don't think we ever were), that would have stopped us. Now, right or wrong, he believes he's "fixed"—or very nearly so. "When I was little, I was autistic, but now my autism's almost all gone." He doesn't want me or anyone else tinkering with him anymore or running interference for him as I once did.

In fact, I think for a while I sometimes held him back. For example, there was the matter of the house key. Everyone else in the family had one, and Ed wanted one, too. I had gone back to work and couldn't be there when he got home from school. However, I pointed out quite reasonably that two of the other three kids were always home ahead of him, so he

33

really didn't need a key. (He'd lose it; I knew he would. Never mind that he'd never lost anything in his life. If kids lose keys—and it's given that they do—handicapped kids perforce lose more keys and in even less time.) What I had neglected to consider was that he was the last one to leave the house in the morning; to him that had clearly been pivotal. "But what if the bus doesn't come? How will I get back in the house without a key?" Good question! He got the key and still has it—the only one of the four who has never lost one.

There was also the swimming. As much as Ed loved to play in the bathtub or in the backyard wading pool, he was utterly terrified of the big neighborhood swimming pool unless I carried him in and held him in my arms the entire time. As the summers went by, we metamorphosed from the wholesome and sublime to the pathetic and ridiculous. It is quite natural to see a mother bouncing her four year old around the shallow end of the pool; it is quite something else when the child is eight, very large for his age, and makes strange faces at the splashing water.

Gradually I weaned him: first to the side of the pool—his hands on the rim, his legs floating behind him, and my arms under his chest. Then we withdrew my arms; then his hands, but his feet had to touch the bottom. Somehow we just couldn't make that quantum leap to total suspension in the water without contact with the pool. I gave up—consoling myself that at least he could now move about in the pool independently.

Almost the full summer went by before the miracle happened, and I didn't even see it. (I had managed to wean myself, too, from unremitting vigilance when Eddie was in the water.) A friend ran up to my pool chair shouting, "He's swimming! Eddie's swimming!" *Swimming* may have been a somewhat complimentary description of what he was doing, but his improvisation of the crawl was nearly as effective as the real thing. There he was—face down, arms churning, legs kicking, moving forward, limited only by the time he could hold his breath. (He never has learned to coordinate his breathing with his strokes, so now he just swims with his head out of the water; it's not graceful, but it works for him.)

There is an obvious significance to an event such as this in the life of any child, but I saw a more subtle and more meaningful one as well. He had accomplished it when I was not involved. It made me think back to similar but less dramatic events that had given me pause: how normally he had talked to a neighbor child once when he thought I was out of earshot; how fearlessly he had played with his sister's turtles when he didn't know I could see him (Ed's fear of water was surpassed only by his fear of animals of any kind or size).

I felt sad, as though I weren't needed by Ed anymore or, worse yet, as though I had been somehow holding him back. My suspicions were confirmed a few days later, again at the pool. His newly won skill had led me to impose what I felt was a necessary restriction: if he wanted to swim in the deep end, he had to come and get me to accompany him. Of course,

Mary S. Akerley

this soon proved more a restriction on me, since he wanted to spend most of his time in the deep end and I wanted to spend most of mine sitting in the sun reading and chatting. Nonetheless, that new rule was probably a good idea at first: autistic kids do not have good judgment and often don't perceive obvious dangers. However, I let it go on too long, and he let me know so very effectively.

The pool is L-shaped: the horizontal base of the L is the deepest part; the vertical top, the most shallow. We had just swum the length together that afternoon and were resting in the deep corner when Ed took off diagonally across the deep end, swimming like a windmill at full tilt. I froze in terror and then took off after him, both of us disrupting the orderly progress of several swimmers doing laps. He got to the other side well ahead of me and was laughing when I reached him. I got the point.

Not that I always remembered it. There have been other times when I did not let go soon enough, but I like to think that they were few enough to do no real harm. Besides, Ed has become very effective at letting us know when he no longer needs us.

John: Ed, did you use my ax today?

Ed: Yes, Dad. I wanted to chop some logs.

John: Well, that's fine, but I don't want you doing it when no one's home. You might have an accident and need help.

Ed: I can take care of myself.

John: [*irritated and sure he's got Ed cornered*] O.K. What would you do if you cut your leg off and couldn't walk? You'd have to lie there bleeding till someone found you.

Ed: No, I wouldn't. I would crawl to the house and dial 911.

And that's exactly what he'd have to do if he were living alone, which is the point of all this. Someday he will be living alone— he'll have to be because John and I are going to die, and probably long before Ed does.

But suppose not; suppose Ed dies first. That is the more subtle lesson I've learned from Ed's first swim: *I* will then have to live without him. His dependence on me was obvious, and it had to be responded to and then diminished. My dependence on him was insidious, life-threatening to both of us if unrecognized and unchecked. It's the danger others have warned us of: the swallowing up of our individual identities by the disabilities of our children. Because of Ed's autism I acquired community prominence, then statewide recognition, and finally national identification. My presence in this book is proof of that. It's heady stuff—sometimes even remunerative—but sometimes it has made me feel just a little slimy. Here I was at some nice conference, rubbing elbows (and bending them as well!) with the stars of the disability circuit, all because I had turned my child's handicap into a personal asset—damned near a career!

This dependence is the polar opposite of the disabled child's; his was cause, mine was effect. His was inhibiting; mine, reinforcing. In the normal course of development (and there is a normal course even for abnormal people) his would diminish, mine would grow. It would be growth so long as it was productive; when it became an end in itself, it would be malignant.

Thank God I had a son whose own self-confidence forced me to see that. He did better when I was not on the scene, and he still does. He came home from school recently and announced; "Well, I did at school today what the law says you have to do when you turn eighteen!" I was positive he had registered for the draft, but no—just to vote. He may have thought voter registration was mandatory because we are such a politically active family, but his party selection was his own.

I think his gratifying self-management is the result of two fears: (1) if something is very important to him and he has assistance the first time he tries it, he believes he will never be able to do it independently; and (2) he's afraid a well-meaning mentor, especially his mom, won't let him try something because he might get hurt. But whatever—I have been told implicitly and explicitly to back off. I got lots of early warning signals from Ed (most of them pretty blatant in retrospect) and more than a few from my own perceptions of other parents who could not let go of their kid and their parent organization, even when it became obvious that the relationship had become stifling for both. The parent had stopped growing, and the subsequent development of both kid and club was stunted because that parent was in the way.

Tomorrow I will graduate from law school, a dream I've had since I was nineteen. When I enrolled, everyone assumed I would specialize in disability law. They looked astonished or hurt, depending on their perspective, when I said no, I was going to do something else. For ten hard but good years, I overdosed on disability. It was my family, my hobby, my career. I think the only way to avoid certain death is to quit cold-turkey before I break my own rule of "do no harm." I did my best to "fix" Ed as he had asked, knowing all along that the most I could do was help him learn to cope with his limitations and maybe change the world a little so he wouldn't have quite such a hard time when his coping wasn't enough. Now he thinks he's "fixed," and so far his coping skills have carried him through more often than not.

We've been lucky, he and I. When we do things together now, it's because we want to, not have to. He came to my mock trial at school and thoroughly enjoyed it; I went to a supper club sponsored by his teen group and proudly watched him perform as the maître d'. We can admire each other's accomplishments and criticize each other's failings. Now we are both job hunting and facing discrimination—I because of age, Ed because of disability. We are genuinely on equal footing, and it's a nice place to be.

Mary S. Akerley

QUESTIONS TO CONSIDER

1. Review the questions on page 31. How accurate were your predictions?

2. How has Mary's role in Ed's life changed over the years? What factors have accounted for this change? Do you predict that the nature of Mary's relationship with Ed will stay the same or change during the next six years?

3. Mary suggests that the recognition she obtained from her leadership role in parent organizations resulted from her turning Ed's handicap into a personal asset. Do you believe that the many parents in similar situations are exploiting their handicapped children for their own gain? Do you expect Mary to withdraw totally from disability-related advocacy activities during the next six years?

Elizabeth Boggs, a parent advocate for mentally retarded people since 1949, chose full-time involvement in issues of legislation and public policy in preference to the career in applied mathematics for which she had originally prepared. In 1950 she became one of the founders of what is now the Association for Retarded Citizens of the United States and in 1958 became its first woman president. She has served on many of its committees over the past thirty-five years but is best known for her work in governmental affairs.

Since 1957 she has received appointments from four different presidents to serve on four different national commissions of various sorts, most recently the National Council on the Handicapped. Like most other ARC/US leaders she has remained active in state and local affairs and was recently cited in a resolution of the New Jersey state senate. As of 1984 she was involved with the ARC/Hunterdon in creating a small residence on property near her own home for six non-ambulatory adults with moderate to mild retardation.

Elizabeth and David Boggs

Her son, David, is profoundly retarded and multiply handicapped; he remains a resident of Hunterdon Developmental Center in northwestern New Jersey, about five miles from Dr. Boggs' home. David's father, Fitzhugh W. Boggs, was also a leader in the ARC, but died in 1971.

Who's Putting Whose Head in the Sand?

(Or in the clouds, as the case may be)

Elizabeth M. Boggs

As this tale unfolds it will be increasingly clear that my son is not only handicapped but disabled by anyone's criteria, including those of the Social Security Administration. Thus, my qualifications as a parent are unimpeachable. My qualifications as a professional in the field of mental retardation, however, are a matter of courtesy. Unlike Phil Roos, (see page 245), I was not a professional in the human services field before I was a parent; unlike Elsie Helsel (see page 81), I did not go after another degree in special education; unlike Rud Turnbull, (see page 109), I did not have a profession I could turn directly toward the field to which my parenthood called attention. Only indirectly did my training in the discipline of science (my doctorate was in mathematical chemistry) help me in the early days to understand the limitations and constraints on the methods of the biological sciences and hence to serve for a while as an interpreter between those scientists and the parents who were eager for miracles from the laboratory.

In these days when certificates, diplomas, and guild membership cards are so often required as passports to participation in decision making, I am heartened to be able to report that I have only rarely been put down or excluded from human policy deliberations in which I judged myself competent. Moreover, I have been permitted to sit and learn in many situations where I would not presume to speak, except to ask questions. To the ever-increasing body of professionals, especially those in universities and in government, who have permitted me to be productive in roles for which my credentials were distinctly unconventional, I owe, and warmly tender, sincere thanks. This is one respect in which my relationships with the professional community over the past quarter century have been exceptionally gratifying.

I am also fortunate to be old enough to have escaped the overbearing coercion of modern feminism which tends to judge productivity by the standards of the marketplace. I am proud to be the only person who has been continuously active in some volunteer capacity within the National Association for Retarded Citizens since I participated in its founding in 1950. I believe that NARC has a unique role to play, and that the existence of a strong lay advocacy group which continues to recognize and respond to the great diversity of need among persons called retarded is the single most essential element in securing their future. I have jealously guarded my amateur status within the association even when positions as a consultant and lecture fees have come my way on the outside. In the early days I carried out many unbudgeted assignments which are now executed by paid staff. In recent years I have been able to accentuate multiple linkages with other agencies and movements that no one with ties to a paid position could have made. The cause has taken me to forty-four states, plus Puerto Rico and ten foreign countries. It is hard to put a job title on the role I've played. One could say that I've been a social synergist with a predisposition toward communication and collaboration rather than confrontation.

That's the public or "professional" side. What of the private, the personal, the parental side? As we are all fond of telling each other, each person, each parent, each family experience is unique; yet there are common themes. How many of us were told that we were overanxious, that our child's tardiness in meeting milestones was within normal limits? How many of us who founded local associations and organized the classes and recruited the executive directors now feel, with Janet Bennett (page 159), that local ARCs are no longer places where parents feel useful? How many of us have seen the doctrines swing and now speculate about the potential orthodoxy of the eighties? Is still another perspective of any value? In an effort to give some integrity to this essay, I've selected some personal vignettes which I relate to three themes of concern to me: first, the discrepancy between the intents of public policy and the actualities of life for retarded individuals and their families; second, the mismatch between research findings and both public policy and private practice (these themes are related, as it happens, to the work of the two NARC committees on which I have had the most extended service); third, the recurrent professional and societal denial of the differentness of the most disabled, and their resultant need for their own ergonomic environments.

This derogation of deviance may isolate unnecessarily and inappropriately those people who come face to face with this deviance as immediate care givers. It's not for nothing that a new magazine of growing circulation is called The Exceptional Parent or that George Tarjan, director of the Neuropsychiatric Institute at U.C.L.A., considered it a major victory when the attendants at Pacific State Hospital were no longer reluctant to reveal where they worked.

Out of my personal experience, I've picked four vignettes to illustrate these themes. They deal with the crisis, daily living, the right to education, and the institutionalization of deinstitutionalization. I still live with the last theme as a current issue; my personal experience with the other three goes back a quarter of a century, but something tells me things haven't changed all that much.

The Crisis

Jonathan David Boggs was born on August 25, 1945. The date is significant for two reasons. It was the second Saturday after V-J Day and, as such, was the first Saturday on which my husband, Fitzhugh Boggs, had not put in a full day at the laboratory. Therefore, when I began having early labor pains about six o'clock that morning, it was not necessary for us to grapple with the decision as to whether or not he would go to work.

Some eight weeks before I had resigned my own research job at the Explosives Research Laboratory at Bruceton, Pennsylvania. That was after V-E Day and after our group at the laboratory had completed its technical contributions to the design of the implosion device being put together at Los Alamos. At the Westinghouse Research Laboratories in East Pittsburgh, Fitzhugh had researched some of the radar jamming technology which had helped the Britons to win the Battle of Britain. At the time, neither of us knew what the other had contributed to the war effort.

We congratulated ourselves on our timing. It may have been more critical than we realized. With the end of the war, penicillin, which had previously been limited to use in military hospitals, was released for civilian use. When David was ten days old, he became very ill. He had a high fever and a nervous twitching referred to as tetany. Several hypotheses were advanced as to the cause of the illness. Our pediatrician later told us that in all his considerable experience he had seen only one similar case. That child had died. An autopsy had shown an infection entering by way of the umbilical cord. David was treated with penicillin and survived. Many years later I was to address the Ways and Means Committee of the U.S. House of Representatives in support of extended authority for the Maternal and Child Health Program. My theme was "Survival Is Not Enough." Since then a collaborative perinatal study supported by the National Institute of Health has yielded a technique for examining the discarded cord in the delivery room to detect such infections.

It was a harrowing three weeks. Dr. Gerald Caplan (1960) at Harvard has studied family crises of which ours was undoubtedly a classic example. As a crisis it was, I believe, well handled by the professionals. We were permitted to express our worries. No one denied the gravity of the situation. The physicians gave us their full attention and took care to explain the reasons for their several tentative diagnoses. They described the treatments, including a period of continuous lavage. A cousin of mine who is a registered nurse saw us through the transition from hospital to home, which otherwise would have been still more frightening to me. David began to regain weight, and the doctors foretold no aftereffects.

But that was not the real crisis. The real crisis unfolded over the next twenty months. David first approached and then gradually— almost imperceptibly at first—fell behind the normal developmental timetable. When he was eight months old, our pediatrician asked us, apparently casually, whether we thought he could hear. We said we did not know. In fact, we were not sure until he was more than two years old, when he responded to the sound of running bath water.

In the spring of 1946, David spent a month in the care of an aunt while Fitzhugh and I vacationed in Cuba, where my parents were living at the time. Fitzhugh was between jobs, and it was the only opportunity we ever had for four consecutive weeks of vacation. If I had known then what I know now about critical periods of separation for infants, I would have arranged things differently. However, while we were away, David learned to roll over.

During the next ten months we were nomads. This was the immediate post-war era, and housing was at a premium. We had purchased a house in Upper Montclair, New Jersey, but were unable to evict the tenants (our legal effort to do so was put off by a technicality). As a result, David and I saw a succession of pediatricians. Each of them responded reassuringly to my description of his slow progress. When he was a little over a year and barely standing, the pediatrician with whom I had hoped to settle down answered my query with "Well, he's prehensile, isn't he?"

In the face of being told repeatedly that David's progress was satisfactory, I did not share my own misgivings with Fitzhugh. As it turned out, he had his own. I seldom dream or, to be more accurate, recollect the dreams I have. Fitzhugh, by contrast, used to have consistent recurring dreams whenever he was confronted with a continuing problem. As he told me afterward, he had been having such dreams, always about David. They stopped immediately when we found a pediatrician who, without prompting from us, indicated that we had a problem.

It was only a partial resolution, however. Having delivered himself of the judgment that David might be self-supporting in a lowly occupation, that pediatrician was not willing to assist us in obtaining further medical consultation. I suppose he saw us as shopping parents. If so, it was a misjudgment on his part because we were very grateful to him for admitting to the reality which we ourselves had observed; namely, David was not developing at a normal rate. However, he resisted our request for a psychological evaluation and for further consultation on the medical side. Because of our appreciation, we felt considerable loyalty to him, and it was hard for us to break away. But eventually we did so, in order to obtain a comprehensive evaluation at Babies Hospital, the pediatric hospital associated with the College of Physicians and Surgeons in New York City. The doctors there recommended institutionalization. By this time David was nearly three.

Following the findings of Dr. Caplan's studies (1960) of families in crisis, I see that this crisis was not well handled by the professionals involved. One would like to think that times have changed since then. Unfortunately, the word still has not gotten around. A young attorney friend of mine, well-acquainted with the field of mental retardation professionally, gave birth recently in a major Washington hospital. There was tentative suspicion of Down's syndrome on the basis of inspection, but she had to fight to get a confirming cytogenetic study carried out. We also still hear reports of routine advice for instant institutionalization at birth.

Daily Living

We accepted the findings of the physicians' and surgeons' group as to the severity of David's impairment, along with its nonspecificity. We also accepted the notion that the underlying organic cause was not directly remediable. (While putting himself through college, Fitzhugh had worked as a lab technician in a research department of neurology, and he had a rather vivid firsthand understanding of the effect of lesions in the central nervous system.) We did not, however, accept the group's advice to proceed with institutionalization. We were reinforced in this decision by David himself who gave us his response to the three or four days of hospitalization. As we got into the car, preparatory to leaving the hospital, he stood between us on the front seat and, speechless as he was and is, gave us in unmistakable body language the message, "Let's get the hell out of here!"

He lived with us until he was nearly seven. Those were trying years in which we were largely on our own. Nevertheless, our efforts toward toilet training and self-feeding were rewarded to a considerable extent. But those were also years in which we could find no means to convey instructions or guidance to him about behavior which was either dangerous to him or productive of chaos in the household. His destructiveness did not convey a sense of rebellion or anger, but rather a total lack of comprehension that it was unacceptable to us. One had to be present physically to deter him from running into the street, destroying the neighbors' flowers, tearing up the magazines in the living room, removing the contents of the refrigerator, or getting up at night and pounding on the window just to hear the noise. Unfortunately, the neighbors also heard the noise and complained to the police.

I do not want to suggest that his motor development was normal. Indeed, by the time he was four, it was apparent that he had mild cerebral palsy. Since then, this disability has become more apparent, and his contractures are now so severe that he walks a hundred feet only with considerable difficulty.

The problem at that time, however, was one of accommodating extraordinary stress in the family's daily activities. Until then I had been a fairly meticulous housekeeper. However, the work of tidying and cleaning could be undone in thirty seconds by David's activities. In addition to caring for David, cleaning up after him would have been a full-time job, had I elected to do it. However, I saw the necessity for maintaining some time for my own intellectual pursuits as well as some outside activities, and we began to tolerate a high degree of disorder in the house. We removed most of the bric-a-brac and became resigned to scarred furniture.

I had, by this time, postponed more or less indefinitely the notion of going back to professional work. I joined the League of Women Voters, a step that turned out to be particularly useful since it taught me some important things about the operation of state government in New Jersey. I also began taking occasional courses at what was then the Newark State Teachers College, now Kean College of New Jersey. The clinical psychologist who gave the course Introduction to Tests and Measurements in the summer of 1949 told me about a clinic being organized by the brand-new Essex County Unit of the New Jersey Parents' Group for Retarded Children. This was truly a self-help group, and its dynamics were very different in those days from the way they are now that the professionals have largely taken over. But that is another story which I shall not tell here.

Rather, I wish to make some retrospective observations about this period from the point of view of parental support and prevention of parental burnout. Michael Bayley (1973), in reporting some sensitive British studies, documents the effects of the daily grind on families who retain a retarded member at home for many years. These deleterious effects can, in part, be mitigated. Christine Maslach (1976) has recently reported studies on burnout among various types of professional personnel who give direct care or service. These include social workers, child-care workers, attorneys, and others who constantly confront the insoluble problems of other people. Generally speaking, the confrontations of the professionals are limited to working hours. Even so, Maslach's research indicated that uninterrupted hours of direct contact, along with isolation from peers having similar duties, contributed to stress. She points out that when the stress becomes intolerable, the professional is likely to respond in one of two ways. He or she either cops out or begins to depersonalize the clients or patients and to blame them for their own misfortunes. Cop-out is possible, for example, when the social worker goes back to graduate school and takes a degree in administration. Both copping-out and depersonalization tend to reduce professional productivity and are detrimental to those being served. Maslach's findings suggest that limiting exposure through planned direct contact and opportunities for peer group interactions can help to reduce burnout and thus enhance humanization for both care giver and care receiver. Although these studies did not include parents as subjects, it is fairly clear that there is a lesson to be learned and applied.

In retrospect, I can see that we had managed to apply some of these principles in our situation. We had what we referred to as a built-in babysitter. Having bought an old house with a third floor, we took advantage of a temporary post-war lifting of one-family zoning restrictions to create a small apartment there for a service man and his family. The apartment was rent-free to them as long as they were available on an intermittent and irregular but mutually agreeable schedule to look after David in our absence.

Elizabeth M. Boggs

This permitted us not only to go out for an evening (which included participating in parent-group meetings) but also to intersperse daytime routines with brief absences.

This model of respite care is, I believe, closer to the mark for both mother and child than is the all-day day-care center or the occasional fortnight of residential care which is more likely to be offered today. Quite frankly, I believe that we have not yet reconciled what we know about the need of a child for a continuing and uniquely identified parent figure and the need to prevent burnout and to foster personhood in parents, especially mothers. I am speaking particularly of the first three or four years of the child's life. The National Collaborative Infant Project developed by the United Cerebral Palsy Association, with the cooperation of NARC and others, has demonstrated a model of early intervention which could displace group day care for most very young handicapped children (Haynes, 1977). Quite aside from the services to the child, it combines assistance to mothers to enable them to be more effective parents, with brief spells of relief from the extraordinary demands of parenting a handicapped child. Both natural parents and foster parents need these supports. The high turnover already being noted among house parents in group homes should be studied against this hypothesis.

The Right to Education

The charter members of the Essex Unit were a remarkably foresighted lot. By the time Fitzhugh and I came on board late in 1949, they had organized an interdisciplinary diagnostic clinic, to which a hardy band of professionals were contributing their time. The initial applicants were accepted by age groups so that the needs of a group could be identified for service planning. Soon there were enough six to nine year olds identified as trainable to justify organizing some classes. This was my first volunteer organizational task. Two classes were opened in October 1950—one in a Sunday school room, the other in a neighborhood house.

These children had been denied admission to local schools. However, we had a social mission in mind, so we, too, had some eligibility criteria. The children had to be toilet-trained and able to understand simple commands. Our mission was to persuade the county superintendent of schools, and through him the local superintendents, that such children could respond to skillful teaching in a classroom setting and should be accommodated in the public schools.

We were, in fact, going backward to the practices of 1911 to 1930 when "imbecile" children had been accepted and provided with an approved curriculum in the larger communities in New Jersey. A state Department of Education publication of 1918 prescribes sense training, speech training, manual training, and "exercises of practical life." It then goes on to note "while results with this group are crude, the improvement in children is marked" (Anderson, 1918). It is hard to recreate now what these classes developed by the Essex Unit meant to parents as well as children.

In connection with my duties I enjoyed my first experiences of professional acceptance. I was permitted to sit in on the clinic team conferences at which recommendations were made relative to those children to be referred to me for class placement. I learned a lot from this experience, particularly as I was able to review the individual reports and watch the children they described over a period of time. It did not take me long to conclude that David would not be eligible for these classes.

About this time the neighboring local unit (Bergen-Passaic) organized a summer day camp. Its admission standards were not as demanding as our classes. They claimed they could handle anyone. The director urged me to send David, implying that my reluctance was an expression of overprotection. We agreed to give it a try; but some weeks later when I visited, I found David off by himself, doing the same things that he did in the play yard at home.

But meanwhile I was also caught up in the group strategy to obtain legislation which would admit the children in our classes to public school, with a program suited to their needs. I became chairperson of the state ARC Education Committee. We studied the state constitution (". . . a thorough and efficient system of public schools for the instruction of all the children in the state between the ages of 5 and eighteen years . . ." Art. VIII, Sec. IV, Par. 1) and the law (". . . courses of study suited to the age and attainments of all pupils . . ." N.J.R.S. 18:11). Exclusions were permitted for contagious disease or behavior dangerous to others, but there was nothing about excluding pupils based on their IQ. Here again was that invisibility—that denial of the existence of exceptions. Suffice it to say that our strategy worked. In 1954 the governor signed a mandatory special education law (N.J.R.S. 18:46), replacing the one enacted in 1911 (the first in the nation), which had been rendered inoperative by the school administrators. They had done so by labelling children with IQs below fifty as ineducable. Our use of the word *trainable* enabled us to accentuate the positive without getting into a confrontation on the issue of the three Rs. Our efforts were paralleled in other states.

A national movement was under way. By 1952 I was chairperson of the NARC Education Committee. In 1954 NARC published a policy statement recommended by the committee, which I quote in full:

> Every child, including every retarded child, is important and has the right to
> 1. opportunities for the fullest realization of his potentialities, however limited, for physical, mental, emotional, and spiritual growth;
> 2. affection and understanding from those responsible for his care and guidance during his years of dependence;
> 3. a program of education and training suited to his particular needs and carried forward in the environment most favorable for him, whether in the public schools, a residential center, or his own home;

Elizabeth M. Boggs

4. help, stimulation and guidance from skilled teachers, provided by his community and state as part of a broadly conceived program of free public education.

And his parents have the right to determine for themselves, on the basis of competent advice, the course of care, training, and treatment, among those open to them, which they believe best for their family, and to have their decisions respected by others, (NARC, 1954).

When I was president of NARC (1958–60) and Gunnar Dybwad was the executive, I suggested that we republish the preceding statement and give it a bit more play. When this did not happen and I asked why, I was shown a letter from the chairman of the Education Committee, who claimed that the statement was unrealistic, that the schools would not accept the most severely and profoundly retarded, and that we were jeopardizing our chances for the trainable by making such sweeping demands. Perhaps she was right; despite the burgeoning literature about schooling for the profoundly retarded and zero reject, I still perceive some invisible children. In fact, when the director of a recent federally funded project asked for nominations of innovative programs for the very severely and profoundly retarded, he had to reject about half of them as not dealing with what the project had in mind. Even NARC once sponsored a film in which a typical child with Down's syndrome was described as profoundly retarded. Anyway, Dr. Dybwad felt constrained to refrain from reissuing the 1954 policy.

The Institutionalization of Deinstitutionalization

Let me now skip, chronologically, to the present day. David is now thirty-two. He does not understand instructions, let alone any conversation which might enable him to anticipate what is going to happen. He has learned, however, to recognize a variety of situational clues. For example, certain observable activities precede mealtimes. The regularity of routine in daily living is therefore of considerably more significance to him than it would be were he able to receive oral or written alerts anticipating changes in that routine. He cooperates in the activities of daily living in which he is not entirely self-sufficient. It is thus important for him to be assisted by people who are well acquainted with his capabilities and his signals since he cannot tell them how to help him. Consistency by care givers and continuity of staffing are especially important for people whose disability includes the absence of communication skills. This is the best protection against "learned helplessness" (DeVellis, 1977).

David likes to eat, rock in a rocking chair, swing in a playground swing, ride in an automobile, and get into water, whether it be a shower or a swimming pool. There is a limit to the amount of time he or anyone else can spend in these activities, and therefore, I must assume that he is bored or tuned out a good deal of the time, especially in the winter.

At the 1977 American Association on Mental Deficiency convention Dr. Burton Blatt gave an exquisite illustrated talk on the current state of affairs in institutions as contrasted with the state of affairs ten years ago (Blatt, 1977). There has been considerable progress, but his final message was that the people in institutions are lonely. One got the impression that loneliness is a function of the institution and that people in the community are not lonely. Subsequently, I made some observations in the hotel lobby. All the seats were occupied, but with one or two exceptions, no one was talking to anyone else, and all of the people looked as solemn and as lonely as those in Dr. Blatt's film. There are a great many lonely people out in the community; many of them are in foster care, group homes, boarding homes, nursing homes, and even in families. I would be lonely myself if I did not have the motivation, skill, energy, and independence to seek out contact and communication with other human beings. I think I would be particularly lonely if I were assigned to live with a small group of people not of my own choosing.

David's group is not small, however. Most of the members of the group of men with whom he lives are more capable in one or another respect than he. Some can talk a little; others can take advantage of the craft instruction which is offered. David does not participate, not only because he does not have the manual dexterity, but because conceptually the product does not have meaning and the process is not pleasing. The more capable men may leave the cottage alone and move about the grounds of the institution on their own recognizance; David must be escorted. On his own he would soon be on the highway or in the woods. One of the more capable men has selected David for paternalistic attention. Charlie sees to it that David gets his own chair back when it has been usurped by another. Charlie's advocacy is both expressive and instrumental. David benefits, but he does not really reciprocate. Indeed, there are very few people for whom David reserves his own enigmatic but gleeful smile. One of these is a young woman who worked as a cottage training technician while putting herself through college. It is a mark of the improvement in our institutions that she was permitted to express a little favoritism towards him.

She is now raising her own son. Recently she visited David while he was in the local hospital following some surgery. As the two of us watched him together, she mused, "I often wonder what he is thinking about, how the world looks to him." That thought is too infrequently pondered. If he were his own architect, how would David design his environment?

There are some parents who like the idea of normalization (Wolfensberger, 1972) because it is useful in glossing over the realities of difference. I sometimes think there are professionals who like it for the same reason. Rather than trying to create a normal environment for my son, I try to think of how the world must look from his point of view and what kind of environment would not only minimize his boredom and loneliness but enhance his sense of dominance. When I try to put myself in his skin, I

Elizabeth M. Boggs

realize that David, like me, has an immediate environment—a home—where he sleeps, eats, and spends his leisure time with certain associates and an immediate external environment which is called the community. His home environment could be improved from his point of view by reducing the noise level of the daytime living space and the number of people using that space (i.e., subdividing the space appropriately) and by reducing the total number of people (staff and fellow residents) with whom he has some recurrent interaction over a staffing cycle, such as a month. However, this woud have to be done in such a way as to retain in his "family" those people he would most like to have with him, while at the same time increasing autonomy and reducing the risk of burnout for the care givers. (The particular residential facility in which he now resides still maintains an overly hierarchical, as distinct from collegial, pattern of organization of the direct care staff.) All this could be done equally well in any residential unit, whether on a campus or in the community.

But what of the community environment? The community surrounding David's home is the campus of the state school. It is an ergonomic community; that is, one which has been planned to suit the inhabitants. Its swimming pool is designed so that anyone can stand up in any part of it. There is a twenty-mile-an-hour speed limit on all its roads. Its doctors make house calls. Respite care is always available; that is, when the surrogate parent has an emergency, another one is available. There is a restaurant where no one stares at the sloppy eaters. Nobody there thinks that it is inappropriate for a thirty-two-year-old man to use a swing on the playground; it is not considered dehumanizing to let a man act like a child if he wants to. David is not restricted by any such environmental taboos.

From his point of view this community is more facilitative and more enhancing than the town half a mile down the road. There were times in the past when I deliberately escorted David into my community. Because he does not like to be in water where he cannot put his foot firmly on the bottom, the area of the community swimming pool actually available to him was very small. On the public beach he would trample the neighboring family's picnic because he wanted their banana. The nurses in the general hospital put him into an enclosed crib (normal for children) which was too short for him. Being integrated into the community means nothing to him. Perhaps we should consider ways of making the community more aware that people with his extreme problems exist and need special care and attention. But first, I think we have to persuade the armchair policy-making professionals of their very existence.

How can we describe their extraordinary need for an adaptive environment structured to their requirements rather than ours? We need some new terminology, it seems. In a recent large meeting a well-known superintendent who runs a facility in which there are residents like David remarked that they had recently placed a number of profoundly retarded adults in the community, and that when these profoundly retarded adults were asked whether they would like to return to the institution, they all said no. I am sure that the adults to whom he referred were successfully placed, and I do not doubt their capacity nor the lack of coercion in their response. However, if people who could make such a conceptual choice, who could understand the question and express an answer are called profoundly retarded, then we need some new term for those who cannot do any of these things.

Richard Willis (1973) did a time-sample study in the late sixties of the interactions of the men residing in a residence hall for the severely and profoundly retarded. These men were able to move about; a large number of behaviors were coded. Unexpectedly, Willis observed that the men seemed to fall into two groups: those who exhibited a variety of behaviors scattered over all segments of the range; and those who failed to exhibit a large but discrete cluster of behaviors, many of which hinged around the area of communication. Willis observed that the absent behaviors appeared to be those which psychologists generally ascribed to homo sapiens but not to other primates. He called this group of residents noncultural. For this honest observation he received at least one derogatory review.

In discussing normalization, Wolfensberger (1972) has emphasized that many norms are culturally determined. Normal behaviors and normal settings are therefore not absolutely meritorious. Even the rhythms of life may vary from one society to another. Since cultures are created by and for the convenience and comfort of the members of a particular society, it would appear that subcultures are not only permissible but, for some purposes at least, ought to be encouraged. Successful societies understand ergonomy; they fit the habitat to the inhabitants. If the inhabitants differ from one another, then so should the habitats and even the subcultures, ethnic or otherwise. In an era of divergent life styles, it seems particularly ironic that we place such stress on normalization for the retarded. Somehow the gap between public policy and private preferences seems great at times. Social reforms based on theoretical constructs are still pursued with the same missionary zeal as was the eugenics movement in times past.

I spend a great deal of time in Washington pondering the language of legislation and the rubrics of regulations. Most of the time I am working for *the* disabled, *the* retarded, the majority, but sometimes I try to relate what goes on there during the week with what I see when I bring David home on the weekend. Of all the things I have done to influence federal programs in the last twenty-two years, there are very few from which I can trace any improvements in my son's well-being, although there have been improvements. There is one exception. In 1969 I helped to initiate the sequence of activities which led to the Intermediate Care Facilities/Mental Retardation (ICF/MR) legislation in 1971, and thus eventually to the controversial ICF/MR regulations of 1977 (Note 1). It seems likely that within the next two or three years the facility where my son resides may become an ICF/MR.

Ironically enough, I do not anticipate that this will bring about the improvements which I believe would be most conducive to his well-being.

Elizabeth M. Boggs

The regulations do not take into account significant recent research findings by a number of investigators working in various settings on aspects of organizational structure and staff-resident interactions. (See, for example, Zigler and Balla, 1977; Raynes, 1977; Pratt et al., 1977; Moore et al., 1976; Wheeler, 1977.) The ICF/MR federal regulations deal with ratios of beds to rooms and staff to residents; although they may increase the direct care staff by a few additional positions, they will not change the way in which the staffing is organized or supervised. If the number of beds in David's bedroom is reduced from six to four, it will not make any difference to him. It will not change the layout of the day room or improve its acoustics (Gentry & Zimring, 1977). He will acquire an individual written habilitation plan. His case will be reviewed on paper somewhat more frequently, and this will raise the per capita cost, but little will change back at the cottage. Charlie will probably be classified as eligible for community placement in a group home, and he will leave. He will not have David to be concerned about. David will miss his defense against the more bossy residents, who will remain because their behavior will not be found acceptable in a group home.

Recently I was invited to give a talk at the NARC convention. I aired some of my concerns as a parent of a multiply handicapped, profoundly retarded adult son (Boggs, 1976). Nothing I have said or written in the past thirty years has occasioned such an outpouring of letters and comments by other parents. Some have adult children at home; others are parents of retarded persons who reside elsewhere. Several of these parents pointed out that they had spent many hours during the last ten or twenty years serving on local or state ARC boards, working for community services for children younger than their own, or working for legislation to aid the more numerous and more able retarded, while the different needs of their own profoundly handicapped sons or daughters received less insightful study and attention. As Tot Avis (see page 185) has pointed out, it is difficult for parents who have accommodated themselves (perhaps reluctantly) to one professional doctrine to reverse directions when an apparently new doctrine supercedes. The parents who wrote to me, however, are not defenders of the status quo, nor are they sheep. Emotionally, they would like to see the son or daughter they know so well miraculously exhibit the capacity to move like his or her siblings into a life of "freedom and participation," to quote Burt Blatt (1977).

But what is "freedom"? What is "participation"? Is it freedom to be placed in a group home? Is it freedom to be allowed to make by default a vital decision that has consequences foreseeable by others but not by the maker? Is it participation to work for a wage you do not earn on a job where your fellow workers are politely tolerant but quickly exhaust any common interests in conversation? Is it freedom to be forced to have and follow an individual habilitation plan?

These are questions to be addressed honestly by self-styled advocates for the retarded. But there is also the question of freedom and participation for their families. What parents are saying is "We are being ostracized, segregated, put down, for thinking unorthodox thoughts, for expressing the idea that an environment designed for normal people may not be the optimum for everyone."

In the early fifties, when NARC was very young, it still took courage for a parent to admit to having a retarded child, so great was the stigma. Although some professionals knew better, the public still thought that the child reflected some sinister bar on the family escutcheon, a streak of degeneracy (Note 2). One of the great contributions was made by Pearl Buck and Dale Evans Rogers, each of whom wrote books about their experiences as mothers of retarded children. If these celebrities admitted without shame to having retarded children, then so could lesser folk. Although not in that league, my husband and I both recognized in the mid-fifties that we could fend off the blows fatal to other more vulnerable parents by using those Ph.D. degrees as shield and buckler. But it required some stamina, even so, to uphold a minority position that retarded children can be helped. Twenty-five years later it still does, even though the majority view we challenge may be different. Now the shield and buckler is not a rather irrelevant doctorate, but a personal examination of the right of one individual to be different, and of one parent to differ — and to be heard.

NOTES

1. The term *intermediate care facility* was introduced in 1967 when Congress sought to define a level of institutional care less than skilled nursing care but more than room and board. In 1971 Congress permitted public institutions for the retarded meeting certain specific standards to be eligible for medicaid reimbursement under this rubric.

2. In the early part of the century, the great leaders in the field of mental retardation—Fernald, Tredgold, Goddard—perceived feeblemindedness as a discrete entity, but they also observed a more than chance coincidence in the same families with drunkenness and promiscuity. In the early fifties, it was customary to write off their observations as methodologically unsound. In the past five years we have discovered that there is indeed a fetal alcohol syndrome; some observers are also concerned that an increase in unmonitored teen-age pregnancies may once again make congenital syphilis a significant cause of mental retardation.

REFERENCES

Anderson, M.L. Curriculum for classes for defectives. In State of New Jersey Department of Public Instruction, *The teaching of children three years or more below the normal.* Trenton: State Gazette Publishing Co., 1918.

Bayley, M. *Mental handicap and community care—A study of mentally handicapped people in Sheffield.* London: Routledge & Kegan Paul, 1973.

Blatt, B. The family album. *Mental Retardation,* 1977, *15,* 3–4.

Boggs, E.M. A volunteer's story. *Mental Retardation News,* 1976, *25*(10), 4–5.

Elizabeth M. Boggs

Caplan, G. Patterns of parental response to the crisis of premature birth: A preliminary approach to modifying the mental-health outcome. *Psychiatry*, 1960, *23*, 365–374.

DeVellis, R.F. Learned helplessness in institutions. *Mental Retardation*, 1977, *15*, 10–13.

Gentry, D., & Zimring, C.M. Acoustics and noise affect speech discrimination. R.C. Knight, C.M. Zimring, W.H. Weitzer, & H.C. Wheeler (Eds.), In *Social development and normalised institutional settings—A research report*. Amherst, Mass.: University of Massachusetts, Institute for Man and Environment, 1977.

Haynes, U. *Review of the collaborative project—Monograph #6*. New York: United Cerebral Palsy Associations, 1977.

Maslach, C. Burned-out. *Human Behavior*, 1976, *5*, 16–22.

Moore, H., Butler, E.W., & Bjaanes, A. *Careprovider characteristics and utilization of community opportunities for mentally retarded clients*. Riverside, Calif.: Center for the Study of Community Perspectives, 1976.

National Association for Retarded Children. *The educator's viewpoint*. New York: NARC, 1954.

New Jersey. Constitution of the State of New Jersey, 1949, Article VIII, Section IV, Paragraph I.

New Jersey Revised Statutes, 1952. Title 18, Chapter 11 (now Chapter 33).

New Jersey Revised Statutes, 1955. Title 18, Chapter 46.

Pratt, M.W., Raynes, N.V., & Roses, S. Organizational characteristics and their relationship to the quality of care. In P. Mittler (Ed.), *Research to practice in mental retardation—Care and intervention* (Vol. I). Baltimore: University Park Press, 1977.

Raynes, N.V. How big is good? The case for cross-cutting ties. *Mental Retardation*, 1977, *15*, 53–54.

Wheeler, H.C. The direct care staff. In R.C. Knight, C.M. Zimring, W.H. Weitzer, & H.C. Wheeler (Eds.), *Social development and normalised institutional settings—A research report*. Amherst, Mass.: University of Massachusetts, Institute for Man and Environment, 1977.

Willis, R.H. *The institutionalized severely retarded*. Springfield, Ill.: Charles C. Thomas, 1973.

Wolfensberger, W. *The principle of normalization in human services*. Toronto: National Institute on Mental Retardation, 1972.

Zigler, E., & Balla, D. The social policy implications of a research program on the effects of institutionalization on retarded persons. In P. Mittler (Ed.), *Research to practice in mental retardation—Care and intervention* (Vol 1). Baltimore: University Park Press, 1977.

QUESTIONS TO CONSIDER

1. Elizabeth writes that she tries to think of how the world appears to David and the kind of environment that would minimize his boredom and loneliness and enhance his sense of dominance. From her description of David's characteristics, how do you think the world looks to him? What type of environment do you believe would minimize his boredom and loneliness and enhance his sense of dominance? Do you think his environment is likely to change in the future?

2. Trace the changes in disability ideologies and public policy caused by Elizabeth's advocacy activities over the years. What policy positions do you predict she will work to advance in the immediate future?

3. What has been the impact of the "institutionalization of deinstitutionalization" on David and Elizabeth? Do you think the future impact will be the same or different?

4. Consider Elizabeth's statement, "In an era of divergent life styles, it seems particularly ironic that we place such stress on normalization for the retarded." How will our current interpretations evolve into future realities for retarded people?

UPDATE:

Whose Head Is in the Clouds?

Elizabeth M. Boggs

Our editors have asked for an update after seven years—one-third of a generation—an update on our lives, child's and parent's, and an update on our thoughts and responses to changing themes in professional doctrine and lay enthusiasm.

Jay Turnbull, who was ten in 1977, is seventeen in 1984, a big difference in anyone's life. David Boggs, who was 32 in 1977, is not yet forty, not so spectacular a difference. His cousin, a Vietnam veteran a few months younger, has one more daughter, the same good job, the same attractive, steadfast, and capable wife, with whom he lives in the same house. To the casual observer, David's life appears to have stayed on course also. He still does not speak or understand spoken language; he still has almost the same self-help skills, although I am told that he is learning to brush his teeth "with manual prompting." His ambulation has deteriorated markedly although he still makes an effort to get around independently, on all fours if necessary. He still has occasional seizures despite modern medication.

But there have been other changes with subtle but significant effects. Late in 1977 the New Jersey Division of Mental Retardation (DMR) made a major decision to enter the ICF/MR program. The decision was based on a careful assessment of the financial and programmatic advantages to the state and its retarded citizens, and it entailed and extended negotiations by DMR with the commissioner of its Department of Human Services, the state Budget Bureau, the legislative leadership, the governor's office, the labor unions representing state employees, and representatives of the federal Health Care Financing Administration. Thereafter, a complex ten-year plan was put in place to enable about half the space in various residential facilities operated by the Division to qualify for medicaid reimbursement under the ICF/MR standards and to create an array of alternative living arrangements in the community for more than half of those persons projected to require care in 1987. The plan was based on several basic assumptions:

1. Then current federal ICF/MR standards, where realized in any of the state residential facilities, would advantage the residents assigned to certified units.

2. Many residents could benefit from community placement, provided care was exercised and resources developed on their behalf over a period of time. Their departure would permit new occupancy standards to be met in existing buildings after renovation.

3. Since most of the clients would qualify for supplemental security income (SSI) and medicaid coverage on the basis of income and disability, the necessary modifications and expansions in the community as well as in the institutions could be accomplished at no net cost to the state (at least for the first few years) if the federal medicaid reimbursement for persons in newly certified beds could be plowed back into the DMR system on a continuing basis, while maintaining the level of appropriations from the state tax base.

New Jersey thus profited by the experience of other states in which ICF/MR reimbursements earned by institutions were not channeled back to them but made their way into the state's general treasury. By placing all federal reimbursements into a state escrow account (known as the control account) dedicated to compliance, DMR enjoyed budget increases in a period when new state appropriations were hard to come by. From 1978 to 1983, 120 group homes were opened, housing 836 people with mental retardation. In 1983 some $12.5 million was committed to group-home operation from the control account. In addition, in 1983 the control account allotted $8.7 million toward the support of over two thousand adults in day programs. In 1984 the control account will be further augmented by medicaid funds earned under the community care waiver. The governor's budget for fiscal year 1985 includes $27 million for community services from the control account and state tax dollars. Between 1977 and 1984 the total population of public facilities declined by 25 percent, and community placements quadrupled. Recidivism has been low, and the majority of the parents of those who have left the state facilities are pleased but still a little uncertain about the future. Most of the people who have gone out have been ambulatory with some ability to communicate, even if not verbally.

In 1977 when the first edition of *Parents Speak Out* went to press, this plan was in the offing. Getting the process started required (1) upgrading staffing patterns at the state schools, (2) renovating the physical plants, and (3) developing the day and residential programs in the community to receive those institutional residents who would most profit from transfer. Reducing the institutional population to increase the space per resident was the strategy preferred to construction of new facilities.

Hunterdon State School (now called Hunterdon Developmental Center) was selected as the first to initiate these three complementary thrusts. The changes there were substantially completed by the summer of 1982 and

Elizabeth M. Boggs

involved a 34 percent reduction in population, resulting in a typical cottage population decline from 56 to 32. As of late 1983 David has had six annual team meetings to formulate or revise his individual habilitation plan (IHP). The direct care worker most responsible for David's daily program participates in these meetings, as do I. About half the members of this team, including the individual program coordinator and a needed physical therapist, have been hired with control account funds. As a result of the renovations David now indeed does sleep in a four-bed room, and the vast areas of the day room have been subdivided (with some improvement in the acoustics) to accommodate the smaller groups now formed for the more active and diversified daily programs. Off-grounds excursions have increased.

Depopulation has indeed meant that Charlie is gone, not all the way to the community, but to a new geriatric center programmed for senior citizens who are retarded, including those with heart problems such as his. It has also meant a major reassignment of most remaining residents, including David, to different cottages with different social as well as physical environments. His is less competitive but not less stimulating. As all of this has been happening, the basic advantages to David of the congregate community have become more clear than they were in 1977.

In short, contrary to my earlier forecast, the application of ICF/MR standards at Hunterdon Developmental Center has made a very significant difference for David as well as others. There is more to do; he gets more individual attention; although I'm sure he misses Charlie, he has less need for protection from other residents; he appears less lonely. Despite staff turnover the IHP process has steadily improved as the clinicians and direct care givers gain experience in working with each other and with me as a member of the team. As a result his program seems to me increasingly relevant; David is still happy to go out with me and just as happy to return.

Again, however, I find a great disparity between the realities of what David enjoys and seems to profit from and the ideologies that the professional avant-garde in the universities promote. I still feel that the current paradigms of normalization and least-restriction are inappropriate as applied to the most profoundly retarded. I have always favored small groupings with interactive staff (with low turnover), but I do not see that dispersing these small groups in far-flung residential neighborhoods creates integration or promotes socialization for people with David's severe limitations. In fact, what I observe is quite the contrary. Profoundly retarded people can be very lonely in group homes, even good ones, and they are not all good. Moreover, as a person whose arthritis makes long trips by car less than comfortable, I am appalled to see people who are profoundly retarded and have contractures which prevent their sitting erect being transported by bus for two or even three hours a day to and from their day program. This is not yet happening in New Jersey, but it is being hailed as the way to go in "more advanced" states.

As for least-restriction, I am certainly in favor of self-advocacy for many people who have been denied this opportunity in the past, but much of our current rhetoric simply denies the existence of persons whose message is, at best, muffled. How can we know what they prefer? Why must we impose on them our own standards of what is appropriate? How can we understand what gives them a sense of autonomy? Given the many natural limitations of their conditions (such as inability to move independently or to convey their thoughts), what restrictions do they perceive as being unnecessarily imposed by us? I try to be receptive to David's views in these matters.

I am thoroughly convinced that a degree of autonomy appropriate to one's capacities is necessary to the mental health of each of us, not least to David. That is why I persist in trying to keep David as mobile as possible since confinement to a wheelchair, which he could not operate at will, would mean significantly greater restriction for him. That is also why I try to take note of his favorite foods and defend his right to retain something viewed by others as a toy.

I owe to Penelope Brooks of the Kennedy Center at Peabody College a fuller understanding of the meaning of "having choices," and especially of "feeling that one has choices," and of the importance of choices to development in childhood and good mental health in old age and before. She brought to my attention relevant research findings and sharpened my perceptions. In order to be enjoyable and beneficial, choices must present a range of opportunities, even challenges, which are neither too easy or trivial nor too difficult or overwhelming. Both success and failure must be possible (and experienced), but reducing the probability of a fatal or devastating outcome is a legitimate societal concern. Not all risk has dignity. These matters are discussed briefly in the American Association on Mental Deficiency monograph on least-restriction, on which both Penny and I worked hard (Turnbull, 1981).

The range of growth-promoting comfortable choices which enhance one's sense of automony, one's "internal locus of control," is different for different people and for the same people at different stages. It is related to capacity. Having the right kind of options and learning to exercise them increases that capacity incrementally, but being presented with choices one does not understand (being asked to sign on the dotted line, for example) erodes the capacity. All of us are occasionally confronted with choices which we find oppressive; they make informed consent a double-edged privilege. When most of our choices fall in this difficult category, the effect can be debilitating. As for trivial choices, most us retain them and enjoy falling back now and then on such a risk-free choice as that between vanilla and strawberry. Others which we find tedious we learn to routinize by developing habits. The breakfast menu is a case in point. But for some people such choices are not tedious, and making them afresh each day may be exhilarating.

Making sure that each retarded person has opportunities to make choices for himself and to take care of himself within an appropriate range is one important way of respecting basic rights. The importance of small considerations in David's life may be illustrated by tracking his rubber duck. Where others finger a cigarette, or knit, or play with worry beads, David has for many years preferred to hold and squeeze a rubber duck. His preference for a duck is unmistakable. A frog cannot be substituted. He does not perceive this as childish, nor does he recognize the duck shape as such.

Shortly after the first ICF/MR survey, David's rubber duck disappeared. On inquiring, I was advised that the duck was not "age appropriate." When I questioned the use of age appropriateness in his case," I was advised that the decision could be reversed if there were a programmatic purpose to be served by the object or apparatus. For instance, holding a tambourine during music therapy was approved. As it turned out, a programmatic purpose for the duck was soon discovered by the direct care staff, who observed that, in the absence of the duck, David found other things to do with his hands such as untying his shoes. The duck, or rather a replacement, reappeared. Now the psychologist has incorporated the duck into the behavior management program. The duck is removed while David addresses a task, such as hand washing, and is returned to him on completion of the task. I doubt that anything other than cantaloupe or butterscotch pudding would motivate him more.

Now that David senses that his autonomy in the matter of the duck is being respected, his behavior has changed in subtle ways. Recently when David was driving with me, he quite unexpectedly extended his hand, holding the duck out to me. I, in turn, put out my upturned palm; he dropped the duck into my hand, then quickly retrieved it. This social behavior, giving and retrieving, is quite characteristic of infants of David's mental age (under one year), but I had never seen him do it before. It was a gesture of confidence that his property rights would be respected.

Of course, there are other matters which are outside his range of decision making and/or communication. It is up to me as his guardian to make any weighty choices. Those who discuss the ethics of surrogate decisions distinguish among various criteria for making a choice on behalf of another person. The best-interests test is the most familiar. What-would-I-do-in-this-situation is clearly less appropriate, especially in a case where he and I are so different. Even the reasonable-man test has to be used with discretion. Each of us has the right to be a little unreasonable at times, even if it means not always acting our age. The test I prefer, although it is the hardest to apply, is the shoes test. What would he do, standing in his own shoes (which, in David's case, means being profoundly retarded), if he could understand for the brief period of decision making the consequences for him, *as he is*. This paradoxical model requires an effort of imagination and is hard for most people to act on, but it has been the basis for several important judicial decisions. To act, using this test, one has to know the individual personally and be prepared to act unconventionally if need be. Robert Edgerton and his colleagues (1984) have spent many years sharing the lives of people who are retarded, both those who can speak a little and those who cannot. They remain humble about our ability to comprehend how it feels to be severely or profoundly retarded. Likewise, even the most empathetic professionals, who are not themselves parents of handicapped children, are discovering that they do not really *know* what it is like to live intimately with a person who is profoundly retarded.

When important decisions must be made for such a person by a surrogate, the availability of options is especially important. If choice has any meaning, there must indeed be alternatives— alternative lifestyles and living arrangements, alternative ways of spending time, alternative means of support, and even alternative ways of arriving at important decisions— not just for people who are retarded but for all of us.

It has been recognized that the right to treatment is not a true right unless it can be exercised freely, and unless there is also a right to refuse treatment. A mandated duty, whether it be a duty to vote or to drive on the right side of the road or to associate with persons not of one's own choosing or to accept treatment, is not a right. Such duties may legitimately be mandated in the interest of maintaining the rights of others, but such obligations do not contain the essential element of choice.

Forced segregation or quarantines, except for individuals who have been duly determined to constitute a danger to self or others, is now clearly established as unconstitutional. Forced segregation of people who are retarded was abolished in New Jersey in 1966. This is not to say that retarded people or their families suddenly acquired real choices just by virtue of that repeal. The opposite of forced segregation is not forced integration, but rather equal access—having the choice to associate or not to associate, to live here or to live there. The right to live in a community is not a true right unless it is accompanied by the right to choose whether and where to live in that community and with whom, or to live somewhere else—in a monastery, for example. Indeed, the right to freedom of association certainly includes the right to join or form intentional communities such as retirement villages or college campuses, where rational selectivity is acceptable.

As David's surrogate decision maker in matters of this kind, I believe I should have similar options to exercise on his behalf. There will always be limitations of resources, but I find it troubling that many leading professionals as well as some parents wish to constrict those choices deliberately, allegedly in the interests of all retarded people including David, whom they have never met. They wish to limit his choice of living arrangements to some stereotype which they will prescribe, to an arbitrary family size, for example. They seek to integrate by mandating that any such housing be isolated from any other residence having a similar purpose. A comparable prohibition, applied normally, might prevent an Italian family from moving next door to another Italian family. We are rapidly substituting a new set of restrictive rules for the old set that we have just repudiated on behalf of people who are retarded. These new rules are based on generalized stereotypes about what is good for people, rather than on true respect for individual differences.

I have contributed my share to the current rhetoric on rights and theoretical models of delivery systems. Like dwellers in the groves of academe, I don't have to go out and "do it" each day; however, I remain wary. In a recent article Bogdan, Biklen, Blatt, and Taylor (1981) of Syracuse University provide a challenging analogy between the present status of persons who are developmentally disabled and the status of former slaves in the post-Civil War era. They see recent judicial pronouncements as affecting the handicapped much as the Emancipation Proclamation affected slaves.

> After the Emancipation Proclamation, we passed the time of questioning whether or not people should be held in the bonds of slavery (except penal slavery) even if they chose to live under those conditions. The law of the land was absolute despite the indefinite hardships that the newly freed and the never enslaved had to endure. (p. 236)

When I think of David, I do not find this analogy very reassuring. It is now over 100 years since the Emancipation Proclamation, and the present status of those who would otherwise have been born into slavery in this century is still ambiguous. The "indefinite hardships that the newly freed and the never enslaved had to endure" turned out to be severe, indeed, especially for the former slaves, and were not limited to their lifetimes, as *Roots* so graphically documented. Proclamations are not enough. Moreover, history can repeat itself. The nineteenth century carpetbaggers did many former slaves great disservice; now modern carpetbaggers are moving in on the newly freed of the twentieth century. Who will pay the personal and social price for reconstruction this time, and how many decades will it take? What will be the status in another hundred years of the successors of those freed in this century?

Douglas Biklen once remarked with conviction that those who happen to be mentally retarded today have a right not to be made the subjects of our social experiments. Is their right being respected? As David's guardian I am not legally permitted to give my informed consent for him to participate as a human subject in any social or other scientific experiment unless it can be shown that he is likely to benefit personally. Nevertheless, I foresee that he is likely to be such a subject without my consent or his.

To put the normalization principle into a class with the Emancipation Proclamation is to canonize a concept that was very useful ten years ago in combating certain negative notions about people who were retarded, but one that now perpetuates those very notions by protesting too much. As Angela Novak (1980) puts it, "the focus of normalization is minimizing the projection of deviancy by an individual, . . . rather than changing the process of what is valued and what is devalued" (p. 206). Wolfensberger (1983) himself has recently responded to such concerns by substituting the phrase "social role valorization" for normalization. The more things change . . .

Freedom de jure is not freedom de facto, and the Syracuseans do suggest that new concepts are not self-executing. They do not propose to let the political forces take their natural course this time around. They propose to guide the conversion through research based on "the new paradigm."

> Deinstitutionalization has come to be thought of as a goal and a process that simply designates getting people out of institutions. Such usage of the term is a distortion of the new paradigm signified by the terms "least restrictive alternatives" and "normalization." The goal of deinstitutionalization is not simply to move people out of one setting and into another but to transform a dehumanizing system of service delivery. The existing principles of exclusion, segregation, and labeling should be changed to a zero-reject, integrated, noncategorical, community-based system. The problems surrounding that change and the barriers to it should be the central thrust of any research endeavor. (Blatt et al., 1977)

Perhaps there are a few things wrong with our assumptions; perhaps they are part of the problem; perhaps we should apply a researcher's skepticism to the hypothesis that so-called principles such as integration, social role valorization, and noncategorical systems are not to be challenged or at least more creatively and sensitively interpreted.

> Research concerning the movement toward community programs should be conceptualized in the context of the conversion of a system. Thus, the transformation of a society rather than the deinstitutionalization of individuals should be studied. (Bogdan et al., 1981, p. 237)

Increasingly, there are other voices now calling for a transformation of society, a never-ending need. But as Blatt and his colleagues tacitly admit, we do not yet really know how to do it; moreover, no one is going to wait for more research. So a transformation of sorts will take place anyway. Would that it could be orderly, and would that its paradigm could be more enduring than a universal application of the already dated and sometimes dehumanizing notions of normalization and least-restriction, so often erroneously equated with integration.

REFERENCES

Bercovici, S.M. *Barriers to normalization—The restrictive management of retarded persons.* Baltimore: University Park Press, 1983.

Blatt, B., Bogdan, R., Biklen, D., & Taylor, S. From institution to community: A conversion model. In E. Sontag, *Educational programming for the severely and profoundly handicapped.* Reston, Va.: The Council for Exceptional Children, 1977.

Bogdan, R., Biklen, R., Blatt, B., & Taylor, S.J. Handicap prejudice and social science research. In H.C. Haywood, and J.R. Newbrough (Eds.), *Living environments for developmentally retarded persons*. Baltimore: University Park Press, 1981.

Edgerton, R.B. (Ed.). *Lives in progress:* Mildly retarded adults in a large city. Washington, D.C., American Association on Mental Deficiency, 1984.

Novak, A. & Heal, L.W. (Eds.). *Integration of developmentally disabled individuals into the community*. Baltimore: Paul H. Brookes, 1980.

Turnbull, H.R., III (Ed.). *The least restrictive alternative: Principles and practices*. Washington, D.C., American Association on Mental Deficiency, 1981.

Wolfensberger, W. Social role valorization: A proposed new term for the principle of normalization. *Mental Retardation*, 1983, *21*, 234–239.

QUESTIONS TO CONSIDER

1. Review the questions on page 80. How accurate were your predictions? predictions?

2. How does Elizabeth operationalize the concept of choice for David? Take the shoes test on David's behalf. Describe the lifestyle you think he prefers. Is it consistent with his present lifestyle? Is it achievable in the future?

3. Do you know anyone who is handicapped in the way and to the degree that David is? Do you think we have enough empirical knowledge to design social environments that would be most enhancing for persons with such disabilities? If you were authorized to make decisions for David and were asked to give consent to his participation in a social experiment, what criteria would you expect to be met in order to protect David's rights?

Leah Ziskin, a public health physician, was the director of Parental Child Health Services in the New Jersey Department of Public Health in 1978. In that capacity she was in charge of planning and organizing programs to prevent mentally and physically handicapping conditions and to serve handicapped children.

Since then she has become the assistant commissioner of Community Health Services in the state Department of Health. As such she administers federal and state programs in the areas of maternal and child health (including handicapped children), chronic diseases, emergency medical services, and consumer health. She is a fellow of the American College of Preventive Medicine and has published in the maternal and child health fields.

Her sixteen-year-old daughter, Jennie, is severely mentally retarded, ambulatory, and nonverbal.

Leah and Jennie Ziskin

The Story of Jennie

Leah Ziskin

Jennie is our third child. She was planned and very much wanted. I had taken care to practice personal preventive medicine before my husband and I decided to have Jennie. I was thirty years old, visited an obstetrician, and was told that I was in good physical condition to have a baby. I was concerned because my husband and I had known ABO incompatibility, and we were also Rh incompatible, I being Rh negative. Our first son did not have any problems; however, our second son had jaundice related to our ABO incompatibility. I also checked with a pediatrician at the hospital where I would deliver, and he assured me that the hospital was equipped to handle a hematological problem which any infant of ours was likely to have. Having checked out my health and potential known problems of our infant, we very happily proceeded to have our third child.

My husband, a physician with a master's degree in biomedical engineering, was working on an Air Force base in audiologic research. I was a physician working in the occupational health division of the base. My duties included examining airmen coming back to work following sick leave, handling on-the-job emergencies, and examining dependents who were staying on the base. I was also becoming involved in true occupational health problems related to workers on the base. I worked from 8:00 A.M. till noon, at which time I went home and cared for my two sons, who were three and one and a half years of age. I was involved with the neighborhood where we lived because we were away from our family; so I felt more like mother and homemaker than I have at any other period in my life.

I remember being acutely aware when I knew that I was pregnant that much of a homemaker's exposure to infectious disease comes through her children. She is directly and intimately exposed to her own children and to other children coming to her home who may have infectious diseases. She may be caught in the secondary spread of diseases which her children pick up in nursery schools or day-care centers. She is directly exposed to infectious disease in supermarkets, on public transportation, in department stores, and in theaters. My own anecdotal view of the situation was that a home-maker who is probably thought not to be at much risk, compared to those in occupations such as, a nurse and teachers, from an infectious disease standpoint had every reason to be concerned; and the medical profession had every reason to be concerned about the homemaker.

Nevertheless, my pregnancy would be considered uneventful; I felt very well, and I remember thinking that this baby must be all right because I did feel so well. My life was not overly stressful because of my limited professional hours and my complete satisfaction at being with my two children without being pulled from them by professional responsibilities. I therefore looked forward very much to the birth of our third child.

The baby was delivered without difficulty. I was awake, and the obste-trician told me that although the baby was small, she looked healthy. The pediatrician would watch her very closely, but the medical staff were not overly concerned. Her weight was five pounds eight ounces, a pound smaller than my two previous children. The one very disconcerting fact the obstetri-cian told me, without alarm, was that the placenta was small although he did not elaborate on any details. Jennie was small but appeared normal to my professional and maternal eyes.

Within a few weeks after Jennie was born, we were scheduled to leave Ohio and the Air Force behind us and return to our home and families in New Jersey. Jennie had a stormy course those first few weeks of her life. She had severe respiratory-tract infections, to the degree that early one morning I insisted that my husband drive us to the base hospital because I was afraid Jennie might need a tracheotomy in order to breathe. In retrospect, a great deal of her problem may have been due to small air passageways. But at that time we did not suspect and the physicians were not cognizant of any unusual congenital difficulties. She recovered without a tracheotomy, and we were able to move the family back to what we considered our permanent civilian home.

Once we were settled and unpacked, I began to be increasingly con-cerned with my new infant. She just wasn't as active as my previous two children. She was not smiling as early as I would have liked. She just wasn't right. I measured her and was concerned at her head size. I took out my textbooks and studied tables of growth and development. When it became obvious that Jennie's head size was below that expected for a baby of her chronologic age, I tried to console myself that it was because her birth weight was low. I started making my own ratios of head size to birth weight and head size to length, which were statistics I could not find in any pediatric growth and development tables. I also excused her slower rate of development as a slow recovery from the respiratory syndromes which she had had.

I took Jennie to a pediatrician when she was eight weeks of age. He was a friend of mine, and I distinctly remember saying that I was greatly concerned that Jennie was microcephalic. The pediatrician examined Jennie in a routine fashion—including measurement of her head, her chest, and her length,—looked up at me, and said, "Gee, Leah, you really don't have anything to worry about." This somewhat offhanded reassurance made me feel better for two or three days, after which time all my own inner doubts and fears returned.

Every day I looked for Jennie to smile a little, to start turning, to squirm more in her crib. She was fussy, she was colicky, she had trouble moving her bowels, but all these things I could overlook. I was deeply distressed, however, because what I was expecting to see as developmental landmarks was not appearing.

At this time I was also job hunting. I finally decided that I would work in the city of Camden in public health clinics. At these clinics I worked examining children, giving immunizations, giving advice and recommendations to mothers of preschool children. Every time I went to a clinic, I would look at these poor, mostly healthy babies and other preschool children, and I would compare them to my newborn daughter. I would pick up a bouncing baby two to three months of age and would be so acutely aware of the deficiencies of my daughter's development that it was hard not to think of my deep personal concern. I kept thinking that at home I had a baby who would be offered nutritious food, who would be adequately clothed, who would have a room and a crib of her own, who would have prompt medical attention when she needed it. Here I was looking at babies whose mothers had love for their infants but had to struggle to provide clean baby shirts, formulas, cereal, and solid foods. I would rush home from clinic sessions and examine Jennie, again looking for signs of development which would somehow assure me that Jennie was as healthy as the lovely babies I had just examined. I was always disappointed. I finally called another pediatrician with whom my husband and I had gone to medical school, described my fears, and ended with "What should I do?"

This friend recommended that I take Jennie to the pediatric neurologist at one of the children's hospitals in Philadelphia. I knew this neurologist and saw him shortly thereafter. He examined Jennie very thoroughly and, when he finished the exam, looked at me and said, "We may have a problem." At that point all my hidden fears of the past few months were realized. Even though he had put it in the realm of probability, for me he was validating all the nightmares and the fears I had tried in vain to believe were imaginary. It was the start of the year and a half that I refer to as my grief period.

The laboratory tests which the neurologist ordered were not extensive. Taking Jennie for the tests, however, I viewed for one of the first times since her birth other abnormal children in a group, and I kept thinking, "Jennie is not like them. Jennie does not belong here." But I knew or sensed that Jennie was like them and that she did belong there. The tests and the neurologist concluded that Jennie was microcephalic. The tests, however, did not delineate any causes.

It was a difficult period of time then to tell family and friends that our lovely daughter was not normal and could never be expected to be. What was extremely difficult was explaining that we did not know the extent of the abnormality and that even the specialists to whom we took Jennie would not predict the extent of her abnormality or what deficiencies we could expect. I, therefore, taught myself to expect the worse. I imagined that she might live in a crib, that she might be completely dependent. I thought back to severely retarded and abnormal children I had taken care of during my internship and at other times, and I had nightmares of what my child would be.

The worst statement for me was "Don't worry, dear, everything's going to be fine." It took every ounce of will power and every lesson in tact that I had ever learned to contain myself and not shout back that I had reason to worry and that things were not going to be fine.

During this period I went back over my pregnancy. I mentally reviewed what I had done, persons I had been in contact with, what types of exposure I had possibly had to things that could not be tested for. I tried to calculate how much radiation I might have been exposed to. We had bought a large order of meat from a supermarket, and I theorized that the meat might have had preservatives which might have affected my child. I had used cyclamates which had not been removed from markets at that time, and I thought these might be the cause of my child's abnormality. None of my theories could be proven, and I was enough of a scientist to know that I was just torturing myself.

I reminded myself that I had taken great care in being prepared for this child, and I then tried to blame my husband in some way. My husband let me do this for a very limited period and then smartly reminded me that we were in this together and that it was no more his fault than it was mine and that he was not going to carry the blame or the guilt any more than I should.

In an attempt to get me away from my problem, my husband took me along on a convention trip to Toronto. On that long drive through the mountains of New York State and Canada, I remember feeling that I had become a completely different person. I felt that my ego had been wiped out. My superego with all its guilts had become the most prominent part of my personality, and I had completely lost my self-esteem. Any credits of self-worth that I could give myself from any of my personal endeavors meant nothing. Graduating from college and a first-rate medical school, surviving an internship, practicing medicine, and having two beautiful sons and a good marriage counted for nil. All I knew at this point was that I was the mother of an abnormal and most likely retarded child.

It took about a year until I came home from working in a clinic and said to my husband, "Today I had a problem that was greater than Jennie." My very wise husband said, "That must mean you're getting better." It did mean that I was getting better, but it took a few more very painful months, and easily another two years, until I believed again that I was more than the mother of a retarded child. I decided that I did not want the major distinction of my life to be the fact that I was the mother of a retarded child. I finally was able to pick up the pieces of my life and proceed.

Once I knew Jennie was retarded, I actually resisted going to organizations or other people for help. I don't know why I felt this way. I did think that they might not understand my particular situation or I would not feel comfortable in a group. Perhaps some of these feelings resulted from my being accustomed to giving advice in a professional capacity and much less accustomed to receiving counseling. Thus, although I knew organizations existed, I refrained from joining them.

When Jennie was about fourteen months old, I attended a pediatric seminar at a local hospital. On the program was an internist who described a school for trainable retarded children. He came to this pediatric meeting not only to make physicians in the locale aware of this resource but also to look for physician volunteers to participate in a school health program. I took this opportunity to introduce myself to the speaker and volunteered to participate in the school health program. I then mentioned that I had a child who had a problem and asked for more information about the preschool program he had briefly described. The doctor was perceptive and proceeded to tell me that he was involved because he and his wife also had a retarded child. The school helped both Jennie and me greatly. It had one of the few infant stimulation programs in our area, and it was held on Saturday mornings, which made it possible for Jennie and me to attend. While volunteers from local high schools, colleges, and the community worked with the children, the parents met separately. We heard lectures on various topics related to retarded children. Some of the topics concerned genetics, feeding practices, and delayed growth and development. Some of the parents had special concerns or looked into the latest medical literature. One of the theories of the time was that high doses of vitamin B_6, pyrodoxine, were very beneficial to children with Down's syndrome.

The school was run by an extremely dynamic priest and a core of brothers, all from Ireland. Their brogue was delightful and their spirit, comforting. We all hoped our children would learn to speak with Irish accents.

The group attending the school was largely Catholic; however, there was no attempt to limit any of the activities of the school to one religious sect. However, the general philosophy of this school was Catholic. I learned that our children were special, that God granted special strength and had special concern for these children and their families. I thought this was a beautiful philosophy that was comforting to many people, although I did not feel I should be chosen for any special strength. I looked for similar philosophies in other religions but did not find it as clearly defined.

About this time I recalled that Pearl Buck had had a retarded child and that she had written a book about her own experiences. I found her book,

The Child Who Never Grew, and read it. What impressed me was that it took her so long to accept the fact that her child was retarded and that she had consulted physicians throughout the world in an attempt to find a diagnosis that she could accept. I had to compare my own experiences with Pearl Buck's because many of our family and friends had questioned my husband and me about why we hadn't sought more medical opinions. Why hadn't we gone to New York, Boston, Texas, California, or the Mayo Clinic to seek a more favorable prognosis for our child or to seek the best possible care or treatment to improve what she might be? The only way that I can explain why we did not seek multiple consultations regarding Jennie's diagnosis was that we actually perceived something was wrong with our child. We then sought a reputable medical facility and reputable physicians highly qualified or specialized in this field. We tried very hard to listen to what they said and to understand what they told us. I truly believe that the physician we did consult could not tell us exactly what was in store for us or how Jennie's life was going to be because he did not know. I can understand that professionals do not know and, that very often parents think that professionals are trying to hide things from them when, in all honesty even the most knowledgeable professionals cannot give clear-cut, well-defined answers. I personally feel now, although I did not at the time, that parents will have to see their own child evolve to appreciate his unique growth and development.

There are many schools of thought concerning intensive therapies, many of which are done in the home. Our philosophy was that we wanted our home to remain a home. We had two other normal children to consider, and these children did not deserve to have their home and their world revolve around another child who was different. We thus consciously elected that nothing special, that no elaborate therapies be done in our home. We also consciously elected to put the needs of our two normal children first. We felt that their potential in life warranted more of our time and more of our effort. I realize that all families with retarded children or children with special problems cannot make this decision as easily as we could or as consciously as we did. We were aided in making this decision and by highly qualified and specialized professionals who told us that if we provided a stimulating environment for Jennie and if we gave her love, care, and consideration, she would grow and develop at her pace and reach her potential. Therefore, our conscious decision was perhaps easier. We wanted to believe what the professionals told us.

There was a time when I was haunted: if Jennie was to be dependent all her life and eventually might have to be put into an institution, why was I waiting for this time? Why was I allowing myself to grow to love her, to care for her? Why shouldn't I give her up now before these ties of love developed? A very dear psychologist who tested Jennie finally helped me resolve these questions. She explained to me that she thought our home environment gave Jennie a sense of well-being. She could also learn social

Leah Ziskin

skills there which would serve her well throughout her life, whether she remained with us or eventually had to be cared for outside our home. This psychologist explained to me that children who were ambulatory, who could eat by themselves, who were toilet-trained, or who could dress themselves probably received better care and more attention than children who could not do these things if they ever had to be cared for in an institution. The fact that Jennie knew how to smile and knew how to love other people would serve her very well in any situation. This way of thinking about what we were doing for Jennie would thus be very valuable preparation for her graduation from home. It gave me a better outlook and made me think that her staying at home was meaningful to her total development.

Jennie has learned to walk. She started walking when she was four years old, and it was more than just her own accomplishment. The school helped, her brothers helped, our housekeepers helped. Jennie climbs stairs, eats with silverware, sits at the table with us, and drinks by herself. Jennie is now nine, and we hope her next major achievement will be that she gets toilet-trained. In return for our efforts, Jennie gives us love and a sense of patience. She makes us see that all people do not learn or progress at the same rapid rate. She makes us appreciate the gift of speech, the gift of communication. She makes us marvel that she communicates with us in her own way—by going to the drawer where the cookies are, by going to the refrigerator when she wants a drink, by perking up when she sees her coat.

Our life style is different because of Jennie. I felt that I had a problem that I had accepted to the degree that I was not paralyzed or impeded by it. The days of getting up in the morning and wishing that she were not there were gone. I had become aware of sudden infant death syndrome—when infants with no prior illness are found dead in their cribs and autopsies reveal no definitive cause of death—and I almost wanted to experience it as a mother. I wished it would happen to my child. After I realized that it was not going to happen, that every morning when I woke up and went into Jennie's bedroom she was going to be there alive, I realized that the family and I would have to compensate and compromise and learn to live with Jennie. It didn't turn out as badly as I thought it would in those early days. We were able to have outside help because both my husband and I worked. The outside help proved to be beneficial because I could return to my profession without worrying about my normal sons and my abnormal daughter during the day.

I think that Jennie influenced my decisions to go back to school and specialize in public health because I was more aware that people with special problems needed support from government-sponsored programs. The problem need not be just that of a retarded child. Poverty, the lack of accessible health care, and inadequate housing were problems that I felt I wanted to help alleviate. Public programs have certainly benefited Jennie. She/ now attends a state-sponsored day training center. She is picked up about nine in the morning and brought back about four in the afternoon in a mini-bus. At her school she is taught social skills that we help her carry through at home. She is taught to improve her walking and table manners; she is also being toilet-trained. She is taught sit-ups, tumbling, and other exercises. It is a great thrill to me that when she is absent for a period of several weeks because of an especially resistant cold, I get a note that Jennie is missed at school. She gets report cards which are funny because they so often mirror her behavior at home.

We have had to adapt our lives because of Jennie. We have rationalized that these adaptations are good for the family and that we are happy with them; we don't even think we have made them because of Jennie. One example that comes to mind is our acquisition of a cabin or summer house as we call it. Our favorite vacations used to be finding a cabin in a wooded area away from civilization. It was always difficult to take Jennie because we had to cart cribs and other paraphernalia, not knowing what we would find wherever we settled ourselves. We therefore decided that it would be much easier for us if we had our own cabin already stocked with the equipment we all wanted. After diligent searching, we found a cabin in a woods an hour from our home. It is now one of the main forces that keeps us a united family and is a great source of inspiration and joy to all of us. In a sense, we have to thank Jennie for making it more difficult to travel and for prompting us to find our own cabin.

Jennie's brothers requested that I include their thoughts.

My name is Daniel. I'm twelve years old, and we live in a nice neighborhood in a fairly large house. I think Jennie knows our house and recognizes things in it. She has a great capacity for associating things with activities. For instance, if she sees somebody get a coat from a closet, she will know that they are leaving the house. If she sees me, she starts giggling because she knows that I like to tickle her and play with her. If she sees different bottles, she'll reach for one beside the other even if I switch the bottles around. I think Jennie is very cheerful most of the time, except at night she is sometimes cranky.

My name is Alan. I am ten years old. I am very impressed and proud of my sister's accomplishments in walking, going up and down the stairs, eating at the table with the rest of the family, and especially understanding simple commands. You can also tell her feelings by her expressions. For instance, if someone puts his coat on to go outside and leaves without taking her, she gets very upset. Also, you can tell if she likes some foods or if she doesn't like them by her expressions—if she spits it out, you know she doesn't like it!

QUESTIONS TO CONSIDER

1. What are the values (or philosophy) of Leah and her husband in relation to Jennie's role in the family? How have these values influenced family priorities? Do you think their values will stay the same or change in the future?

2. What have been Jennie's positive contributions to her family? How do you think her mother, father, and brothers will benefit from these contributions? What do you think Jennie's future contributions might be to her family?

3. What types of adaptations has the Ziskin family made to accommodate Jennie's special needs? Do you think they will make the same or different adaptations in the future?

UPDATE:
Transition— From Home to Residential Care

Leah Ziskin

I wish to share my philosophy concerning the transition period between the times when our daughter, Jennie, lived at home and when we placed her in a residential care facility. I write specifically for those families that feel it best, for whatever reason, not to keep their child at home; they must know that others have made this choice and have made it with a good conscience.

As a profoundly retarded child grows older and her demands upon the family change, it is necessary for the family to rethink its attitude and to plan for the near, if not the distant, future. When Jennie was chronologically between six and ten years of age, we found that we were seeking out ways of coping and meeting her physical needs, working out legal and financial plans for the future, and considering long-term placement.

As Jennie grew older and bigger, it became increasingly more difficult for her care givers to bathe, dress, toilet, and generally take care of her at home. In addition, because she was more active (and we encouraged her activity), she could also get into more things around the house, thus increasing her potential for harm. One Sunday morning, for example, I set out on the table three Styrofoam cups, two of which were to be filled with cocoa for Jennie's brothers; the remaining one was filled with hot coffee for Jennie's dad. In the short time that it took to carry the cocoa from the kitchen counter to the table, Jennie (who was then nine) had pulled the cup of coffee down on herself. The hot coffee soaked through her shirt and burned her chest. Most of her skin suffered first-degree burns and healed rapidly. But one area, about the size of a quarter, suffered a third-degree burn and remains heavily scarred to this day.

This incident made me reflect on my own actions. Of course I found several ways in which, if I had altered my behavior, the harmful incident most likely could have been avoided. However, the thought that persisted was that Jennie could not learn from this accident. If the same set of circumstances were presented to her again, she would grab the cup and burn herself as badly or worse. I was extremely discouraged about this prospect and I was beginning to realize that home was not the best place for Jennie. My husband and I also felt that Jennie had reached a developmental plateau. We saw no progress in toilet training or eating. In thinking about my talks with the psychologist who had evaluated Jennie during the early years of her life, I recalled that she had told me that family life would provide Jennie with social skills. I felt we had done this. Jennie was lovable and unafraid of interacting with people. However, we did not appear to be advancing any of her daily living skills.

When Jennie was almost ten years old, the family had an opportunity to accompany my husband to Australia on his sabbatical leave. We obtained guest-placement status for Jennie at a state institution during the four months that we were away. From all reports Jennie's adjustment was uneventful; she did well. However, we missed her. Someone didn't always have to be watching her or feeding her; in other words, we felt suddenly unburdened. When we returned to New Jersey, we brought Jennie home. But our attitude had changed—probably mine most of all. I realized that our family had interacted better when Jennie was not always there. In retrospect, it appears that we did not realize how we were functioning as a family when we were dealing with Jennie on a full-time basis.

My husband and I decided it was time to begin proceedings to place Jennie in a residential care facility. After looking at both public and private institutions and comparing costs and eligibility requirements, we finally filed forms with the state. This did not mean that care would be free. Our income was reviewed, and our share of the cost was assessed. Looking back over this transition period between Jennie's early years at home and her moving away prompts me to list some of the major factors that families must assess in making the decision:

1. Is the child's care becoming easier or more difficult at home? Are care givers coping?
2. Is the child progressing at home?
3. How are all family members, including siblings, really feeling?

Placing Jennie in an institution caused our concerns and problems to take on a new focus. The daily burden of physical care was removed; however, we were left with questions of how Jennie was being treated and uncertainty about what was happening to her. We think this must be true of all parents. Depending on the child's needs and the ability of the institution to fulfill them, placement will achieve varying degrees of success and satisfaction. Perhaps key to a parent's peace of mind, once the placement decision is made, is to identify the major goals that one hopes to attain. One must then expect to have some trade-offs. For example, if one wants a child to be safe from physical harm and thus asks for an arrangement where there are few nonfood objects available to place in the mouth, the

Leah Ziskin

surroundings will be more barren or sterile and thus much less stimulating. If one wants a child safe from infectious disease, then the child must be more isolated. Of course these examples lead to extremes in thinking, and it is often best to try for a middle-of-the-road approach at first and later strive for a situation more suited to the child's capabilities and needs.

Some of the major problems that have upset me since Jennie has been away from home have been the health and medical care she has received. Because the institution was renovating its buildings to meet federal requirements for intermediate care facilities, Jennie was moved from her usual residence cottage. Shortly after this move an outbreak of hepatitis A (formerly known as infectious hepatitis) developed; she was exposed and became ill. During the course of her illness, she was catheterized for urine specimens and had her blood taken far more than I felt necessary. When her illness subsided, I was asked whether I would sign a release for her to be put under general anesthesia for a skin biopsy and cauterization of other skin lesions. I discussed this request with a local dermatologist, who felt it was extreme. I asked that the institution obtain a second opinion on the proposed therapy. The new consultant was able to treat the skin lesions far more conservatively and with no need for anesthesia. What had emerged, from my perspective, was a pattern of overzealous medical care: care and therapy that far exceeded that for a normal child and exposed Jennie to additional risks.

Another continuing problem has been late notification of an acute situation—after action has been taken. This is frustrating because I am left feeling, "What can I do now that it is over, except take an adversarial position, and how can I best prevent situations like this from happening again?" My approach has been to talk. I talk to the medical director; I attend the annual team conferences to plan Jennie's care; and I talk to persons involved with her care. It helps, but only to a degree. I sense that I am trying to make exceptions to the rules and procedures by which the institution operates most of the time. The degree of flexibility in addressing situations is frequently proportional to the size of the facility and the degree of individual decision making permitted at the care-giving level. For example, when Jennie was bitten by another child, I was not called because the immediate care givers are instructed to report these incidents on a special form. A level of administration outside the residence cottage decides whether or not the incident warrants parental notification.

In summary, my major impression of our decision to place Jennie in a residential facility for these last five years is that our reprieve from providing for her daily physical needs cost us our control over her interaction with her environment. I did not realize how innate this sense of control was to me as a parent, nor could I articulate the concept as clearly before placing Jennie. However, examining the advantages and disadvantages of out-of-home placement in our case, I would be prepared to repeat our decision and will accept the consequences, anticipating that there will be a continual need for mental and emotional adjustments in our response to interaction between Jennie, her care givers, and her family.

QUESTIONS TO CONSIDER

1. Review the questions on pages 72–73. How accurate were your predictions?

2. What were the catalysts for the Ziskins' decision to move Jennie to an institution? What family support services would have been necessary for the Ziskins to be able to keep Jennie at home? How does institutionalization influence the type and degree of stress in a family?

3. If Leah were to write about Jennie and the Ziskin family in six years, what would be her major theme?

The Helsel Family is composed of Elsie and Bob, Bill, and Paula, Marjorie (nee Helsel) and John DeWert—and Robin. Robin, now 38, is disabled by cerebral palsy and mental retardation. He lives at home with Elsie and Bob.

Elsie is a professor emeritus in the College of Education at Ohio University. Before retiring in 1981, she served as director of the university-affiliated Center for Human Development. She is deeply involved in volunteer work, serving as vice-chairperson, President's Committee on Mental Retardation; vice-president, United Cerebral Palsy Associations, Inc.; chairperson, Governor's Special Education Advisory Council, and member, Ohio Developmental Disability Planning Council.

Bob is a professor emeritus in the Department of Mathematics at Ohio University. He is spending his early retirement years hiking and backpacking in the Cascades, the Rockies, the Great Smokies, and along the Appalachian Trail. In the late fifties and early sixties he worked diligently, first for the Association for Retarded Children and then for United Cerebral Palsy.

Robin Helsel

Bill, three years Robin's senior, received an M.A. in special education at Ohio University and is teaching EMR students at Athens High School. He is married to Paula, who also completed an M.A. in special education, taught EMR students at Athens Middle School for two years, and then returned to teaching seventh and eighth grade math and science.

Marjorie, seven years Robin's junior, completed an M.A. in special education in 1975. After teaching LD and EMR adolescents for three years, she enrolled at the University of North Carolina at Chapel Hill, where she is completing an interdisciplinary Ph.D. in computer science and special education. Marjorie is also on the staff of the North Carolina Reeducation Center, a short-term residential treatment facility for emotionally disturbed children. For the 1983–84 academic year she served as the coordinator of microcomputer services, for the Division of Special Education in the School of Education at the University of North Carolina at Chapel Hill.

The Helsels' Story of Robin

The Helsels

Elsie's Perspective

Saturday night

Dearest Mother and Dad,

I wish I didn't have to write this—you have worries enough now. But we may as well all know the facts and then meet each day's problems as they come. We can still hope, too, and those who can, can pray. Somehow little Robin's brain has undergone injury—whether through disease, degeneration, or developmental accident, the doctors can't say. Nor can they give any very encouraging prognosis. They think the impairment may not be progressive; they also think it is partial (i.e., he will learn to walk eventually); and there is still hope that he may develop sufficiently to fall into the normal bracket in intelligence. If during the next year or so the impairment remains the same, then he will probably continue to develop according to a normal pattern but with this much retardation. No one knows how much brain tissue is necessary for normal development, and certainly no one uses all of the intelligence he has. Everything else seems to be normal, and he is in perfect health except for his adenoids which must be removed.

Robin and I went into the hospital last Monday night. I stayed with him the whole time. Here at Children's they prefer that the mothers stay, and they have lovely rooms, lounges, and dining rooms to take care of guests. Tuesday morning resident doctors and interns performed routine lab analyses and many examinations. Tuesday afternoon Robin had X rays. Wednesday morning they did a spinal tap for examination of the spinal fluid. From then on Robin felt bad. A neuropsychiatrist checked him Wednesday afternoon. I would not put too much faith in his prognosis (which was not good) because Robin screamed the whole time and didn't respond to his simple tests. This was the weakest

81

part of the examination and, in one respect, the most important. Thursday morning Robin went into surgery with an anesthetic for the removal of all the cerebrospinal fluid and its replacement with air so that an aeroencephalogram could be made. A Mayo-trained surgeon did this job—he was the only one who took time to explain what he was doing and why. Also, he warned me that there was a certain amount of danger in the operation, and he wanted me to know about it beforehand. Since this was just like any other operation, Robin was and still is quite sick. We must give him plenty of fluids and keep him quiet and resting for a week. This was the part of the examination that showed the unusual brain condition. All of these tests and the specialists' opinions will be sent on to Johns Hopkins when we go. As soon as Robin recovers from the shock of this hospitalization, we shall write Johns Hopkins and ask when we can come. Dr. Baxter thinks it would be best to wait for summer. Then we could get some picture of change if there is any.

My fingers feel like lead and my heart, too. This is the hardest time because people keep calling and dropping in. When we get through this, we plan to ask our friends not to talk with us about it. We shall attempt to set up as normal a home atmosphere as we can because that will give Robin the best chance to develop. No matter what lies ahead, we shall love him and try to keep him as healthy and happy as we can. Then we can always hope.

Don't feel too sorry for us. Life has been very good to us and if we can't rise to meet this problem, then who can? This is a real test of our long period of training, yet we have much to learn of humility and everything to learn about faith. Robin may bring some fine things into our home.

Love to you both,
Elsie

P.S. Robin and I came home Friday night—I have been too exhausted to write. Now that we are home, Robin is much happier. He didn't like the hospital and, as usual, someone was always coming in for something and waking him up.

That letter was written thirty years ago. As I sit here at breakfast with my thirty-year-old cerebral palsied, mentally retarded, epileptic son, I still recall with anguish that week when my world collapsed. What I could not know at that time was that, as a consequence of this tragedy, all of the events and experiences that would bring meaning, direction, and purpose to my life were about to begin.

I remember vividly the details of how I found out that Robin was seriously impaired. He was a second child, and from the time he was six months old, I had been questioning my pediatrician about his lagging development. For about a year the pediatrician had been turning aside my questions and delaying any unusual procedures. Finally he agreed to a diagnostic work-up at Children's Hospital. When the hospital orderly brought Robin back from one of the procedures, a pneumoencephalogram, he inadvertently left Robin's hospital charts in the crib. I picked them up and read, "Entering diagnosis: mental deficiency." Before being discovered, I had read all of the reports. Soon, however, a harried nurse entered and snatched the charts from my hands with a stern admonition that I had no right to read their contents. In no time at all, a small group of white coats and dresses came bustling into the room to talk with me until my pediatrician could be summoned. When he came, they respectfully withdrew and left him with the awesome task of explaining why he had not leveled with me earlier, what the prognosis was, and why I shouldn't rush off to John Hopkins, where I had a pediatrician friend on staff. The only thing I really remember from that encounter is a garbled explanation of mental deficiency and the doctor saying, "We can't all march in the parade!"

To his credit, he did not recommend institutionalization or some other unusual disposition. He did advise me to take Robin home, love him, and treat him as a normal child, providing as normal a home life for him as possible. I packed up my baby and my hopes and dreams for him and tried to do just that. The discharge diagnosis was mental deficiency at a profound level.

I began to read everything I could lay my hands on about mental retardation. I found the Gesell Developmental Scales and quickly picked up the aberrant motor patterns and the other indicators of delayed development. I also contacted my friend at Johns Hopkins. I told her about my findings on the Gesell and suggested that Robin might have cerebral palsy. This seemed more acceptable to me than mental deficiency. In making my appointment with Johns Hopkins, I asked to see Dr. Winthrop Phelps, who was the authority on cerebral palsy at that time. However, the doctors there refused to schedule me with him, stating that there were no indicators in the report from Children's Hospital that Robin might have cerebral palsy. It wasn't until four years later that we finally got to Dr. Phelps. He confirmed the diagnosis of cerebral palsy and asked why the child had not been referred to him earlier.

Our story is not atypical—lots of parents have told me similar ones. Yet it has something to say to professionals concerned with the diagnosis and assessment of multiply handicapped children today—listen to the parents. They are frequently giving you the diagnosis.

Tears still come to my eyes as I look at this handsome, blue-eyed, blond son of mine and think what he might have become had not something damaged his brain. I can rationalize that his life has had tremendous significance through his influence on our family, but the hurt is still there. Certainly he has changed our lives and has prompted us as a family to contribute significantly to the whole movement affecting severely and multiply handicapped individuals.

By the time Robin was born, my life style and career plans were fairly well set. I had completed my Ph.D. in genetics and was playing out the role of faculty wife and mother. Vaguely, at some undetermined point in the future, I planned to return to the university and continue my research on chromosome mapping. To be honest and blunt, I was a smug, self-centered intellectual snob. Robin's birth and the problems attendant to finding services and adequate care for him abruptly changed the pattern of my life, my attitudes, and my plans for the future. Suddenly I was thrust into a totally different world with people from all levels of society. We had common problems, and our children had common service needs. Through working together, we learned to know and appreciate each other for what we were and not for professional, financial, or social status. My attitudes changed not only toward people with handicapped children, but toward all people with problems. I knew what it meant to be stared at, shunned, avoided. People became embarrassed when we brought Robin out in public or when we explained his condition—especially when they learned that he wasn't going to grow out of it or recover from it.

In the neighborhood where Robin was born and his problems were known, we had no difficulty with acceptance. Our neighbors learned about mental retardation and cerebral palsy right along with us. They helped with our door-to-door campaigns and our projects to get services for Robin. However, when we moved to a more sophisticated, more affluent neighborhood, the problems of explanation and acceptance had to be faced anew. Our teen-age daughter asked if we could keep Robin in the house because she really didn't know how to explain his condition to her new friends. Our neighbors raised their eyebrows when the school bus for retarded children pulled up at our door.

An interesting event came to our rescue, however. The police in our neighborhood had spotted Robin laboriously plodding around the block with his special canes. They stopped to ask him where he lived and Robin, who has no speech, pointed out his house. The policemen wanted to know if it was safe for Robin with such an obvious disability to be out alone walking around the block. "What if a child or dog should topple him over? What if he should get out into the street and get hit by a car?" After getting reassurances from us that Robin could manage very well, the policemen left but sent the fire officer. He wanted to know the location of Robin's room and our plans for fire evacuation. He also asked permission (apologetically) to put a small decal on our window so that in the event of fire, the firemen would know there was an invalid in the house. He told us it was difficult for them to find handicapped and elderly individuals in the community because most people did not want their neighbors to know about any incapacities their family members might have. When we suggested a PR campaign to explain the obvious advantages of such a service, he asked if we would be willing to let them take some pictures of Robin for an article in the local paper. We agreed, and a few days later the fire chief, in full regalia and followed by the hook-and-ladder truck, pulled up at our door. Pictures were taken of Robin with the firemen and were published in the village paper.

Overnight Robin became a celebrity, and there were no more questions about "What's the matter with your brother? Why can't he talk?"

In working to get services for Robin, I developed skills and knowledge in a totally new field. This led me into a new career of program consulting, writing, and lobbying in Washington and eventually into an administrative and teaching position at Ohio University. Now at a time and an age when most people are thinking about retirement, I must make choices concerning which job opportunities to pursue. Robin has indeed brought direction, purpose, and meaning to my life. I have achieved a degree of personal fulfillment that I think I would never have attained in my former career as a bench scientist. I have seen more of the world, had opportunities to meet saints and sages, been part of the glamorous Washington scene, and worked side by side with top people in our national government. I have been on the cutting edge of the action in legislation and programs for the handicapped. Best of all, I have had the opportunity to earn the respect of my peers and colleagues, and I have had the intense satisfaction of leading my own son and daughter into professional careers in working with the handicapped.

On the minus side, I have had to come to terms with the obvious fact that Robin was not going to make it intellectually or educationally. Hardest of all, I have had to sit back and watch him slowly lose functions over the years, slowly lose incentive to try, slowly become more and more frustrated and unhappy. Seizure problems have now come under partial control, but each episode is a reminder that the old basic problems are still there.

Despite all the services, the knowledge, the counseling, and the emotional support, living with a problem for thirty years takes its toll. I get tired dragging Robin around, making all the special arrangements that must be made before I can go anywhere or do anything. I get tired lifting that heavy wheelchair in and out of the car. It would be nice just to be free to take off on a moment's notice and not have to plan ahead.

Professionals are constantly probing and asking questions concerning how Robin's constant presence and problems affect our marriage. Once again, there are pluses and minuses. I really don't believe any one factor in a marriage can be pinpointed as a strengthener or strainer. There are too many variables affecting a marriage for such a simplistic explanation. The temperament of the individuals; the physical, emotional, and financial strengths; the problem-solving and coping skills the commitment people bring—all have some bearing on the strain a handicapped child places on a marriage. From my point of view, Robin has added more strength than strain. At least my husband and I are still living together after thirty-seven years of marriage! For one thing, at those points in a marriage when you are contemplating divorce (intellectually, emotionally, or actually), the presence of a child such as Robin is a major deterrent. The focus quickly changes from your own needs, wishes, and desires to your responsibilities, commitment, and the needs of the child. Somehow this helps you work through a problem, and you find another way. I have never bought the argument that the presence of an adult person in a family, handicapped or not, is a disruptive factor. I feel society has lost a mooring with the breakdown of the extended family. Romantic twosomes are great for novels and certain periods of our lives. I do not see such a pattern as essential for a successful marriage. My husband and I will not have a footloose, carefree, romantic retirement life style, but we will have something else—the opportunity to feel needed.

Bob's Perspective

The following section is comprised of a conversation between Bob and his daughter, Marge. They are discussing Bob's perspective of being Robin's father.

Marge: When you first found out that Robin was mentally retarded or cerebral palsied, what kind of gut reaction did you have?

Bob: I didn't have a strong gut reaction. We realized when Robin was less than a year old that he didn't show the normal physical reactions and abilities. It is my impression that I accepted this, even the brain damage. Elsie didn't respond that way and dragged us around to various clinics and authorities for diagnoses and prognoses. I went along with that, but not because I was expecting to find some cure or some hope.

Marge: So it sounds like you had a pretty realistic outlook toward it, or at least you felt you had.

Bob: At least I felt so at the time, and I still feel so, although I might have been more emotionally involved and up-tight about it than I realized. But my impression is that I accepted it, and there it was.

Marge: You couldn't do much else?

Bob: That's right.

Marge: Do you remember some of the initial reactions of our grandparents? Were their reactions just like those of other people as you told them about Robin? Can you remember anything about that?

Bob: Three of the grandparents were living then—my mother and Elsie's mother and father. I feel that, like Elsie, her parents weren't too accepting, and they hoped against hope that we would find something to cure Robin. As I recall, my mother was more accepting. But she was the kind of person who put her trust in God, and she didn't get too upset.

Marge: Did that make it harder for you, having them have a real emotional reaction?

Bob: No, I don't think so. I think at times I was irritated by the attitudes of Elsie and her parents. To me, it looked like their desires to have a normal child and grandchild were clouding their thinking. This can be irritating, but it didn't affect my attitude toward Robin. He wasn't the one profoundly affected.

Marge: So you don't really think that it was such a bad thing necessarily?

Bob: No.

Marge: How about other people, like neighbors? I suppose when he was younger, there wasn't that much contact.

Bob: Robin was a very loving baby and young child. Our neighbors responded positively to him. I guess we were fortunate in that. There were no instances of neighbors shunning Robin or being upset by him. Quite the contrary. It was a good experience, I would say, in that respect.

Marge: So Robin's nice personality kind of helped out?

Bob: Yes, it did. He was nice to be around. He was good-natured and loving.

Marge: How about my brother Bill and me? Did you see any early reactions in us. Were we pretty much unaware?

Bob: Within the family, I didn't notice any adverse reactions. Again, Robin's personality played an important part there. He was a member of the family, and he joined in, and you and Bill responded and accepted him. Now, how you felt about Robin when you related to your peers, I really don't know. I assume you had a certain amount of shame and guilt, but I didn't see this because it occurred in contacts outside the home, and I wasn't part of that. But inside the home Robin was one of us and was accepted and loved. And he responded to this. He joined in our love and concern.

Marge: He wasn't a disruptive influence, then?

Bob: Not internally. I do think that you and Bill probably had difficulties outside the home because of Robin, not necessarily because of anything that anyone said or did, but simply because you feared you would be criticized, ostracized, or made fun of because of a handicapped brother.

Marge: How did you feel about the educational services he received and how his teachers reacted? You were in sort of an interesting situation since you were involved in the parent organizations [ARC & UCP].

Bob: We were the beginners, the people who formed the first classes for such children and who struggled to gain the proper services for them. As far as the actual class experiences and the way I felt about them, the teachers, of course, had no previous experience or training, so they tended to teach as they would teach normal children. This irritated me because I felt there was nothing that such a child as Robin needs less than the three Rs. What they needed and what such children still need is training that will enable them to get along to the best of their abilities. And there really isn't any need to do spelling or arithmetic—although you could argue that they could use arithmetic to make change and so on. But this wasn't what they were teaching. When I was in charge of the classes for retarded children, I wasn't happy with the teaching. But I didn't try to impose my views although I voiced them often enough. I don't know whether the situation has changed greatly or not. I think there is still probably the tendency to try to give these children too much formal education and too little of what they need to get along at home and in the street.

Marge: So you think his education left a lot to be desired as far as meeting his needs?

Bob: That's right. And because of its formal character and his inability to respond in a manner acceptable to the teachers, it was extremely frustrating for Robin. It was a bad experience for him. He rebelled against it because he couldn't measure up. As I said, it disturbed me because I felt this wasn't relevant to his future life and wasn't what was called for.

Marge: What eventually happened?

Bob: He just wouldn't go to school anymore.

Marge: At what age was this?

Bob: Oh, I don't know if I can give you the age.

Marge: Just a rough estimate.

Bob: We had him in classes of one kind or another, I suppose, for a period of ten years or more. This would mean that when he finally rebelled to the extent that we stopped pressing him to go, he was perhaps sixteen years old, something like that. But he never had had what I considered a satisfactory experience for him.

Marge: You feel like other people were trying to say, "This is what he should do," and weren't looking at him as an individual and saying, "This is what he needs"?

Bob: Or "This is what we hope to have him achieve." You're quite right. They never tried to measure his abilities and interests. They tried to impose preconceived notions about what people should learn in school. He didn't learn what they taught, and so he was unhappy, and the teachers, of course, weren't particularly happy with him.

Marge: Do you feel this early experience with education has affected where he is now?

Bob: It's been a factor in his growing frustration. I mentioned that Robin was a very loving child who was enjoyed by, I think, all of the people who knew him. But his personality has changed over the years and reflects his growing frustration. Certainly his inability to do what was expected of him in a school situation was part of that frustration. I think it wouldn't be fair to blame it all on the schools and say that that is why he is now a frustrated individual, but they added their bit.

Marge: Or they didn't add the right bit or something. Robin's had a lot of illness—how has that affected you? I know it's upsetting for any parent to have a sick child. Did his illnesses place a special burden on you, or did they help you in any way?

Bob: Well, they didn't affect me any more than the illnesses of my other children. A parent is sick when the child is sick. These things, I suppose, eventually leave their mark on the parents' health and well-being. But I don't feel that Robin's illnesses have been any more traumatic for me than the illnesses of my other two children.

Marge: Are your reactions toward Robin different now as opposed to when he was younger?

Bob: Well, I've mentioned that Robin's personality has undergone great changes as he has matured and has come to know his limitations and has been frustrated by that. And in the same way, my reactions to Robin, my personal attitudes, have changed over the years. I think I enjoyed Robin very much when he was quite young, and I didn't feel as bad about his handicap as I do now. As I see his growing frustration, my sympathy and empathy for him increase, but at the same time the manifestations of his frustration—tantrums and such things—cause my tolerance to wear thin. At least, the limit of my tolerance is approached. In other words, he's harder to live with now—much harder to live with.

At no time have I regarded Robin as a burden. I always felt and still feel that I'm fortunate to have a handicapped person in my family. It is through him that I've learned tolerance for other people of lesser and different abilities. I know that my teaching has been deeply affected by him. I no longer judge a student on the basis of what he can do in mathematics. I try to look at him as a person. I don't think less of an individual who can't do mathematics or one who lacks some physical ability, like high jumping seven feet. So Robin's handicap has been a very constructive influence in my life.

Marge: That's a nice thing I hear you saying—that he's broadened your awareness of individual differences or whatever you want to call it and made you more accepting of other people.

Bob: That's right. And I have also realized through Robin that every individual has a contribution to make to the people around him. And Robin has certainly made contributions—earlier because of his loving nature, and more recently as I have become more fully aware of his frustrations. There is also another reaction to Robin that I might mention, which is highly personal. Probably no other member of the family shares it. Since I enjoy getting out in the woods and roaming around, I often stop when I am out hiking to think of how much I wish that Robin could have such an experience. I suppose that my desire to keep in good physical condition and remain active is in part a reflection of his physical incapacity. I wish somehow I could do it for both of us—see nature, love it, and enjoy it not only for myself but for Robin, too.

Marge: I'm sure it makes you sad that he can't share that. I know how important it is to you.

Bob: As I said, I think part of the impact is that because I am so aware of his incapacity, it is all the more important for me to enjoy it fully.

Marge: But knowing you, I don't think you have ever forced Robin to do things that he couldn't do just because you wanted him to share an experience with you. Do you have any feelings about this?

Bob: No, I think I've been a fairly reasonable father as far as not pushing Robin—although in some things I would have been stricter than the other people around him.I would have been inclined to make him toe the line a little more and behave in a more acceptable manner.

Marge: So you think other family members were a little too lenient?

Bob: Yes. But I don't know that I would have been right, and I am glad that I didn't insist because I could have been wrong. But I did feel that because of his handicap and because he was not the oldest member of the family, he probably was permitted to misbehave and show his anger and frustration more than he should have, more than was good for him. He has a very low threshold as far as going into tantrums is concerned. This isn't to his benefit. But perhaps it is part of his condition, too.

Marge: Returning to what you said about the increasing frustration that he feels, are you worried about it?

Bob: I'm not worried. It's just that it moves me deeply, and I feel frustration because I can't relieve his frustration. So my feelings about Robin and my attitudes toward him are certainly much different from what they were when he was young. Simply, as he has changed, I have changed, not in a way that makes me less accepting. As I just mentioned, I feel more frustrated about Robin now than I ever did before.

Marge: Can you tell me more about the frustration? Do you have concerns about where he is going and what he is doing right now? Or is it just sort of an aching, all-over feeling, not really specified?

Bob: It's a general condition. I just wish I could help him recapture the kind of attitudes that he displayed as a youngster. I wish I could relieve his frustration. I wish I could make him a happier person. But I don't know how to do this, and I don't know whether anyone can do it. It just bugs me; it is a constant thing.

You mentioned worrying about the future. I suppose this is the biggest worry that a parent of a severely handicapped child has—what happens when I die? And there is no answer to that. As far as I know, there is no way to provide properly for him in that eventuality—at least, I don't know of any way.

Marge: So you know the problem is there, but you're not sure what to do about it.

Bob: You can't amass enough capital to set up a private home. There just isn't an answer or a way to provide properly for such a person after your death.

Marge: That's a real heavy thing to think about anyway. How would you summarize Robin's impact on you? You said some things about how he has opened up your awareness of other people and about your love of the outdoors and wanting to share that with him. Are there any other ways that Robin has had a direct influence on you?

Bob: I can't think of specifics. I'm convinced I'm a better person because of Robin's presence in the family. He has made me into a better parent, a better teacher, a better person.

Marge: How did he make you into a better parent?

Bob: Well, I learned a lot of tolerance, forbearance, love, and acceptance. These are qualities that make a good parent.

Marge: So all in all, you feel that Robin's being in the home has been a good experience for everyone involved?

Bob: Certainly. In some sense every home should have a handicapped person in it just to heighten their awareness of the needs and limitations of other persons.

Marge: Can you think of any special problems that Robin presents, has presented, or will present to you?

Bob: Well, I would say in the past he didn't present any special problems with respect to limiting my life although I certainly put lots of time into a lot of activities for various groups trying to set up and maintain facilities for handicapped people. But he was a member of the family. We had other children, so taking care of Robin didn't place any special burden on us.

But it seems to me as I approach retirement age and would like lots of personal freedom, he will present a problem in limiting my ability to go where I want when I want. I'm not worried about this, but it is a fact. I don't know whether a solution will be found to give me the freedom that I would like to have or whether we'll just continue to be somewhat limited because of Robin. There are facilities opening up to take care of handicapped persons on a short-term or long-term basis which we might utilize. Such facilities would give us the freedom to travel or go on more hiking and backpacking trips. I am aware of the possible limitations on freedom to leave home.

Marge: A freedom which most parents of normal children have when their children are out of the nest.

Bob: Or if they aren't out of the nest, they are at least old enough so that the parents can say to them, "Take care of yourselves; I'll see you next month!" But with Robin, we can't do that.

Marge: You said that now you're wondering about there being some limitations on your freedom, but when he was growing up, you didn't.

Bob: Oh, I didn't feel limited because I didn't have any freedom to speak of. I had a job to go to every day, and there were the other children, so he didn't place any particular restrictions on me. But now the situation is different.

Marge: But it sounds like you're beginning to think through some solutions, like maybe a group home.

Bob: I'm sure that whatever develops will be satisfactory for all concerned.

Marge: But it's a valid point that it's a situation that should be dealt with.

Bill's Perspective

On several occasions while growing up, I remember my mother saying that she had planned for my brother Robin to be a companion for me, apparently feeling that his handicap prevented this from occurring. However, when I recall childhood days, many fun-filled occasions which we shared together come to mind. I don't think I really thought of Robin as a handicapped person—we just naturally designed play activities in which we could both participate.

Our Columbus, Ohio, home had a den area which was our domain. Many times we constructed elaborate forts, complete with labyrinth-like passages and secret gates. Robin could adeptly maneuver his way through all of these constructs; he especially enjoyed demolition procedures when it was time to redesign our surroundings.

Similarly, at our summer home in Pennsylvania, we would pass hours building sand castles and roads—I, doing most of the building and he, the tearing down. We also perfected wonderful sand pies and paving cement—recipes now lost to posterity. On one occasion we built a road through the adjacent woods, a project deemed foolhardy by our parents; yet in later years our rustic trail became a main thoroughfare when our family constructed a larger home nearby. We would now be rich if we had collected a nickel toll for each traveler using our thruway.

Robin has always demonstrated great resourcefulness when addressing a problem situation. As a very young child, still unable to crawl, he perfected a unique rolling technique for locomotion. On the occasion of one adult gathering at our home, he rolled upon the scene and proceeded from guest to guest, emptying all beverage bottles left on the floor.

Another time he took the gun-cleaning rod used by my father to administer spankings to both him and me, bent it up like a pretzel, and carefully replaced it on the proper closet hook. I, unjustly, was accused of the crime and duly punished. Perhaps my collaboration was assumed because of previous occasions when I had instructed Robin in such activities as dismantling his bed. I recall his being an able learner, needing only one demonstration to master this and similar tasks.

Robin's capacity for remembering things has always amazed me. As a child he would bury toys in the woods around our summer home and return to excavate them the next year, proceeding to the correct location without hesitation. Likewise as an adult, we have learned never to mention anything casually in his presence, assuming that it will either pass him by or be forgotten.

Although unable to speak, Robin has developed his own effective language system, consisting of self-created gestures and sounds. At times he has stumped all of us trying to figure out what he wants to say (we often resort to our own version of twenty questions). Despite speech limitations Robin understands all of what he hears being said around him, including the subtle points of jokes and stories. On more than one occasion, he has surprised house guests by reacting to something they were saying which they apparently felt he would not understand.

Robin's favorite vice is drinking beer, for which he acquired a taste as a young child. I really don't know what his capacity is, but it is more than enough to put me under the table. At social gatherings in our home, Robin can usually monitor himself and not overdo it; however, when he has been angry and alone in the house, he has consumed all of the beer in the refrigerator, somehow managing to get the tops off the bottles, which we felt he couldn't do for himself. When asked if he drank all the beer, Robin put his finger to his lips and made a shushing sound.

The first significant change in my perception of Robin occurred when he became too large to be included in those family activities for which he had been carried or transported in his carriage previously. At our summer home Robin dearly enjoyed going swimming in the nearby creek, but the rough terrain prohibited our carrying him there once he became a teenager. Father and Mother bought Robin a large plastic swimming pool, which was set up next to our house. In it we enjoyed many a water battle—but it was somehow different from before. Similarly, Robin's participation in other family activities away from home lessened as he became older.

I have observed that adolescent children in many families tend to become very independent and ignore family activities, so I can't be sure that our family would have been one in which many activities were shared even if Robin had not been handicapped. Today Robin has his own interests as I have mine. It is easy to look upon his routinized life style and prescribe changes for his betterment. Still, I don't think his life is substantially less happy or satisfying than my own. Despite our different life styles, we share many common joys and frustrations.

Someone outside the family could easily look at my life and infer some causal relationships from the fact that I grew up in a home with a handicapped person. Certainly there has been some influence, but it has been more indirect than direct. By this I mean that Robin and I share an interpersonal relationship based primarily upon personality and only secondarily upon physical circumstances. Living with Robin has made me more aware of and sensitive to persons with special needs, but we are all persons with special needs—each asking for attention and understanding. However, Robin's presence has not meant that I am always at ease with handicapped persons or can always look at them in an objective way without feeling distressed or disturbed.

Probably the most significant difference between me and another person is that living with a handicapped person is neither strange nor unusual to me. It is sometimes hard to remember the difference between my perspective and that of another person. To this point, I recall my wife's telling me how nervous she was the first time that she met Robin, not so much because of him, but because I was not providing her with information to help her relate to him. While handicapped persons do not wish undue attention called to their situations, individuals unaccustomed to being with them may appreciate some guidance.

Marge's Perspective

As a young child, I cannot recall considering Robin to be retarded or in any way different from me or the other members of my family. He was simply my brother—an affectionate presence during my early years and a welcome playmate during the summers my family spent at our somewhat isolated country home in Pennsylvania. I remember Robin as a willing guest at afternoon tea parties beside the small stream that ran through our property. I remember evenings filled with giggling and pillow fights in the room he and I shared in our cottage.

When we returned to the city in the fall, I can recall accompanying my mother each morning to the rather grim-looking building where Robin was enrolled in a volunteer-run school for retarded children. Even then I did not think of him as being different. In my mind he was just going to school as I knew all children of his age did.

I cannot pinpoint exactly when I first became aware of Robin's handicaps. Several incidents come to mind, all of which occurred around the time I was eleven years old. One involved a trip to the shoe store where Robin was to be fitted for orthopedic shoes; another, a trip to the town near our country home for dinner at the YMCA. On both of these occasions I can remember being acutely embarrassed by the ill-concealed stares as we pushed Robin in his wheelchair. I was certain that everyone was looking at my brother with his obvious handicap and then wondering what was wrong with the rest of us. As a result of these feelings, I began to refuse to go out to dinner or shopping with my family and took precautions to avoid being seen on the street or in the yard with Robin.

These avoidance tactics brought an accompanying sense of guilt. I knew that it was wrong for me to be ashamed of my brother. I loved Robin dearly and realized that the opinions (real or imagined) of others should have had no bearing on my interaction with him.

Looking back, I think I would have benefited from some counseling during this period. As an adult, I now realize that my reactions to Robin's handicaps were not unusual, but I certainly did not know this at the time. It would have helped me to be able to talk with an adult other than my mother or father about the feelings I was experiencing; I think it would be extremely difficult for any youngster ever to admit point-blank to her parents that she is embarrassed by her brother. Yet I also believe most children growing up in a society which places a great deal of emphasis on so-called normalcy will come to a point when they are ashamed of or may even reject outright a disabled sibling. It is at this time that they should be given a concise explanation of the disability (i.e., what it is, why it happened, what the prognosis is), be permitted the opportunity to explore their feelings about their sibling, and be given some guidance in problem-solving and coping skills to help them deal with their feelings in a constructive manner.

Following my period of avoidance, I entered a phase of false pretenses. I forced myself to appear in public with him—but only if I felt I looked my very best (freshly washed hair, make-up, a snazzy outfit). My specious reasoning was that if people were going to stare, they weren't going to find anything wrong with me. Also, though I am reluctant to admit such a selfish thought, I suppose I wanted to encourage people to think, "Oh dear, look at that sweet young girl pushing her poor crippled brother around. What a wonderful child she must be." This period extended into my college years, at which time several events occurred that led to an abrupt change of attitude on my part.

Robin has periodically undergone hospitalization following seizures which have left him in a comatose state. I recall vividly my sense of dismay the first time I awoke in the morning to find my brother's room empty and no sign of him anywhere in the house. I remember rushing to my parents' bedroom to find them lying in bed, fully clothed, and my mother's tearful explanation that Robin had become ill during the night and had been taken to the hospital. Because I was too young to visit Robin, at the times of his early hospitalizations, these episodes did not really have too much impact on me. Robin always came home after a few days, perhaps a bit less alert, a bit less his enthusiastic self; and our family life resumed its usual course. One day when I was a freshman in college, I drove out to my parents' house for a visit. I went into Robin's room to say hello only to find it once again empty and to hear my mother tell me that Robin was in a coma at the hospital. I remember the shock of the news and my sense of urgency to see my brother. I recall the agonizingly slow drive to the hospital, the walk down the long, forbidding corridor to his room. There my brother lay in bed, connected to all sorts of tubes and looking quite pale and helpless. My heart went out to him. I rushed over to the bed and picked up one of his hands. I felt that if I could only get him to give me some sign of recognition, he would recover. I stood by that bed and called Bucky—our pet name for him— over and over, praying that he would hear me and respond. After a seemingly interminable period of time, he finally did open his eyes and weakly squeezed my hand. I felt I had been given the best gift in the world. What really hit me hard then was how much I did love Robin and how very precious he was to me just the way he was.

After the experience in the hospital, my parents encouraged me to become involved in several volunteer programs serving the developmentally disabled. Through programs at the local mental health center and a state institution for the mentally retarded, I began to come into contact with special educators and other individuals who genuinely accepted and cared for persons like my brother. These people taught me the value of viewing everyone, developmentally disabled or not, as a unique individual filled with potential and worth. Gradually, I found myself talking more about Robin to others, introducing him to my friends, taking him places. In short, I had finally learned to accept Robin for himself.

Having Robin as a member of our family caused me to undergo a great deal of introspection, which led me to insights into certain aspects of my character that needed to be changed. My contact with him, coupled with some sound advice from my parents, also unquestionably influenced my decision to pursue a career in special education. I had originally intended to enter the field of chemistry, and indeed I completed a bachelor's degree in that area. However, something about my choice bothered me. I enjoyed the lab work and the excitement of scientific discovery, but something was missing. It wasn't until one of our what-are-you-going-to-do-with-your-life discussions that my father pinpointed the problem when he quoted the following statement of the philosopher Kierkegaard: "The door to happiness opens outward." What this meant to me was that one could only find true happiness through serving others. The choice of a career then became obvious to me. What better way was there to serve others than to enter the field of special education, where I could help people like my brother lead more fulfilling lives?

I do not mean to imply that life with Robin has been all goodness and light. I have seen the strain that his constant care has placed upon my parents. I worry about the increasing frequency of his seizures and about what would happen to him if my parents became unable to care for him. Robin himself, like all brothers I suppose, can be truly irritating. It makes me angry to see him try to weasel his way out of doing things that I know he is capable of doing. Just the other day I was scolding him for not clearing his place at the table. I guess my sisterly bossing was too much for him: he pointed at me and angrily made the sign for handcuffs— his way of indicating that I should be put in jail.

All in all, though, I feel that Robin has brought much good into our family. He has taught us a great deal about acceptance, patience, individual worth, and most of all love.

The Helsels

Having shared how we feel about Robin and how we perceive his impact on our family, what can we say to other professionals that may give additional insight into the needs of families with handicapped children?

First, the old concept of parent counseling must go. The needs extend far beyond the parents, and they certainly require a great deal more than counseling in the traditional sense. A handicapped person places stress on the whole family, so the whole family needs support and help in understanding the handicapped child's condition, his needs (both present and projected), and the extra demands his presence will place on the family. The entire family needs help with feelings. They need to know that it is all right to feel resentful, embarrassed, uncomfortable, inadequate. They also need to be told about the joy, love, challenge, and opportunities for growth and fulfillment that such a situation can offer. As new children join the family, they particularly need help. The fact that they have been born into a family with a handicapped person will not automatically equip them with the facility to explain their sibling to peers or to accept their feelings without trauma. Much of what a family needs does not fall into the realm of counseling. Members need information, skills, knowledge, management techniques, individual and group therapy. We would like to replace the old notion of parent counseling with family supportive services.

In view of the needs outlined above—and they are only some of the needs families will have over a lifetime—professionals should recognize early that they, too, are going to need help. The thought that one professional or one clinic or one service can supply all the support a family needs is absurd. Trying to assist with problems of the magnitude, complexity, and duration of a family member's handicap will require a team effort. No one person has God-like powers to know what is best for a particular family, yet countless professionals assume this role. Above all, what families do not need is the professional BIA (Big I Am). They need professionals who are well qualified in their fields but who have humility and empathy in the face of tragedy. Parents do not need to suffer professional putdowns. They particularly do not need professionals who are off on their own ego trips. Professionals should be objective and should not lay their own hang-ups or preconceived notions on the families they are trying to help. Through the years we have become more and more convinced that some professionals should not presume ever to counsel parents.

Furthermore, professionals dealing with families with handicapped children should constantly remind themselves that families are different. They come to this situation with all kinds of backgrounds and experiences, all kinds of coping skills, all kinds of strengths and weaknesses. Families are not all guilt ridden, overprotective, and emotional. No pat answers, clichés, prescriptions, or labels fit all families.

In addition, professionals should be current in their knowledge. They should obviously keep up on handicapping conditions, but they should also be knowledgeable about services available in the community, legislation affecting the handicapped rights of parents, community attitudes toward handicapping conditions, realities of financial costs, and feasibility of service plans. For example, during the past few years there has been a complete turnabout concerning institutionalization and placement in the least restrictive environment at the community level. There has also been a quiet revolution concerning the rights of the handicapped to services. Professionals, particularly those preparing other young professionals, have a particular responsibility not only to be current in their knowledge of today, but also to be aware of trends for tomorrow.

Finally, but perhaps most importantly, professionals should accept parents as full-fledged members of the management team for their child. Parents have much to contribute from the moment a child's atypical development is suspected. They spend more time with the child, have more opportunity to observe the child, and are more sensitive to the nuances of a particular condition. They also have lifelong responsibility for an impaired child. The courts are mandating their involvement in the programming for their children.

We hope our experiences can contribute something to the professionals of the future who will touch the lives of new parents of handicapped children, helping them to find the joy mixed with sadness, the hope mixed with despair, the opportunities mixed with disappointments.

Pearl Buck (1950) said it best so long ago,

Parents may find comfort, I say, in knowing that their children are not useless, but that their lives, limited as they are, are of great potential value to the human race. We learn as much from illness as from health, from handicap as from advantage—and indeed perhaps more. Not out of fullness has the human soul always reached its highest, but often out of deprivation. This is not to say that sorrow is better than happiness, illness than health, poverty than richness. Had I been given the choice, I would have a thousand times over chosen to have had my child sound and whole, a normal woman today, living a woman's life. I miss eternally the person she cannot be. I am not resigned and never will be. Resignation is something still and dead, an inactive acceptance that bears no fruit. On the contrary, I rebel against the unknown fate that fell upon her somewhere and stopped her growth. Such things ought not to be and because it has happened to me and because I know what this sorrow is I devote myself and my child to the work of doing all we can to prevent such suffering for others. (pp. 57–58)

REFERENCES

Buck, P.S. *The child who never grew.* New York: John Day Co., 1950.

QUESTIONS TO CONSIDER

1. Elsie's letter to her parents at the beginning of the chapter concludes with this sentence: "This is a real test of our long period of training, yet we have much to learn of humility and everything to learn about faith. Robin may bring some fine things into our home." What were the lessons the Helsels learned about humility and faith? Did Robin contribute fine things to the family? If so, what were they and what impact did they have on Elsie, Bob, Bill, and Marjorie? Do you think Robin's positive contributions will be the same or different over the next six years?

2. All of the Helsels, in one way or another, describe the increasing complexity of meeting Robin's needs as he grows older. How would you characterize the impact of Robin on the Helsel family life cycle? What are your predictions about the impact Robin is likely to have on his parents during the next six years?

3. What are the special needs of siblings as described by Bill and Marjorie? How have these needs changed over time? What needs are likely to occur as Bill and Marjorie marry and establish their own families?

4. Describe the characteristics of a professional who would be especially helpful to the Helsel family.

The Helsel Family Today

Marjorie DeWert and Elsie Helsel

Marjorie's Update

Soon after the first edition of *Parents Speak Out* was published, I married and moved away from my hometown. Consequently, my contact with Robin over the past four years has been limited to holiday visits and occasional telephone conversations. (Robin has no speech, but he's a master at sending loud, smacking kisses over the phone.) The physical distance between us has not prevented Robin from continuing to have an impact on my life, however.

The first example of Robin's influence that comes to mind is the warm, loving relationship that has developed between Robin and my husband, John. Like many newly engaged young women, I was a bit apprehensive about how my family would react to my husband-elect at first meeting. In particular, I was concerned about how best to introduce John to my developmentally disabled brother. Fortunately, I recalled that my older brother, Bill, had faced a similar situation several years earlier with his wife, Paula, so I went to him for advice. Acting upon his opinion that much of Paula's initial uneasiness with Robin could have been eliminated had he provided her with more information concerning Robin's condition, I made a conscientious effort to teach my archaeologist fiancé about developmental disabilities in general and Robin in particular.

John proved to be an enthusiastic pupil, bombarding me with questions: "How can I communicate with him if he can't talk?" "Will he be able to understand what I say to him?" "What should I do if he has a seizure?" "Is it OK to touch him?" After a crash course in charades à la Helsels, our family's special method of communicating with Robin, I took John to my parents' house, introduced him to Robin, and crossed my fingers. I needn't have worried. After an initial handshake John asked Robin about one of his favorite subjects, drilling oil wells, and soon the two of them were concocting a hilarious scenario centering around the discovery of ten gushers in my parents' backyard and the subsequent formation of the Robin Helsel Oil Company. Now, five years later, my husband and my brother are great friends, and it is a joy to see Robin's face light up whenever John walks into the house.

John and Robin's friendship has taught me two important lessons. First, the interaction of handicapped individuals and persons unaccustomed to being with them should not be left to chance. The literature on the topic is full of articles touting the virtues of allowing handicapped and nonhandicapped individuals to interact freely in educational, vocational, and social settings. Yet all too often these articles ignore the question of just how such interaction is to be accomplished, given the general public's discomfort with disabled persons. Families with a handicapped member should be alerted early-on to probable public reaction and should be provided with the information and skills necessary to foster positive interaction between the disabled family member and other persons in his environment.

The second lesson I have learned from watching John and Robin is that, as a professional, I must be careful not to let the disabilities of those I serve overshadow their abilities. In particular, I must not overlook the uniquely human capacity of Robin and others like him to give and receive the special kind of love that comes from a close, enduring friendship.

I would like to share one other observation in the hope of encouraging more professionals to become involved in my area of special interest—the utilization of computer technology in special education. One upshot of having a close family member who is developmentally disabled is that I invariably scan the special education literature with the question "Would this help my brother?" in the back of my mind. Of late, I have been particularly excited and encouraged by the number of articles describing the potential of low-cost microcomputers to assist disabled individuals with communication and environmental control. Imagine what it would mean to my brother to be finally able to speak to us via a portable, programmable speech synthesizer or to be able to choose his own cable TV channel (something he cannot presently do because he lacks the fine motor control necessary to manipulate the small buttons) through a customized selection system involving a microcomputer and a digitizing tablet.

In his book *Special Technology for Special Children*, Goldenberg (1979) introduces the concept of the computer as eyeglasses to extend the abilities of handicapped persons in much the same way that eyeglasses extend the visual acuity of much of the population in general. He states, "My ultimate intention is to present a picture of a social and technological environment within which such vast improvements in the quality of life of a handicapped individual can be realized that we, and, importantly, the individual, can begin seeing his life, like that of persons with eyeglasses, as normal" (p. 5).

The environment proposed by Goldenberg need not be a pipe dream. Much of the necessary technology is available now. It remains for us as

Marjorie DeWert and Elsie Helsel

professionals to become actively and knowledgeably involved with the development of this technology so that the needs of exceptional individuals are adequately met. The alternative—remaining uninvolved—undoubtedly will result in the continued production of technological devices of questionable efficiency by computer experts who do not understand the nature of special education.

Elsie's Update

Robin, now thirty-eight years old, continues to live at home with his parents in Athens, Ohio, a university town in the heart of Appalachia. This rural area still has nothing to offer Robin by way of appropriate or acceptable day programming. The local workshop is struggling to accommodate wheelchair clients from a thirty-two bed intermediate care facility in the area, and the work available requires fine motor skills that Robin does not have. The clients in the adult activity program are ambulatory but have behaviors that upset Robin, so he does not wish to attend. We feel that, at age 38, he has the right to make this decision.

Robin's day starts around 8 A.M., when he gets up, gets dressed, and makes his own coffee in his automatic coffee maker—a ritual he dearly loves. After breakfast and a short devotional period, we read to Robin from whatever book he brings to the table. Right now we are reading Jimmy Carter's *Keeping Faith*. During the past year, Robin has been very interested in the baptism of the Holy Spirit, and we have read several books on this subject.

He spends the rest of the morning exercising on a stationary bike and a rowing machine while he listens to the radio. He then takes a leisurely bath before lunch, watches the noon news and a couple of favorite soap operas, looks through the mail, and takes a nap. Examining the mail is another ritual Robin enjoys—and we get a lot of mail. He carefully sorts through it and takes out anything addressed to him. He then lays aside anything that looks as if it came from a political or religious source—letters from congressmen or party fund raisers, newsletters from the governor's office or the White House. He gets very excited if he spots mail with the White House or the governor's crest. He watches carefully while such mail is being read and then appropriates for his bulletin board anything that can be shared. He also examines carefully magazines, catalogues, or newspapers that come in the mail, especially the *Washington Post*, from which he collects pictures and articles about political figures he recognizes.

Robin has a 4′ × 6′ cork bulletin board on the wall beside his bed, and he keeps it covered with articles, pictures, cards, and snapshots. He changes the items and the configuration daily and loves to call attention to new pieces of particular interest. He usually works on the board after dinner and the early evening news. Then he rides his bike and watches TV in his room or joins the family to watch a program of mutual interest. Robin usually stays up after we have gone to bed and seems to enjoy this private time alone. He has a snack, takes another bath, checks the locks and lights, and then goes to bed.

This routine is varied by regular attendance at church and church functions and trips to local restaurants, his brother's home, doctors, and the dentist. At home Robin enthusiastically joins any social event, committee meeting, or business conference. If the visitors are friends, he shares new items on his bulletin board. If it's a big party, Robin likes to be the doorkeeper.

Robin's interests are a mixture of fantasy and reality, little boy and grown man. However, his capacities for self-direction, judgment, responsiblity, and dependability are mature and reasoned. He establishes his own life within the limitations of his disability and his membership in the family. We feel he is well aware of the limitations of his life and finds them frustrating. However, he has found ways to cope, and he has his own ways of poking fun and then laughing uproariously at a humorous situation.

Since Robin is independent in his daily living activities, he can manage very well through the day. He does not need a sitter or companion. However, he has made it very clear that he does not want to be left alone overnight. When Bob and I are away, we have Robin's brother or a student stay overnight. On such occasions he also has the choice of going to a nearby accredited facility which has respite beds. However, Robin does not choose to go there even though he does know a couple of the men from the home who come to our church.

We keep Robin's evaluations up-to-date so that he is eligible for admission to an intermediate care facility if or when an emergency or permanent placement is needed. Since Robin can manage so independently, he has not limited our life style, even in retirement. We are both free to come and go as we choose. I am very active in volunteer work, and I travel a good bit. Bob takes extended backpacking trips several times a year.

We feel that we have an adequate plan for Robin's care at this time or in the event that we should both become unable to care for Robin. We are also fortunate in having two normal children who are both working in the field of special education and who could meet any contingencies for Robin as they might arise.

We have considered, but not asked for, court-appointed guardianship of Robin. We really do not see the advantage of this for Robin at this time, but we have asked in our will that Bill and Marjorie be named successor guardians. We also know that Robin would receive some supervision and attention from our church, where he has many friends.

We have lived long enough and through enough that we are not fretting about what will happen to Robin when we die. There is a limit to what can be accomplished by planning ahead. Who knows precisely what will happen ten years from now, or five years from now, or even tomorrow? We

Marjorie DeWert and Elsie Helsel

believe that all of us are in God's care and under His protection. Robin's deep, abiding faith in God has helped him cope with a very frustrating existence on this earth. He truly believes that God is his refuge and strength, and that belief will sustain him as long as he lives.

Pointers for Professionals

So what do we as parents approaching our seventh decade have to say to professionals who are attempting to counsel parents or to train new professionals in their discipline?

1. Be humble. Nothing you have learned from books or experience gives you the right or the privilege to tell parents what they should or should not do. We really do not need any more counseling on what we should do about Robin, and we have—or know where to get—information for decision making.

2. Be supportive. Begin early to train and strengthen parents so that they can be informed, independent, responsible case managers for their children. We have been Robin's only case managers who have had a lifetime of responsibility for him. Even the best of professional relations and programs are time-limited.

3. Be accepting of parents as equal partners. Even the most limited parents have information and insight into strengths, weaknesses, and potentialities in their children that would be helpful in designing more appropriate and effective individualized program plans. Even though we ourselves are professionals and have a lifetime of experience in the field, social workers, physicians, therapists, and facility managers still talk down to us. A professional's job is to find ways, not excuses, to get parents to participate as equals in the planning process and to feel comfortable enough to use their information.

4. Be understanding of changes in parents over time. Even the most enthusiastic of parents burn out. Don't expect all parents to fit into one mold, especially aging parents who have their own problems adjusting to life's changing circumstances.

Challenges for the Future

As we look around and listen to other parents, we see some progress in the quantity and quality of programs available to persons with handicaps. We see very limited progress, however, in the acceptance of these persons as full citizens. We see an overall diminution of the strong, coordinated effort of parents to keep programs in place with adequate funding and to press for new programs still needed to fill existing gaps. We see this as a real threat to the gains achieved over the past twenty years.

We also see some new areas of anguish for parents. First, there is the controversial abortion issue, with parents caught in the middle of a fight between groups with agendas that give no consideration to the feelings of parents. Where is the unprejudiced, objective, and factual counseling for parents when a severe handicap is clearly predicted for their unborn child? Everyone is in favor of prevention up to a point. But where are those points, and who should help parents make those decisions?

In our zeal to promote prevention, what kinds of mixed messages are we sending to parents, to the public, and to the handicapped themselves concerning the value of life of the handicapped citizens already living among us? What are we saying about the quality and worth of that life while, at the same time, promoting full citizenship for persons with handicaps? What are we saying to those parents who have worked so hard to secure appropriate services for their sons and daughters and who are so justifiably proud of their accomplishments? And how are we explaining our positions on prevention to the handicapped individuals themselves who are struggling so valiantly to make it in our society?

These are some of the difficult questions for which the new generation of parents and professionals will have to find answers.

REFERENCES

Goldenberg, E.P. *Special technology for special children: Computers to serve communication and autonomy in education of handicapped children.* Baltimore: University Park Press, 1979.

QUESTIONS TO CONSIDER

1. Review the questions on page 99. How accurate were your predictions?

2. What is Marjorie's advice on how best to prepare a spouse to meet a handicapped sibling? What type of service agency might be most effective in assisting families in meeting this need?

3. What Helsel values are reflected in Robin's life style and routines? How would you characterize Robin's current quality of life? What are your thoughts on the quality of life he is likely to have in six years?

4. Elsie's thoughts on prevention of handicaps are very provocative. What is your view on prevention of handicaps as it comes into conflict with respect of individual differences? Attempt to answer the difficult questions Elsie poses at the end of her essay.

Marjorie DeWert and Elsie Helsel

Rud Turnbull is a lawyer who specializes in special education, mental retardation, and public policy. He served on the faculty of the Institute of Government at the University of North Carolina at Chapel Hill from 1969 to 1980. There he was active in local, state, and national consumer and professional organizations; he was counsel for local and state mental health and mental retardation agencies; and he was counsel to mental health committees and special education committees in the North Carolina General Assembly.

Since 1980 he has been a professor of special education and law at the University of Kansas and a senior officer of the Association for Retarded Citizens/U.S.A. and the American Association on Mental Deficiency, which he served as president from 1985 to 1986. In addition to his extensive writing on legal, policy, and ethical issues affecting citizens with mental retardation, he also has testified several times on such matters before the United States Congress.

Jay and Rud Turnbull

His son, Jay, is now seventeen years old and is in a public school program which includes classes with nondisabled students in Lawrence, Kansas. Jay, who is moderately mentally retarded, has been involved in both mainstreamed and segregated scouting, recreation programs, and church activities. Jay's two sisters, Amy and Kate, are now nine and six.

Jay's Story

H. Rutherford Turnbull III

In many respects, nothing in my life had prepared me for Jay; in other respects, everything had. Jay was born on a glorious, bright, warm Baltimore day in May 1967. His delivery at Johns Hopkins was not quite unexceptional—he was a breech baby and our obstetrician was late in arriving. From that point on, however, the unexceptional was the exception.

"It's Better for You Not to Know"

One of the first things I noticed about Jay was that he had a large, egg-shaped lump on the top of his head where most babies have a concave impression; in photographs at home it is so noticeable that it is remarkable that nobody seemed to pay it much heed. Another early warning sign was his plain dullness—not that he wasn't a beautiful child with an abundance of blond curls; it is just that he didn't turn over, move about, push himself up on his elbows, or do the other things that my friends' children of his age had done. His pediatrician, now the head of the Department of Pediatrics at a large eastern state school of medicine, seemed to pooh pooh my concerns. After measuring the circumference of Jay's head, he simply said Jay was within the high range of normalcy, bordering on a bit slow. When my ex-wife tearfully cross-examined him, giving ample display of our anxieties, his responses became even vaguer.

Had it not been for Jay's hernia in the first year of his life, we might have waited far longer to have our suspicions confirmed. Upon detecting the rupture, the pediatrician admitted Jay to Hopkins for what should have been a fairly simple operation, but it turned out to be rather more than that. The Hopkins surgeon gave Jay a thorough examination the day before the scheduled operation and immediately called off the surgery, explaining to me on the telephone that Jay's retina was unusually flat and he wanted a neurologist to look at him. Later that week, after the pediatrician, surgeon,

109

and neurologist had examined Jay, I learned that they wanted to do more tests before deciding on his surgery.

My antennae were up—I was seeing danger signals in every phrase the doctors uttered. My questions—"Can't you be more specific? Have you had cases like this before? Why is the neurologist involved? Is something wrong with his eyes?"—went unanswered. I was told, "We can't say yet; we're still checking things [not him] out."

On one of my frequent visits to the hospital to see Jay, I saw a nurse I used to date and asked her to come see Jay with me. His curls had been shaved off his head (they are in an envelope in our safe deposit box, remnants of our age of innocence), and he was in a crib next to a child whose chart read, "Nothing by mouth or intravenously," and whose head was far larger than Jay's. While we were visiting Jay, I picked up his chart and asked her to read the neurologist's report. After scanning it quickly, she said, "It's better for you not to know, Rud." And she left, suddenly saddened and taking with her my hopes for knowledge. The nurse in charge of the ward promptly appeared on the scene, admonishing me not to read the chart. "Jay's doing fine, Mr. Turnbull." Of course he was: no worse and no better than at home. But I wasn't doing fine at all.

A day or two later, still ignorant but scheduled for the neurologist to undertake some minor surgical procedure, we waited and waited and waited for him to come to see us before the surgery. When at last he appeared, I turned all my anger and ignorance on him. "Before you so much as lay a hand, much less a scalpel on Jay, I want to know, I demand to know, what the hell's going on! And where have you been all this time!"

"Saving a life down the hall—and you've got the right to be angry, Mr. Turnbull. Let's talk."

Had it not been for Dr. Neal Aronson, the neurologist who leveled with me, the entire staff of Johns Hopkins Hospital might have kept me in eternal ignorance. Simply, deliberately, humbly, and patiently he explained all: Jay's flat retina, the little egg on his head, his slowness, and his "high range of normalcy" were signs of either macrocephaly or hydrocephaly. Jay, I heard him say, was retarded and very seriously so, although the exact degree was hard to pinpoint at his early age and would be hard to fix for several years. He ran a serious risk with surgery for the hernia. To better evaluate the risk, the doctors needed to do an exploratory—that is, take a look at his brain through a very small incision, maybe blow air around his brain, or put fluid in and take pictures, nothing unusual or unusually risky. He let me know so gently that all I felt was absolution, the soft vanishing of my present and past anxiety—not the pain of the future.

Many years later I still feel strongly about that experience. In a remarkable gesture to all the fathers and mothers of all the Jays in public schools, Congress has now made it possible for parents to see their children's school records if the school receives federal assistance. Accountability, parental rights to control children, school-home dialogue and teamwork, due

H. Rutherford Turnbull III

process, misclassification—these are the concepts underlying the Buckley-Pell Amendment. As a lawyer, I am convinced of the correctness of this legislation and of the need for similar legislation in the fields of health and mental health. As Jay's father, I quickly discard "It's better for you not to know" in favor of a principle that I have believed since I was an undergraduate student and that Dr. Aronson believed and acted on: access is not only invaluable to parents and professionals, it is imperative as a course of decent conduct between people and as a weapon against charlatanry, from which I have been largely spared.

Jay's surgery went well, his hernia was repaired successfully, and he came back home with the recommendation that he be put into a behavior program at the Kennedy Institute, an adjunct of Hopkins Hospital. Trusting and hopeful, we duly enrolled Jay and were obliged, as part of his program, to watch a professor of psychology try to get him to say "Aaah" in exchange for a spoonful of banana pudding. "We want to teach him to react to his environment, to control it," we were told. And that's all we were told, even after questioning. We saw failure after failure. And to what purpose—helping Jay? collecting data?

Leaving aside (if one can) the irreparable injury Jay's repeated failures did to my ex-wife and me, and not daring to calculate the almost numberless times parents have had their children's deficiencies so pointedly and callously highlighted by helping professionals, I wonder whether the concern that we attorneys have with consent is sufficiently impressed on all of us. I shudder to think how many programs children have been enrolled in without their parents ever truly knowing the who, what, where, how, why, and how long. When did my trust turn to skepticism? When I first asked, "What's in it for Jay?" That simple question is not asked often enough. Informed consent troubles us all, and rightly it should—we don't have enough of it.

The Search

Gaps exist in Jay's story, at least as it is told here, but they stop in the years 1970 and 1971. In those years for many reasons, not the least of which was Jay (still beautiful, still heartbreakingly retarded, still without programs of any benefit), I began the search—to find a place for Jay. When my ex-wife was hospitalized for treatment of emotional disturbance and determined not to come home until Jay was no longer there, I faced what I immediately recognized as a horribly cruel choice. Which of those whom I loved would I have to give up? Whose immediate future held more promise of habilitation? The chosen one would consign the other to an institution. For reasons not necessary to be told, I chose to place Jay. At first it was easy—Cordelia, a huge, black woman who worked at the day-care center that Jay attended, offered to take care of him. He lived with her in a home I saw only once, where he thrived despite the always tearful, rending visits I made to the center. I made fewer and fewer visits as they became harder and harder for him and me. Both Cordelia and I knew that Jay's being with her would never be permanent, and I was constrained to begin my search for a school that would accept a nonverbal, nonambulatory, non-toilet-trained, almost three-year-old boy.

My search took me from Massachusetts to South Carolina, from expensive, pretty, and small institutions to large, dilapidated, reasonably priced, and overcrowded ones. I saw children whose very existence caused me to wonder (I struggled to reconcile their animal-like treatment with my religious training and "God's mysteries") and whose appearances were horrid to behold (a large head on a tiny body, three times out of proportion to the body; an open spine on an infant whom a Sister cradled, affirming the right of that child to live and to live with love). Later I was repulsed as I saw patients in institution after institution sitting in butterfly chairs all day long, dressed in the same faded denim, in places that smelled of the same stale urine and disinfectant, with the same terrazzo floors, in wards where no partitions separated beds from chairs from toilets-with-no-seats from steel tubs for bathing. I asked myself why the state couldn't do something about these places.

I inspected almost thirty institutions in eight states in a period of three months, and all I could find for Jay was the nonambulatory ward of a state institution nearby (I vowed Jay would *never* go there) and the unclassified wards in two small Catholic schools. How was I to choose between the two schools? Surely by the people involved, since the facilities in one were pathetically overcrowded and the facilities in the other were old. It was my choice to make, and mine alone.

As fate would have it, I chose well. Sister Mary Howard's Pine Harbor School in Pascoag, Rhode Island, no longer exists physically. The diocese ran out of willing sisters and sufficient funds, and the state association for retarded children and the state itself joined hands to condemn the school as unsafe. Yet it still does exist in Jay's life and my heart. It was there that Katie McCarthy and her family "adopted" Jay when they saw him in the Christmas play. It was at Pine Harbor that, in the most wrenching moment of my life, I performed the most difficult act of my life, and handed Jay to Katie, a teen-age volunteer and an utter stranger; crying, burbling, stammering, I managed only to say, "Take him, he's yours now." Jay's screams and his look ("Again? You are leaving me again!") remain with me today—vivid, poignant, immediate.

Pine Harbor closed, and Sister Howard and Katie took Jay to Crystal Springs Nursery in Assonet, Massachusetts. There he made friends with other children approximately his age; now able to stand and walk (Katie had taught him to walk), he toddled after them as they left for their group home. "Would it be all right if he were transferred off campus to the community group home?" the administrators asked. "Oh, by all means," I replied. They elaborated, "It's an old house, but it's fixed up nicely, and there are two wonderful house parents there; are you sure you don't mind?" "Not as long as he can be with his friends and have a chance for love," I said.

Sue and Dom D'Antuono cared for Jay and his friends for two years, until Ann (my new wife) and I brought him home. Now every night he begins his prayers with "God, bless Sue and Dom and Paul Taylor (his roommate) and Johnny Corkle and Elaine Loomis and Michele and Annie Raffle. . . ." He learned love in a community group home.

Nowadays it is sometimes and in some places fashionable to posit that parents and their retarded children have inherent conflicts of interests; accordingly, it is argued that the state, in its duty to children, should inquire into the decision of a parent to place a child out of the home. The method of intervention should be a due process hearing, conducted in court or before a quasi-judicial body, in which the parents and child (represented by counsel of the state's choice) can give evidence why placement in or out of the home is desirable, necessary, inevitable, or whatever.

The argument appeals to me as a lawyer. I am concerned about children, particularly retarded children. I have a fairly good idea about institutions (particulary state ones, since I work with staff in them and serve on the Human Rights Committee in one). And I have an abiding concern, common to most lawyers, with fair procedures producing fair and acceptable results.

But when I look at myself as a parent, I shudder to think about the conditions of my search: my family in disarray; my home divided; temporary care clearly only temporary; many institutions unacceptable for even the most desperate persons; and in, around, and throughout it all, Jay's love for me and mine for him making rational choices difficult. Due process for Jay? For my ex-wife? For me? What role would the courts have had in my search? It's a question to ponder in these days of judicial activism in mental health. The lawyer and the parent in me speak in conflicting terms.

I have no such conflict, however, when I think of the inability and unwillingness of the states to comply with accreditation standards. The public and private places I saw were grim testimony to the urgent need to upgrade the physical facilities and staff of institutions by whatever means are successful, including court action. Standards are minimal and necessary; they are never sufficient. Only good people can make institutions good.

You Can Always Come Home

It may seem incredible, but the day Ann and I took Jay from Sue and Dom and his friends was a sad day. We could feel the breaching of bonds slowly and carefully nurtured by Jay and his friends. It's not as though we had not been in touch with Jay, but telephone calls and a visit at Easter are poor substitutes for physical presence, for affectionate hugs, for quiet moments together on the couch. What is more, Jay had been at school for just over three years, so I had a rather poor idea of what I was getting into. But we were certain of one thing, and it was that Jay must come home.

We knew about his classes, his friends, the field trips, and Sue's and Dom's mothers, who had welcomed Jay into their homes during holiday times. But we were well fixed to help Jay. Both of us had served as president of the local association for retarded children. Both were on the board of directors of the sheltered workshop and the group home. We were advisors in a professional capacity to a host of state and local mental retardation agencies. Both of us had worked hard to get a primary class for the trainable mentally retarded started just in time for Jay to be a charter member. We served on the board of a statewide political action agency for handicapped children. Both of us could draw on a wealth of professionally qualified friends.

Sad to say, neither of us was fully prepared for some of what lay ahead. We learned, for example, that the community could be inhospitable. Some friends and colleagues recoiled when Jay went to shake their hands, as though he were contagious. Others were glad to have their children visit our house, where there were always plenty of cookies and milk, but we had to tell those parents that friendship is a two-way street. And strangers, curious about this lad with the strange gait and large head, stared even as he devoured his ice cream cone, like an ordinary kid.

The battles on Jay's behalf continued and expanded, for now we had an immediate stake in the outcomes. School boards, county commissions, mental health boards, and town recreation departments at first reluctantly and then with some conviction began to heed our pleas: take Jay's class out of the administration building and put it in a regular school, use surplus funds to keep the developmental center open, increase the range of programs for the mentally retarded, try to get the hot lunches to the kids at camp before 1:30 P.M.

Not all was bleak, by any means. Strangers became the dearest friends because they loved Jay, and he loved them back in his unquestioning, unbargaining, unrestrained way. Other people in town remain strangers to us, but Jay is greeted by many people when we take our Sunday outings downtown and in the mall—his circle of acquaintances and friends is large and varied. Jay has changed the attitudes of people who can affect his life; he has given them an understanding and (what is more important) an appreciation of his needs.

A successful farmer in the north end of our county has learned to appreciate people like Jay. The ideologies and life styles of the people in the north end are markedly more conservative than those in the southern end, where the university is. This farmer laughs with us now about the time I asked him to rent a home for use by retarded women. "Will they shoot my cows?" he asked. I assured him they would not shoot his cows or assault people, would care for themselves, and would earn taxable income at the workshop. Not persuaded, he investigated the group home board and later came to board meetings, listening intently as we talked about the program, house parents, residents, and funding. After one meeting I asked, "Mr.

H. Rutherford Turnbull III

Pope, have you any questions?" He replied, "No, I don't think so. Come see me in two days, and you can pick up the lease."

Many months later after innumerable alterations to the rented home and considerable hullabaloo and indecision by local and state licensing bureaus, Mr. Pope's house was ready for occupancy. Two nights before the first residents were to arrive, he attended the board meeting to say he had been talking to his friends in Cedar Grove, the community where the home is. Out of both curiosity and fear, someone on the board asked, "Have you heard any negative comments, any objections to the women?" He paused, smiled slowly, and said with increasing firmness, "No, I haven't. I don't expect to. And I'd better not!"

Some mental retardation and mental health professionals view lawyers as Don Quixotes who tilt at windmills that the professionals have painstakingly created to serve the retarded (and not wholly incidentally, themselves). Surely, that view is justified, but just as surely it is incomplete. Litigation does indeed change social institutions by challenging the forms (facilities, programs, bureaucracies) as well as the norms (the notion that the retarded are best put out of sight and mind) that underlie and support those institutions (law being one of them) that have so unfairly treated retarded citizens. To mental retardation professionals throughout the country, I am happy to say that the courts are coming to the rescue and are prodding other agencies of government, particularly the legislature, to mend its ways and amend its laws.

We are, however, at a crucial juncture in the rights-for-the-retarded movement, and finely attuned thoughtfulness must be the order of the day. Having established the retarded citizen's basic right to, for example, education and treatment, or against involuntary sterilization and peonage, lawyers and lawgivers move into the stage of monitoring compliance and of implementing the rights that are given universally but denied individually. We must be careful to think hard about, for example, the intended and unintended consequences of forcing community facilities down the throats of a largely ignorant and sometimes hostile public. When we deinstitutionalize or mainstream, we must ask, "Whom do we take from what and put where and how fast?" Ann and I thought the answer was easy and now know it is not.

Lawyers know that laws are unenforceable unless they have the weight of public opinion behind them; prohibition and anti-abortion legislation bear witness to that fact. But lawyers also know that public attitudes can be shaped by law. The issue of which comes first—the law that changes an attitude or the attitude that makes the law practicable—is raised in the deinstitutionalization issue. It will take time to effect change so that all the Jays can go home and stay home. But we must make the time brief, for there are many Jays and few ways now of bringing them all home.

I have been fortunate in the past three years to have had the chance to put my professional training to work in the mental retardation field. In these years I have consulted with, advised, helped solve problems with, instructed, and written for a host of mental health and mental retardation agencies at the federal, state, and local levels. Because Jay and Ann have given me a good working knowledge of the deficiencies and capacities of mentally retarded people, I think my advice and counsel have been far more effective than they would otherwise have been.

Several months ago, for example, the Education Committee of North Carolina's House of Representatives was debating the state's second effort at an equal educational opportunities act. During the course of debate, several legislators questioned the meaning of "appropriate education," a phrase used in both the federal and the proposed (now enacted) state law. Directing their question to the deputy superintendent of public instruction, they were told, in effect, that he did not know what it meant and that, in any event, the public schools could not afford to provide it to handicapped children and their teachers were not trained to give it. Astonished by this very blunt and negative reply, some of them turned to the sponsor of the bill, who then turned to me for an answer.

"If your child is nonhandicapped," I began, "and can go to the bathroom by himself when you take him out to dinner and can return to your table having washed his hands and buttoned his trousers, you will think that an appropriate education for him does not consist of training him to do these small but very important acts. But if your son is handicapped and cannot do these things, it becomes very important to you and him that he be taught to do them. His eye and hand coordination, his manual dexterity, and his physical strength become sources of real concern because you do not want to be embarrassed by him in public and you do not want him to embarrass himself. An appropriate education for one handicapped child, then, may consist of teaching him to button his trousers. Does that help?" Indeed it did. Everyone on that committee understood immediately the meaning of the term and its importance. Jay certainly helped me to be a better lawyer that day.

During the same session of the legislature, I was working with a committee consisting largely of lawyers on proposed (now enacted) legislation to enable mentally handicapped people to have limited guardianships. Many of the legislators and clerks of court who opposed the legislation could not understand the concept of limited guardianship. They assumed that a person was either wholly incompetent or not incompetent at all. How, they asked, can we know otherwise?

Using as examples Jay's adult retarded friends, I explained the gradations of capacity/incapacity that mental retardation professionals are accustomed to describing in their own language (i.e., profound, severe, moderate, mild), but I did so with an illustration the legislators would understand. "Suppose you know of an adult who wants to have a friend of the opposite sex. Suppose both are healthy and will want to have sexual relations. Neither wants children. Both have limited understanding of money and how to make their way in the world. The girl has been instructed in alternative methods of contraception and wants to be sterilized. Should she be able to consent to that procedure on her own? If the answer is yes, should she at the same time be denied a guardian to help her make her way in the world?"

The committee members then understood limited guardianship. Jay, Ann, friends in the group homes, friends at the sheltered workshop, and residents at the state institutions had given me the answer to an otherwise difficult question.

Rights to education, appropriate placement, limited guardianship, and least restriction are concepts that have turned the world of mental retardation upside down, have caused us to ask questions and seek answers we did not think to ask a few years ago, and have involved lawyers among others in the turmoil that surrounds the lives of retarded persons. If my experience in giving straight answers in simple terms to inquiring legislators is typical of the contributions that other lawyers are making in courtrooms as well as in committee rooms, I believe that lawyers are making significant contributions and that some turmoil and uncertainty is a small price to pay in exchange for those contributions. To probe, analyze, question, debate, and challenge are lawyers' functions. To provide answers is likewise a lawyer's function. My answers have come from life with Jay, Ann, and our retarded friends.

It has not been possible to write this essay without recalling enormous amounts of pain and an equal quantity of joy. The reader can only begin to appreciate what Jay and Ann have meant to me, personally and professionally. And I myself am just beginning to see the results of their contributions to my professional life as legislation and concept papers I have worked on intensively and extensively survive public scrutiny.

At one point in my life, I knew none of the answers, much less any of the questions. At another, I was fairly sure of knowing many of the questions and at least a preponderance of the answers. But I am older now and wiser. Jay, too, is older and perhaps wiser. Like Ann, I have learned that I still have much to learn. I am wary, then, of certainty and of advocates who say they have not only all the questions but all the answers as well. Do they know Jay? Do they understand, as Ann and I do, that mental retardation is a process?

Jay's life has changed drastically several times in his brief ten years, and he himself has changed and will continue to change. Inflexibility and dialectics would not have helped him or others of us caught up in the process. Rather, freedom in acquiring knowledge about Jay, in being informed about his placements, in having alternative places available for him to live, and in obtaining services that fit his abilities and disabilities as they exist at different times—this should be the moving factor in reform in mental retardation. If the law is to assist Jay and others like him appreciably, it will be because lawyers, lawgivers, and policy makers have given careful thought to what freedom of choice means for retarded persons and their parents.

My present belief is that it is the function of law and those who make and affect it to create more choices for the retarded and their parents. We all cry out with the same message: let us choose, and give us more from which to choose. The felt need of our time has been the felt need of the past, the need for greater choice in responding to the evolving process of life with a retarded person. It is the function of law to shape the institutions of society so that freedom of choice can be increased for all of us.

QUESTIONS TO CONSIDER

1. What have been the positive contributions that Jay has made to Rud? Is it fair to say that Jay's disability has enhanced Rud's ability as a lawyer? As a person? Do you expect this trend to continue in the future?

2. How much faith does Rud have in the law? Will that same attitude continue? Does it cause any conflict for him? How will he resolve it?

3. What type of family support services would Rud have needed when Jay was three to be able to keep him at home and avoid institutionalization? Are such services available today? Are they likely to be available in six years? What about services for Jay once he came home? Does successful accommodation of a child in a home or community require only services? If not, what else is involved?

4. What does Rud mean by "freedom of choice"? When should parental choice give way to choice by the disabled person? When do you think Jay will be allowed to make significant choices?

H. Rutherford Turnbull III

Jay's Story— The Paradoxes

H. Rutherford Turnbull III

Jay has grown up, so to speak. He is now 16 and well through his first rite of passage, puberty. Nowadays, he forces me to come to grips with new and troubling realities and prospects. He has taught me that the greatest disabilities are those we impose on ourselves, that the greatest growth is that which comes from removing our own disabilities. And he inspires me to new personal and professional growth. That is the ultimate paradox: Jay both disables and enables me. I will try to illustrate my point by describing other paradoxes—the parts that make up the sum.

Jay will pass too soon from public school to adult services. He will move from a school system that must serve everyone to a nonsystem of multiple programs with usually inconsistent goals, functions, eligibility criteria, funding and governing authorities, and accountability—programs that need not serve him but must merely practice nondiscrimination. He will go from a relatively protective system to one that may impose responsibilities on him that he cannot meet. And he will graduate from a system in which I can legally and functionally command services and accountability to a system that is far less amenable to my importunings. Will there be a group home for him, a job, entitlement benefits, recreation, and other opportunities for growth and protection? Frankly, the answer is unclear, and the pending transition from some certainty to great uncertainty is profoundly disquieting to me.

Another aspect of Jay's growing older also distresses me. He is no longer a cute or precious little boy. He is a maturing young man with a confused sense of his own sexuality and infrequent but massive outbursts of temper that are sometimes dangerous to him and can be harmful to his younger sisters. Today, those who care for him must be of college age; females do very nicely so long as they are mature, self-confident, and not easily embarrassed since Jay sometimes needs prompting. But I can envision the time when only young men will be able to take charge of him easily and comfortably.

His behavior has become more problematic. Because his seizures occur almost invariably when his routine changes (he barely tolerates our weekend excursions although, ironically, he does well at one-week camps or longer stays away from home), we allow him to opt out of some family activities. We consciously plan our vacations around his summer camp trips now because one extended vacation upset him greatly and triggered a harmful seizure. Life without Jay is sometimes far easier for us and for him, too. But it is a life lived deliberately without one's son, and that is no reason for joy.

When our adult friends occasionally invite Jay to a movie or other special event, I can appreciate their extraordinary kindness. As well-mannered as he almost always is, he is not a child anymore but an awkward, unusual-looking teen-ager; and he usually does not spontaneously respond to their goodness with manifest appreciation. My gratitude for them is all the greater, as is my sadness for his condition.

When I say sadness, I think of the anxiety he experiences about his maturation and the remorse he feels about his difficult behaviors—he is not a child any longer. Family, friends, and the public now regard him differently, sometimes more cautiously. Paradoxically, however, he remains a boy—a physically mature person inside whose strong body is the mind and often the disposition of a child. He is my boy and my child, but he will never be fully my son. The pleasures and disruptions that my parents and I experienced will not be ours; because of his retardation he cannot be my companion in much of life. His disability is not just his; it is mine, too. It twice curses—it debilitates him and me alike—as it deprives us both of normalcy.

Add to this my own, natural sense of mortality (I am feeling the harsh pinch of my own limitations as a father, a professional, and a mortal), and one finds me greatly conflicted. I regard my two normal daughters as my bonuses. I know and constantly tell myself that comparison is not fair to them or to Jay, who has taught me so much about life and who has enriched my life so greatly. But I will not deny and cannot proscribe my feelings or the unresolved conflict they cause. A strong sense of fairness tells me I should feel equally about Jay and my girls, but I do not. It is not that I love them more than him, or him more than them, or that I would do more or less for them or him. It is, rather, that I look on their lives with a different sense of potentiality and fullness; I clearly have different assumptions about how we will all grow older together. The joys Amy and Kate bring are both great and small, and they occur daily. The joys Jay brings likewise are great and small, but they occur infrequently. That may be part of what mental retardation means: it is the delayed development of the normal life of parent and child.

It is hard to demonstrate precisely the causal relationship, but I know that my own sense of mortality and my own differential expectations of the

H. Rutherford Turnbull III

future with my children have caused me to take a new professional direction. I realize now that the law—as powerful as it has been and will be in defining who and what Jay and I are—is a necessary but not a sufficient system for him or me. In the eyes of the law, shock therapy, compulsory sterilization, institutionalization, and other risky, painful, or unvalidated interventions are presumed wrong. And that is how the law should be. But what is right? What is just in the case of the defective newborn child, which Jay was; in the case of the retarded adult without parents, which Jay most likely will be; in the case of the dying retarded person, which he will become? We may know the law's answers, but are they entirely right? I must explore behind today's correct legal answers.

Others are accurate when they observe that retarded children exacerbate their parents' existential quandries. As Jay and I grow older together, the existential aspects of my life grow more important to me, and I more fully realize the truly revolutionary impact Jay has had on me and my life. Like the great teachers (Ghandi or Christ) or the great events (surrender at Yorktown or the Bolshevik Revolution), he and his retardation have turned my life upside down and sent me into entirely different life streams than I had prepared for or anticipated. Reversals of expectations for the future are commonplace perhaps; but Jay has been the catalyst for my existential revolution.

That is not bad. It is good—I am glad for the push to develop, for the new personal and professional directions. But it is different. Most of my friends whose children are not disabled and even those whose children are disabled cannot easily or often travel that route with me. It is my blessing that Ann can and does. And it is Jay who impels me along this unexplored route. That is one of Jay's most important contributions nowadays. It is one aspect of the paradoxical effect of his life on me. I am grateful to him. But the path is hard to forge: the prospects are both exciting and troubling; the law could be right, but it could be wrong. And it may or may not be confluent with my sense of ethical right and wrong. At least for me at this point in my life, the challenges that I face as Jay's parent can be faced—and all of our children's growth and life without us can be met more confidently and comfortably—if we can agree about what is right. After all, the lesson of numerous landmark cases, when stripped of their legal trappings, is simply that certain kinds of treatment are just plain wrong; they slaughter our collective consciences and sense of rightness. The future challenge, then, is to agree on what is ethically right—the law most likely will follow.

Lest I paint too dismal a portrait of my life with Jay, allow me to put another light on the picture. As Jay has grown up, he has developed an uncanny competence. It is one that he either skillfully hides or that we do not see because we do not expect it. By way of example, we concluded some time early in his fifteenth year that it would be safe to leave Jay at home while the rest of us went about our daily errands. We reasoned that we would be gone no longer than an hour or so, and we could lock the house so he could not leave or let anybody enter. There were few ways he could injure himself, (the electric range, the knife rack) and he had not been inclined toward any of them. Knowing that we eventually would have to risk his independence, we planned for him to play his records while we were away, confident that he would do just as he does when we are in the house and allow him to choose his activities. It was with some trepidation but at least equal confidence and determination that we left. And it was with a great relief that we returned to find Jay comfortably ensconced in his favorite living-room chair, music in the air and a dirty plate on the kitchen table along with telltale bread crumbs and a dinner knife with peanut butter and jelly on it. Jay clearly knew what to do when left alone.

On another occasion I became exasperated with our children's constant meddling with my record collection; none of them were prone to handle the records with care. To prevent my collection's further deterioration, I put my most treasured records into a locked hallway closet. But I did so when I thought no one was watching. By happenstance, Jay saw me—only for a few seconds—putting the records into the closet. Several days later he found the ring of keys, selected the proper one from among three others, opened the closet, and chose one of the hidden records to play. That he did this when I was at work is all the more evidence of his abilities.

It is on occasions such as these that Jay's competence delights and surprises me. There is more to him than I am sometimes apt to believe, and that fact is reassuring for the future. I tell myself to be cautious when estimating Jay's abilities and disabilities; I recall that more than a few professionals underestimated him and he proved them wrong. For instance, his long-term memory is remarkable: to this very day he remembers in his prayers the house parents and children in his group home in Massachusetts, where he lived ten to twelve years ago. Perhaps, I say to myself, Jay will indeed have the competence to work in sheltered or even supervised competitive employment and to adjust to life in a group home. Of course, that is my hope, but it is not one that I entertain without mixed feelings.

As I wrote earlier, the hardest day in my life was the day I surrendered Jay to a stranger in an institution. Jay's sense of loss was profound. He suffered from depression for several months, and my later visits to him (after the mandatory time for his adjustment) caused him to cry uncontrollably when I was with him, to cling desperately to me, and to pull savagely at my hair so I could not leave him. My sense of loss was no less great; it is a sense I feel even now. I dreaded the recent day I admitted him to a hospital for one month of neurological and other medical evaluation. I knew he needed it and I knew the hospital staff were extraordinarily competent. But my sense of loss was powerful. Jay adjusted magnificently; I fared less well.

This sense is one that inevitably affects my rational self. I know that out-of-home placement will be appropriate for the adult Jay, his sisters, and his parents. The competing interests balance out—Jay has a right to a normalized adult life (most children leave their parents' homes), his sisters have their own rights to normalization, and so do Ann and I. Indeed, Jay positively delights in his overnight camping trips with the Special Scouts troop and the Special Olympics; he may depend on us, but that does not mean he doesn't get tired of us.

Still, my sadness about Jay's leaving our home is manifold. There is the sadness that I would experience if he could not leave home or if there were no community alternatives for him. And there is the sadness I know I will feel upon his inevitable departure. My experience of surrendering Jay when he was only a child cannot help informing my emotions when it comes time for Jay to go away again. Or when my death approaches. The sense of loss, past and future, is pervasive and powerful.

In a way, I think, that is what our seven-year-old Amy was expressing during two particularly insightful moments. When CBS-TV was visiting us recently for three days of filming for the Charles Kuralt *Sunday Morning Show*, we consented to her being interviewed alone about Jay. The reporter asked her what it meant to her to have a retarded brother. She answered that she wasn't concerned about his being different; after all, she and he both liked music, both danced, and both had a lot of things in common. Pressing the issue, the reporter asked what she thought about Jay's future. And here she blind-sided everyone (particularly us) by saying that she worries about whether he will have a job and nice clothes and a good place to live. The reporter gently asked what she would do if she found out that Jay did not have these things. She promptly and unhesitatingly answered, "He won't have to worry because I'll give him my money. I don't want him to be a bum." Like me, she could not tolerate Jay's loss of material comforts and family.

On another occasion, Amy and Ann were being interviewed by a minister and his psychologist wife on a Topeka television show about differences in a family. When asked to describe Jay, Amy blurted out her concern about his seizures and added that during one of them he had grabbed her and hurt her. Ann was caught off guard by that response; she had expected Amy to describe Jay in any way except that. Amy, too, may have realized that she had unwittingly cast Jay in a very unfavorable light; so as the show was in its concluding minute and the hosts were trying to wind it up, Amy insisted on one last word and squeezed into the final seconds this affirmation: "What really hurts is not the hits but when you lose a friend. I am glad Jay is part of our family."

None of my training or skill enables me to improve on Amy's assessment. What hurts is when Jay has his seizures, when he is depressed, when he opts out of our lives, and when he cannot or will not be my son. What hurts is the prospect that both Jay's disability and society's response to it will render him a bum. What hurts is losing a loved one, however that loss occurs.

Adjustment in our life with Jay means learning to do without; it is learning to cope with many types of loss. Paradoxically, it also means learning to appreciate the great bounty he provides. What is so heartening is Jay's innate sweetness and his secret competence. It is his ability to teach me how to live life. It is the road of intellectual and spiritual growth that he causes me to travel. It is his constant presence in my life, his limited but comfortable companionship. It is his way of helping me overcome some of my own limitations and accept his and mine, thus adding to my personal and professional integrity, endowing me with a reciprocal sensitivity to other people, and showing me how to practice tolerance. He displays and thereby teaches about unconditional love, nonmanipulative relationships, and an essential peace and contentment. No doubt, Amy, we are all glad that Jay is part of our family, paradoxes and all.

QUESTIONS TO CONSIDER

1. Review the questions on p. 118. How accurate were your predictions?
2. How does Jay's presence exacerbate the existential aspects of Rud's life? Do you think Rud will resolve these feelings over the next six years? What resources or processes do you think will be helpful?
3. How does Rud characterize adjustment to life with Jay? Does the meaning of adjustment change at different points of the life cycle—when Jay was initially diagnosed, at the time of institutionalization, at the time of deinstitutionalization, during puberty, and as he approaches adulthood? In six years, Jay will be past the age of majority. Will adjustment mean something different at that time?
4. Rud describes certain paradoxes of his life with Jay. Will the current paradoxes ever be resolved? How? What will the future paradoxes be?
5. Does Rud continue to believe in maximum choice? Why, or why not?

H. Rutherford Turnbull III

Ann Turnbull was a member of the special education faculty at the University of North Carolina at Chapel Hill when she contributed to the first edition of *Parents Speak Out*. She also worked as a regional consultant for special education programs and as a member of an interdisciplinary evaluation team for a university affiliated program at the University of North Carolina.

Together with her family, she moved to the University of Kansas in 1980 and now is associate professor of special education as well as acting associate director of the Bureau of Child Research. In addition to serving as vice-president of the Education Division of the American Association on Mental Deficiency and as a member of the board of directors of the local Association for Retarded Citizens, she has continued to work in the areas of family adaptation, mainstreaming, and individualized education. Currently, her research involves studying how families can be responsive to the needs of all members, not just the member with a disability. Her work in family systems focuses on family strengths, coping skills, and positive contributions that disabled members and their families make to each other.

Ann and Jay Turnbull

From Professional to Parent
A Startling Experience

Ann P. Turnbull

I can vividly recall when I spoke three years ago to an interagency committee in a nearby community on the topic of deinstitutionalization. At the time I was a strong advocate for the quick return home of substantial numbers of mentally retarded persons from state institutions. I was interested in developing an educational program tailored to the needs of mentally retarded children and their families during the transition process from the institution to the community. I was in contact with the interagency committee to solicit the names of families who might be interested in involvement with such a program.

A social worker attending the meeting from a nearby institution reported that a ten-year-old female from the local community had been identified by institutional staff as having high probability for successful deinstitutionalization. Another member of the group stated that this child's parents had no interest in having her at home and that, in fact, they bitterly opposed the idea.

At that point I remarked that it was difficult to understand that kind of parental response. Immediately a mother of a mentally retarded boy flew to her feet and began berating me in front of the group. While shaking her finger in my face, she screamed, "Do you know what it is like to live with a mentally retarded child?" I felt both embarrassed and defensive. After trying to explain my comment, I responded (probably in a somewhat self-righteous way), "No, I don't know what it is like, but in two weeks I will begin to find out. My husband and I will be bringing his mentally retarded son home from an institution." She smiled at me as if to say, "Are you ever in for it!" Yet my confidence in approaching the new parental role and responsibilities was unshaken. I had three degrees in special education with an emphasis in mental retardation, several years of teaching experience in public schools and in a residential institution, and a position on the university faculty with a joint appointment in a university-affiliated facility focusing on the diagnosis and treatment of developmental disorders and on provision of services to the handicapped and the School of Education. Being with mentally retarded children was a way of life for me. I thought to myself, "Just wait. I will show you that it really is not all that difficult to be a parent."

When Rud, my husband, and I first became friends, we often talked about Jay or prepared care packages to send him. From the beginning Jay was very much a part of our relationship. When we decided to get married, I insisted that we bring Jay home. Rud was very pleased that our family would be together. So began Jay's deinstitutionalization.

Rud and I took a leisurely trip through New England and on our return picked Jay up at his school in Massachusetts. We were very happy to see him and, were filled with excitement and anticipation as we packed his things into the car. After a tearful good-bye to Sue and Dom D'Antuono, we started the trip back home to North Carolina. We stopped early on the first afternoon at a motel so we could have a relaxing swim before dinner. As we approached the pool, Jay's temper tantrum started, and it did not end for a seeming eternity. He kicked and screamed and cried. Finally, when he calmed down, he got into the pool but would not budge from the railing on the side. A girl much younger than Jay was swimming laps beside him. Her father, who was beaming with pride and clapping at her performance, turned to me and said, "Do you always have this much trouble with him?" I absolutely froze. I could not muster any kind of response. I wanted to shout, "Give me time. I've been his mother for less than a day." I choked my tears back and insisted that we go back to the room. Throughout the remainder of the trip home, the question kept echoing in my mind, "Do you always have this much trouble with him?"

Jay seemed happy with his new home. We spent the first days getting to know the girls next door and shopping for clothes. Jay was naturally very unsure about his new surroundings and was unable to understand immediately what was happening. He had a new mother, a new home, a new school, and new friends. The only consistent contact in his life was his daddy, and Jay was determined not to let him get out of sight. While on a shopping trip during that first week, Rud went to the bathroom while Jay and I were looking around in a department store. Jay panicked when his daddy left and started flailing around on the floor, screaming at the top of his lungs, "Daddy, Daddy, Daddy!" It was the heartfelt plea of a child who had been left many times before. I ached for him, yet I ached for myself also when crowds of people started peering at us and at my futile attempts to provide comfort. As the screams became louder and the crowds larger, I felt more and more helpless and inept. My image of being a model mother able to handle difficult situations was beginning to crumble.

For one who thought she knew a lot, the last three years have, indeed, been a humbling experience. The twenty-four-hour reality test has challenges far greater than any examination I ever took while earning my three degrees. In fact, the three degrees may have been more a hindrance than a help in meeting my new parental responsibilities. I had always been taught to be objective and to consider the facts of a situation. All of a sudden, I had an ache in my heart, a knot in my stomach, and tears welling in my eyes. It did not take long for it to dawn on me that the mother from the interagency meeting was right—I was in for a startling experience.

Jay was soon evaluated at the interdisciplinary clinic where I headed the Special Education Section. Suddenly, I was thrust into the parent role in my own professional territory. As I sat in the observation room watching Jay take test after test over a five-hour period, I was shocked at how different it was to observe as a mother rather than as a special educator. College students were also observing—it was standard practice at this clinic for students to observe—and were making remarks about Jay's language and motor skills, pointing out his particular deficiencies. I became incensed at how casually they made their comments. One made a comment about some developmental history she had read in the records—the privacy of Jay's past and of family business had been invaded by sheer strangers. Although I had known it was standard practice for students to have access to records, suddenly the issue of confidentiality took on new meaning when it was my family being exposed. After all the evaluations had been completed, several of my colleagues at the clinic went over the results with Rud and me. These colleagues were sensitive, supportive, and helpful; but as I sat there receiving the information, rather than giving it (which was my usual role), I struggled to remain composed. A glaring memory is the jolt I felt when Jay's IQ score was reported; it was much lower than previous tests had indicated. I could easily recite all the reasons that IQ tests are poor predictors of the future adjustment and employability of retarded adults, yet I still ached with the reality of Jay's severe handicap. At home that evening Rud and I wept from the tension of the day and our concern for Jay's future. I wondered then how many parents had left a conference with me in my professional role and had experienced the same reaction.

In Jay's first months at home, I faced many of the emotional reactions that parents typically encounter immediately after the birth of a handi-capped child. Almost all of my friends were professionals whose work related to the developmental problems of children. Many of them reacted to Jay as a patient or client, rather than as a child. I became very angry at their offhand remarks, and as a result, some of my closest friendships were abruptly ended. One friend commented, "I've never seen a child with such a big head." Another said. "Doesn't Jay remind you of an autistic child, the way he stares off into space?" How does a new mother respond to such questions? One unfortunate situation happened with one of my best friends, who was also a special educator. Jay and I went to see her one Sunday afternoon to take a pie we had made for her to serve to her weekend company. Jay was beginning to feel more secure with me and happened to be in a delightful mood that afternoon. He told my friend and her husband about his school, sang some of his favorite songs, and listed the ingredients we had put into the pie. He laughed and played and enjoyed himself. I was so proud of him I could hardly wait to share with Rud the wonderful afternoon we had had together. The next day my friend dropped by the office to thank me for the pie. She commented that her husband had hardly said anything for the rest of the afternoon and evening after we left because he was so depressed after being with Jay. I was speechless. What did she mean? Jay had behaved perfectly at her house. Why was her husband depressed? I was unable to ask any questions or make any kind of response. She left my office, and a friendship was over. It seemed so unfair.

Yes, Jay is different. His developmental level is far below his chronological age. Will he spend the rest of his life depressing other people? Will he be able to find friends who can love and respect him for who he is? I was very confused at that point and felt alienated from many of my professional colleagues who were advising me to be objective and to remove myself from the emotion of the situation. I was getting the message that they thought I was an obnoxious and hostile parent. I had been on the inside long enough to know what professionals think about parents who refuse their advice. I could remember having those feelings myself about parents. That's what really hurt. I felt both parental anger and sorrow over some of my own professional mistakes in previous interactions with parents.

One of the major hurdles in Jay's home adjustment was reestablishing his bladder control. During Jay's first year at home, he went from being dry during the day to wetting his pants twelve to fifteen times per day. He also wet his bed several times during the night. We later found out that his incontinence was caused by medicine he was taking for his eyes, but we struggled with the problem for a four- to five-month period before we identified the cause. Every morning I would send eight to ten pairs of jeans and underwear to school with Jay; every afternoon he brought home a huge sack of urine-soaked clothes. Each morning his bedroom smelled of urine. Keeping up with the laundry alone was almost overwhelming. We were charting his wetting accidents at home, as his teachers were doing at school, but no consistent pattern emerged. We started a program of taking him to the bathroom every twenty to thirty minutes but met little success. He always seemed to wet during the intervals. His pediatrician started giving him kidney and urinary tests to determine whether a medical problem existed; it was through her persistent and committed efforts that the connection between the incontinence and Jay's medications was established. A psychologist was also working with us and Jay's teachers on behavioral approaches. She spent an incredible amount of time reviewing charts and planning reasonable interventions. If all families of handicapped children could be fortunate enough to work with sensitive and competent professionals like Joanna Dalldorf and Carolyn Schroeder, how much easier parenting would be. Joanna and Carolyn worked with us on almost a daily basis

Ann P. Turnbull

through a very difficult period. They were supportive, flexible, and willing to try over and over again when their first efforts were unsuccessful.

We encountered our share of charlatans during that episode. While attending a conference, Rud and I were introduced to a psychologist who told us he was writing a book on managing the behavior of retarded children at home. We asked what suggestions he had for chronic incontinence, as we described our problem. He flippantly replied that a problem of that nature could quickly be eliminated by feeding Jay a couple sacks of pretzels every day. He explained that the salt would soak up the urine, and the wetting would be eliminated. He was completely serious and smiled self-righteously, as if he had the answer to all the world's problems. I suggested to him that he include an obesity program in his book for the retarded children who ate all the pretzels. That type of easy answer to a very complex problem is the type of advice that creates mistrust and alienation between professionals and parents.

Another professional, one who worked at an institution for retarded individuals, also had a solution to the night wetting problem. He recommended that we get up during the night every hour on the hour to see if Jay was wet or dry. If he was wet, he should be made to sit on the toilet and then to walk from his bed to the toilet twenty times. After changing his pajamas and the sheets on his bed, he should be allowed to go back to sleep, only to be awakened again at the next hour. I laughed at his recommendation, and he quickly asked me how committed I was to eliminating the problem. The institutional staff, he reported, was willing to follow such a schedule. However, he failed to acknowledge that the third-shift institutional staff slept during the day. Imagine the havoc and frustration that would be created within a family by following such a regimen. As a professional I felt bitter that some of my fellow professionals were so insensitive and oblivious to their own lack of competence. The credentials and fancy titles were insufficient to mask the fact that they really did not know what to do, yet few of them were able to say, "I don't know."

Jay has had a profound influence on my professional life. Friends have often commented that Jay is very fortunate to have a mother who is a special educator. Really, it's just as true the other way around. There is no doubt that Jay has taught me far more than I have taught him. Some of the many lessons I have learned from being his mother are summarized here.

First, professional behavior must be tempered by humility. It is impossible to have all the answers in the diagnosis and treatment of problems associated with handicapping conditions. It was shocking and humbling for me to come face to face with how much I did not know. I often wondered what my professional colleagues would think of me if I admitted to them that I needed help in solving particular problems. It was important, albeit difficult, for me to learn to acknowledge my weaknesses without apology or shame. Honesty and openness can be the keys to truly professional behavior.

Learning to say "I don't know" can be the beginning point of refining one's skills.

Second, living with problems associated with mental retardation has substantially broadened my perspective of issues which must be addressed by professionals in interacting with families. Most formal training programs are extremely limited in preparing professionals to interact meaningfully with parents of retarded children—i.e., to help them solve very practical, day-to-day problems. In my formal training at three different universities, I cannot recall ever considering how to establish guardianship, or help brothers and sisters of retarded children understand the nature and implications of their sibling's handicap, or help retarded children make friends in their neighborhood and community, or find ways to handle situations in public when strangers stare at and mock a retarded person.

In regard to this last issue, a stranger yelled across a restaurant at my husband and me, "What's wrong with that strange little boy?" When we tried to ignore him, he kept pressing, "I asked you why that little boy looks and acts so strange." Other persons in the restaurant looked back and forth between him and us, waiting for a response. My husband told him that nothing was wrong and he should mind his own business. The stranger replied, "That little boy can't talk for himself. You are an insincere man, and you have a strange little boy." The stranger left the restaurant. My husband and I were in a state of shock. Jay was unaware of the nature of the interaction. As we continued to feel the other customers looking at us and at Jay, we got up and left the restaurant. How is the best way for parents to handle such situations? It was hard enough for the three of us to share that kind of incident; what will happen when Jay encounters that kind of insensitivity alone? How can we prepare him to handle it when we are at a loss in handling it ourselves? I did not realize the extent of negative attitudes and social curiosity toward retarded individuals and their families until Jay came into my life.

As a teacher trainer, I have substantially reordered priorities in preparing students to work with mentally retarded persons and their families. One project which evolved was part of the course Psychology of Mental Retardation, which I taught to juniors. Rather than having students do the routine term papers or journal abstracts, I required them to develop a one-to-one advocacy relationship with a retarded individual and to keep a diary of their experiences, questions, insights, and concerns. The relationship was to be a friendship involving recreational activities, going shopping, riding public transportation, preparing meals together, listening to music, constructing art projects, providing respite care, or simply visiting with each other. The advocacy projects proved to be a powerful training tool (Turnbull, 1977). The students reported learning far more from experiential contacts than from traditional methods of instruction. The firsthand opportunity of getting to know retarded persons and their families as people rather than as students or clients enabled the special education trainees to become aware of some of the complexities of handicapping conditions that are rarely considered in university courses.

What goes on in training programs in the name of education is sometimes shocking. It has become commonplace in special education departments of colleges and universities to offer courses in working with parents. I cringe at the thought of some of the course outlines I have reviewed. In many of these courses, very limited attention is directed toward helping parents solve the day-to-day problems, yet weeks are devoted to the "psychological insight approach to parental guilt." Many such courses are a fraud and tend to insure further conflict between parents and professionals. Extended experience with families of handicapped children and the provision of respite care for families should be standard requirements for courses which purport to prepare students for working with parents.

Third, when professionals interact with parents, respect is a necessary ingredient. For too long, the professional-parent relationship has been characterized by a superiority-inferiority interaction. Professionals often have tended to respond to what they think parents need rather than to the needs stated by the parents. Sometimes this situation results from the professional's unwillingness to listen actively to what the parent is saying. Some professionals immediately give advice rather than spend time getting a grasp of the problem. One of the most meaningful interactions I have had as a parent with a professional was with a psychologist. As I shared some very personal concerns about planning for Jay's future, tears came down her cheeks. We sat in silence for a long time, both considering the course of action which would be in Jay's best interest. The silence was beautiful. It confirmed that she was hearing what I was saying and was sharing my feelings on the subject. There was no easy answer. An immediate response, telling me not to worry about things, would have been an insult. I knew she respected me when she shared my feelings. My respect for her as a professional grew one hundredfold.

Many offhand comments offer insights into a professional's view of parents. One special educator asked me if I knew of handicapped children she might tutor who were achieving two years or less below grade level. She commented that parents of children achieving a lower level probably would not be interested in paying for tutoring, since they would likely be the type that had spent their lives wishing their problems away. That type of callous generalization indicated limited respect for parents of handicapped children. For a period of time I was unsure how to handle this kind of unprofessional behavior. In some cases I was so surprised that I found myself at a loss for words. However, I have come to the conclusion that an immediate response— asking the professional to clarify and support what he means—is appropriate. In most cases I have found that the professional does not really mean what has been said. But bringing insidious comments about parents to the attention of professionals should result in their thinking twice before making such comments in the future.

Fourth, a parent-professional partnership is essential if handicapped children are to be provided with opportunities to reach their full potential. Parents cannot assume all the responsibilities alone. After Jay returned home, Rud and I found ourselves overwhelmed with advocacy responsibilities which we felt were our duty as parents of a retarded child. We had meetings on an average of four or five nights a week. We were actively involved with the Association for Retarded Citizens, the group home and sheltered workshop boards of directors, a day-care coalition, a special education task force for the local schools, and a coalition aimed at legislative impact. We were constantly on the go and had little time for family relaxation. It occurred to us that we had brought Jay home from an institution only to leave him with a baby sitter while we went out and advocated for him. I could not help wondering why I saw so few of my professional colleagues at these evening meetings. Rud and I began to question whether the concept of normalization applies to families of handicapped individuals as well as to handicapped persons themselves. There was nothing normal about our schedules. We were not just consumers; rather we were consumed by the need to establish programs and services for Jay. When we reached the point of exhaustion and frustration, we realized that family priorities had to take precedence over advocacy needs.

Just as parents cannot meet all the needs of their handicapped child, neither can a professional. Often parents do not do their fair share and leave overriding responsibility to the professional. Parents and professionals must work together in mutually defining and sharing roles and responsibilities so that no one becomes overwhelmed with the tasks to be accomplished.

Fifth, too often the need for handicapped children to have personal relationships outside the family is overlooked. In the three years since Jay has been home, he has very rarely been invited by other children (handicapped or nonhandicapped) to participate in activities. Almost all of his recreational alternatives revolve around family activities or neighborhood friends who come to his house to play with him. Parents often need help in knowing how to increase socialization options for a handicapped child who is not automatically accepted by others (Turnbull, in press).

One of the nicest things that has happened to us since Jay's return home has been his relationship with Grandma Dot, a friend living nearby who "adopted" Jay as her grandson. Having no grandchildren of her own, she wanted to spend time with children and asked me if she could act as a grandmother to Jay and Amy, our two-year-old daughter. I was thrilled with the idea. Grandma Dot takes Jay and Amy on outings, makes puppets with them, reads books to them, and has them over to her house to spend the night. It is one of the most enjoyable relationships that Jay has ever had. He loves to be with Grandma Dot and talks about her every day. Especially since all of our extended family live far away, it has also been very supportive for me to have her close by. I can share my feelings very openly with her and know that she understands. Additionally, it is important for me as a

Ann P. Turnbull

parent to have persons other than relatives love Jay and seek opportunities to be with him. It confirms that Jay is lovable to others as well as to us. To the profession's credit I should add that Grandma Dot is also a professional who works with families of handicapped children and trains other professionals for such involvement.

Moving from a professional to a parent role has been a sometimes painful and difficult task for me. It has caused me to engage in tremendous self-examination. Being Jay's mother has also resulted in an extended growth process for me. As much as anything, I have learned how much I do not know. Now, I am ready to learn.

REFERENCES

Turnbull, A. P. Citizen advocacy in special education training. *Education and Training of the Mentally Retarded*, 1977, *12*, 166–169.

Turnbull, A. P. Professional-parent interactions. In M. Snell (Ed.), *Curriculum for the moderately and severely handicapped*. Columbus, Oh.: Charles E. Merrill, 1983.

QUESTIONS TO CONSIDER

1. Ann says that her professional background had not prepared her for her parental role. What were some of the new lessons she needed to learn? What are your predictions about how her parental role will change over time?

2. Ann describes both positive and negative encounters with professionals. What are the professional characteristics associated with positive relationships and with negative ones? What can you infer about Ann's values? Do you think these values will stay the same or change in the future?

3. How might Ann have replied to the friend who described her husband's depression after being with Jay? To the friend who commented, "I've never seen a child with such a big head"? To the stranger in the restaurant? How can parents be best prepared to respond appropriately in such circumstances? Do you think the frequency of insensitive remarks about Jay will increase or decrease in the future?

The Dual Role of Parent and Professional

Ann P. Turnbull

As I reread my earlier essay, I am flooded with flashbacks about our collective lives immediately after Jay joined our family. That was nine years ago. I am amazed at how much has happened to me and to our family since then. Sifting through my memories, I am most strongly struck by the continuum of change. Drastic changes have occurred in some areas and minis- cule changes in others. Learning to live constructively and humanly in both the presence and absence of change is my greatest challenge.

Areas of Greatest Change

Three themes characterized my first essay: (1) it was a startling experience for me to learn the twenty-four-hour reality of being Jay's mother, (2) I had intense emotional reactions to the insensitivities of others toward Jay, and (3) my professional priorities changed as a result of Jay's influence. I have experienced major changes in the first two areas, but none in the last.

The startling experience of parenthood is over; it is now a way of life. Being a parent has taught me that nothing really prepares you for it—certainly not three degrees in special education. The startling factor to me now is my naiveté in initially thinking that I would be so on top of the situation. Competence and confidence as a mother has evolved from my commitment to family relationships, the joyful and painful lessons of experience, and the gift of time. Furthermore, Amy and Kate, our eight- and five-year-old nonhandicapped daughters, have taught me that parenting is challenging with all children—not just with handicapped ones. In many contexts, Jay is the easiest of our three children; in others, his behavior creates great stress. Prior to Amy and Kate, I erroneously attributed many of my parental frustrations to Jay's retardation. My mentor and friend Dick Schiefelbusch once told me that he believes people have their greatest chance to achieve

137

wisdom from the lessons they learn from their children rather than from their professional endeavors. Since Dick has achieved wisdom, I trust his insight. I no longer view parenthood as a startling experience but rather as a source of tremendous personal, emotional, and spiritual growth. I hope the end result will be wisdom, but I have far to go.

In my earlier essay I expressed my intense emotional reaction to the insensitivities of others. I now affirm, however, that over the years the sensitivities of people have far outnumbered the insensitivities. It is interesting to reflect on this reversal and identify the factors involved. Jay treats others with kindness and good manners, and they reciprocate. Also, I believe society in general has become more sensitive to the needs of handicapped persons over the last five years. The sensitivity of our extended family, friends, and neighbors to Jay has been very rewarding. But the heart of the matter is that I am no longer on my guard, waiting for the inane comments or the rude stares. It takes far too much energy to be defensive, and it's not worth the effort. My best coping skills are an obliviousness to what other people think and a sense of humor.

I chuckle now when I recall the incident of Jay's greeting guests at a reception we were giving for a colleague. Jay loves to welcome people to our home and does very well until he becomes overstimulated. At the point of overstimulation that evening, a distinguished professor came to our door. I glanced over at Jay just as he was introducing himself: "This is my son, Jay Turnbull." Seeing the bewildered expression on the professor's face, I dashed over to intervene, whereupon Jay politely turned to me and said what he has so often heard his dad say, "And this is my wife, Ann." By this point the professor was totally aghast. At one time in my life, my reaction would have been embarrassment and emotional upset, but it no longer seemed warranted. Instead I smiled and responded, "It's been a long and wonderful relationship." Our guest was completely overwhelmed.

There have been other areas of significant change. One of the most obvious is my ideological style, part of which is reflected in my previous comments. Over the years I have been placing less emphasis on Jay's retardation and more emphasis on Jay himself. Basically, my response reflects a decreased need on my part to change him in an all-encompassing way, to make him less different. Many professionals are committed to molding the experiences, activities, and life-styles of retarded people according to those of their nonhandicapped peers. For them the ultimate goal for a retarded person seems to be to walk in someone else's shoes, to be normalized.

Jay has taught me a valuable lesson: he prefers his own shoes to other people's. He feels absolutely no need to conform or to replicate the choices of someone else. Increasingly, I have realized the value and necessity of entering his world rather than requiring him to enter mine. I value achievement; Jay values contentment. I value spontaneity and variety; Jay values structure and routine. I value activity; Jay values passivity. On numerous occasions these differences have created major stress and frustration for both of us. But I am realizing that he is just as entitled to his preferences as I am to mine. Why should he have to walk in the shoes of a hypothetical nonhandicapped model? Perhaps a reversal is in order—some of his behaviors should be the model for nonhandicapped people. If we learned from Jay a slower tempo of living, the joy of being alone, and a relaxed need for achievement, then the millions of dollars spent on stress and time management books and quick-fixes could be channeled into something more worthy. Jay has some incredibly fine qualities that I am striving to emulate.

Another significant change surrounds Jay's adolescence. He is physically mature, even more so than most sixteen year olds. Puberty has created tumultuous emotions for him, partially because he does not understand what is happening. His rapid physical changes stand in stark contrast to his slow cognitive growth, and the imbalance has been difficult for me to adjust to.

The final major change is the presence of Amy and Kate in our family. They add zest and spice to Jay's life, as well as to ours. And they have learned lessons from Jay that we alone could never have taught them. Their unfailing sensitivity to Jay and his feelings is inspiring, and Jay derives great joy from gently comforting them when they are hurt or upset.

But here again is another source of conflict and family stress. During Jay's very rare but frightening outbursts, his aggression sometimes has been directed toward his sisters, who are helpless to defend themselves against his uncontrolled strength. I absolutely cringe at the thought of their physical or emotional injury, but at the same time I know that both are possible as long as Jay is living at home. Their presence in our lives adds tremendous joy; it also exacerbates the pull of competing interests.

Areas of Least Change

One of the major themes of my first essay was the change in my professional priorities resulting from Jay's influence. His influence on my professional work has continued and has become even more pervasive. During the last few years I have spent a considerable amount of time analyzing the sociological literature on family adjustment and synthesizing it with the literature on the impact of disabled children on families (Turnbull, Brotherson, & Summers, in press; Turnbull, Summers, & Brotherson, in press). I am intrigued by concepts of family structure, interaction, multiple functions, and life cycle. Jay continues to be the catalyst of my thinking and my ever-present litmus test of reality. So often he is the teacher, and I am the student. This learning process has not changed.

I laughed when I read my first essay's account of Jay's enuresis. My only other alternative was to cry, but I didn't want my mascara to run. When I wrote that account, I thought wet sheets were history, I was unaware of the hundreds of wet sheets still in store for us. Jay's problem gradually returned to the point of nightly occurrences over the last three years. This has been a chronic frustration for Jay and us. Several months ago we once again were blessed with the assistance of very competent psychologists, and I am happy to report that dryness is once again the rule. But I think I have become more tempered in my assessment of our current and future prospects. I have come to recognize that some things may never completely change. Rather they will ebb and flow, appear and disappear over time.

Related to this point is the fact that Jay's dependence on us has changed only minimally. Retardation is chronic; that is one of the fundamental problems for families. I am just beginning to realize the impact of lifelong responsibility and the need to fortify my coping abilities for the adult years. My most perplexing dilemma is learning to deal with the aspects of his retardation that are most debilitating to him and to us. One of those is Jay's overwhelming need for routine. For example, family outings planned for relaxation often become stress experiences for Jay, characterized by his repetitive language, rigid movements, and extreme withdrawal; they become endurance tests for us. His episodic aggressive outbursts with his sisters are something else I would give my right arm to change, if only I could. But I can't, or at least I have not yet been successful. My personal goal for the next phase of our lives is to achieve the perspective expressed in this well-known prayer: "God grant me the serenity to accept the things I cannot change, the courage to change the things I can, and the wisdom to know the difference."

REFERENCES

Turnbull, A.P., Brotherson, M.J., & Summers, J.A. The impact of deinstitutionalization on families: A family systems approach. In R.H. Bruininks (Ed.), *Living and learning in the least restrictive environment*. Baltimore: Paul H. Brookes, in press.

Turnbull, A.P., Summers, J.A., & Brotherson, M.J. Family life cycle: Theoretical and empirical implications and future directions for families with mentally retarded members. In J.J. Gallagher & P. Vietze (Eds.), *Research on families with retarded children*. Baltimore: University Park Press, in press.

QUESTIONS TO CONSIDER

1. Review the questions on p. 135. How accurate were your predictions?

2. Based on Ann's values, do you think it will be more challenging for her to deal constructively with the things she cannot change or the things she can change? What do you predict will be the areas of greatest change and least change for Jay and for Ann in the next six years?

3. Based strictly on Ann's values for herself, what kind of adult life-style might she try to create for Jay if she opted to have him walk in her shoes. Based solely on Jay's values, what type of adult life-style

do you think he would most prefer if he is allowed to walk in his own shoes? Whose values do you think the Turnbulls will use in planning Jay's future? Characterize the life-style you think Jay will have in six years.

Kathryn (Peg) Morton was the director of family and community services of the Montgomery County (Maryland) Association for Retarded Citizens when she first contributed to this book. She had previously served as research associate for *Closer Look* and as assistant director and director of the Information Center for Handicapped Children (funded under a grant from the Bureau of Education for the Handicapped). She was a member of the National Advisory Committee of the Study on the Classification of Exceptional Children.

There are five daughters in the Morton family. Beckie, the youngest, was fifteen years old when this first essay was written. She is profoundly retarded and attends a special school in Delaware.

Jennifer Ackerman, the author of the second essay, is another of Peg's five daughters and is the closest in age to Beckie. Jennifer is currently employed as a researcher by the National Geographic Society in Washington, D.C.

Kathryn Morton

Beckie Morton and Jennifer Ackerman

Identifying the Enemy
A Parent's Complaint

Kathryn Morton

Raising a child who is profoundly retarded hasn't been easy, but on the other hand, it hasn't been as hard as it might have been. In balance, life has been very good to me. But I have encountered some enemies, and they need exposing. One is fatigue, and the other is loneliness.

The first doesn't need any explanation; it just needs to be taken seriously by us parents and by the professionals who advise us. Disabled children use up enormous amounts of their parents' physical and psychic energy. These children require more of everything, and those who take parenting seriously give it to them. Yet all the rest of life goes on and also demands its due from us. And the collective demands must be met within the same twenty-four-hour day allotted to everyone.

But there is more to it than just that. There is an expectation by others that we should live normally, as if, in fact, there were nothing abnormal about our lives. Who—besides another parent of a handicapped child—understands the extraordinary effort it takes to hang onto friends, respond to family, attend back-to-school nights, take children to dentists, entertain for husbands, shop for groceries, do the housework, take the car to be fixed, drop one child off to play with a friend, pick up another after a piano lesson, or, heaven forbid, hold down a job while attending to the needs of a child who is disabled and needs extraordinary care?

It is not a one-time demand. We all know mothers whose children are recuperating from illnesses or other temporary catastrophies. Those mothers get a reprieve from life's daily expectations. Husbands will shop for groceries, a friend can drive the car pool that week, the dentist appointment can be postponed, the piano lesson can be canceled, back-to-school night can be skipped. But there is nothing temporary about the exorbitant demands on time and energy made by a retarded child, and one cannot expect friends and family to respond endlessly to a crisis which is chronic. Each day presents us with the challenge of figuring out how to do everything that would be done if we didn't have a handicapped child, while managing the handicapped child we clearly do have.

That might entail, for instance, grocery shopping with the retarded child in tow. When Beckie was little, such an excursion required only the extra energy needed to carry her on my hip and choose groceries one-handed, or the skill to maneuver her special stroller with one hand and the grocery cart with the other. But when she hit her teens, a completely new ingredient was added to the challenge. I took her shopping with me only if I felt up to looking groomed, cheerful, competent, and in command of any situation, so that when she bellowed and stamped with joy as she always did when we walked through the supermarket door, people who stared could quickly surmise that I would handle the situation, quiet my strange child, and get on with my shopping. To look as tired and preoccupied with surviving as I so often felt would have turned both of us into objects of pity, and that I clearly did not need. If I could not play the role of the coping, competent mother, I did better to stay at home and grocery shop after she went to bed, or ask one of the other children to come home early and sit for me, or leave the big shopping until another day and ask a neighbor to pick up a necessity or two for me, or make do with what I had until I felt more energetic though chances were excellent that I wouldn't.

For parents of handicapped children the fact of life which is least understood by others is this: it is difficult and exhausting to live normally, and yet we must. To take the other route, to admit that having a disabled child makes us disabled persons, to say no to the ordinary requirements of daily living is to meet the second enemy—loneliness. It means drifting slowly out of the mainstream of adult life. In a very real sense, we are damned if we do make the extraordinary effort required to live normally, and damned if we don't.

The sapping of energy occurs gradually. The isolation it imposes does, too. As I work professionally with young mothers, I see them coping energetically with the demands of everyday life. They are good parents, caring ones, doing everything possible to help their retarded child reach full potential, sometimes doing more than they have to; and if they have other children, they are doing the same for them. Most of these young mothers even get out, see friends, attend meetings, volunteer in the community and do all the things their friends and families expect them to do. All this is at least possible when one's child is little, though it demands enormous energy. But to look at the mothers of children who have turned into teen-agers is to see the beginnings of the ravages. Their life-style is changing. They go out less, see fewer people, do less for their children. They are stripping their living to the essentials. And to look at parents of retarded adults still living at home is to see lives that are far removed from those of their peers. The physical and psychic effects of twenty or more years of extraordinary demands on their energies are visible, and they have given up the struggle to be normal.

Kathryn Morton

The enemies are related. In the very long run, energy dwindles and a way of life sets in that is plainly isolated.

There is much about parenting a handicapped child which makes it a lonely business. First of all, there are too few retarded children to give them the advantage of being commonplace. And ignorance about them still abounds—about their diversity, about services which can help them, and about the problems their parents and siblings face. Even the best-intentioned people, trying hard to be helpful on the basis of bits and scraps of information they have gleaned from an occasional magazine article or TV program, can make parents feel very much alone and unhelped. I cannot count the number of times that I have been informed about wonderful schools, dedicated people, heretofore undiscovered cures which can help my child. I have been enthusiastically referred over a dozen times to St. Coletta's in Wisconsin, "where the Kennedy daughter is." It is always painful to deal with the other person's disappointment when I point out that St. Coletta's does not accept children who are as severely retarded as mine. It is as if I am somehow being uncooperative and do not want to be helped. But in all fairness, I should not resent and blame them for their limited knowledge. I must understand that it is only human to feel impotent and impatient with problems which have no immediate cure, no prompt solution, no easy answer.

I can still feel rage for the stranger in the public library who, years ago, commented on the four year old I was carrying, suggesting that I let her walk. I explained that she couldn't walk, that she was severely retarded. The stranger's face softened; her attitude was warm and understanding. "Oh," she said, "they are such wonderful children, and all they need is loving." Perhaps I had a premonition even then of how many years of assistance and training it would take before she would be able to walk, not to mention toilet herself, feed herself, and dress herself, which she still cannot do at age fifteen. One comes out of such encounters feeling very much alone, burdened by the obligation to explain, educate, and reassure others because they know so little about our children and so very little about how to help.

There may be no solution to our dilemma. As one looks down the list of life's other sad happenings, most bring with them a ritual or a tradition which helps people deal with them. When a person is ill, there are cards to send, visits to make, flowers to deliver, gifts that comfort. When someone dies, there are routine ways of informing people of the sad news, funerals where people can grieve together, and a long period of mourning during which sorrow is OK, in fact expected. Friends and acquaintances know their roles—to be sympathetic, understanding, comforting, available when needed, and helpful in managing the mechanics of living during the grieving period. It is only after many months that the surviving family are expected to lay aside their grief and resume normal living. All those rituals and expectations are helpful. The roles of the comforter and the comforted are clear-cut.

The birth and life of a retarded child has no such advantages. It is a quasi tragedy, a joyful event that got spoiled. There is no established way of announcing the time for grief (in fact no real certainty that one is entitled to out-and-out grieving) since it takes a while before anyone can know just how severe the disability is. One should not be gloomy and expect the worst. But there is certainly little reason to feel happy. Family and friends are faced with the same ambivalence. Just what is their role? What words should they say? Can they reassure that everything will be all right? Should they extend their sympathy? bring supper to the family? send flowers? None of the usual comforting gestures are appropriate, so most people, under such circumstances, do and say nothing. The absence of response to an event of such enormous significance and impact on the lives of the parents simply compounds their loneliness.

This loneliness is not a one-time phenomenon. I suspect that the behavior of the members of my family is typical. Most of my relatives do not talk about Beckie with me; from their point of view there is really not much to say after the initial "too bad" has been expressed. But since the concern and care for her goes on and on in my life, leaving the topic unmentioned is to treat a major segment of my mental and emotional life as taboo. And that is very isolating. One hears the disappointment expressed again and again when mothers of retarded children assemble; time after time family members do not provide the ongoing emotional support required. Yet I think we are wrong to expect support to come from them. They may well be the people least able to provide it because their own discomfort is so acute. Each of them is having to come to terms with why a retarded child arrived as the son or daughter of someone they love and care about. It is very likely true, however, that those who have found a satisfactory answer are less uncomfortable, more able to talk about the child, more able to be helpful, than those who have not. Beckie's grandmother's distress and discomfort was acute for years until I turned professional and began writing for and working with families of handicapped children. Then she saw it all in terms of a mission—something intended to happen. It is not an answer I share, but it is her way of accepting Beckie as an important and significant happening, and I find the ease with which she can now deal with the child quite comforting.

The potential for loneliness is present every step of the way. The process of referral to specialists thrusts parents outside the mainstream. For the parent whose child is in a special education class, even such a commonplace event as a PTA meeting can be a difficult experience. Chances are good that not much that's relevant to the special class will be discussed. Chances are also good that what goes on at the PTA meetings will become less and less interesting to the parent of the special child, and motivation to join in will dwindle. Bit by bit it is easy to have less and less in common with parents who do not have handicapped children. Perhaps special classes, special schools, special buses, and even our special parent organizations are ultimately doing as much to segregate and isolate parents from the mainstream of adult life as they do to isolate children from the mainstream of child life.

There is really no solution for us parents except to put out the extraordinary effort it takes to live normally, to keep one leg in the mainstream, to explain, educate, reassure the others, to be up to taking our children wherever we go. It's a lot to ask of a parent whose energies are extraordinarily burdened.

If only new traditions, new rituals could be invented to help others deal with our particular kind of sad happening. If only practical offers of help were a traditional response to handicapped children—offers to baby-sit while we grocery shop, offers to take our children for a walk around the block, offers to take them swimming, offers to give any reprieve, however short, which could give the parents, especially the mother, a chance to relax or tend to other things. Sympathy and pats on the back are nice, but we can get our solace more effectively from fellow parents who do indeed fully understand. From people who are less burdened than we must come different gifts—the practical help, time, and manpower we need to rout our enemies.

QUESTIONS TO CONSIDER

1. From Peg's perspective why is it difficult and exhausting to try to live normally? Do you think that the struggle to live normally will be easier, the same, or more difficult for Peg in the future?

2. Peg discusses the benefits of rituals that help people deal with sad happenings. What types of rituals might be helpful in preventing the buildup of fatigue and loneliness?

3. When this essay was written, Beckie was fifteen years old, profoundly retarded, and still without basic self-help skills. What are some residential alternatives for Peg to consider as Beckie moves toward adulthood? For each alternative identified, specify a likely outcome for Beckie and for Peg.

4. Do families have the right to normalization? Does Beckie's placement in the least restrictive environment (her home) result in a highly restrictive environment for Peg? How could this highly restrictive environment affect Peg?

UPDATE:
Preparing for Separation

Jennifer Ackerman

I'm the fourth of Peg Morton's five children. Beckie, my profoundly retarded sister, is the fifth and youngest. I was asked to write this essay because Peg died of cancer, quite suddenly, three years ago. Her death was a shock to all of us, and we feel her absence as an insurmountable loss. I cannot offer a substitute for Peg's expertise as a professional, nor for her wisdom and understanding as a parent. I would like simply to describe the impact on our family of two events: Beckie's placement in residential care and Peg's illness and death. Both involved preparation for difficult separations: the first, by Peg, for leave-taking from Beckie; the second, by all of us, for the loss of our mother and Beckie's primary care-giver.

Peg wrote her essay about the fatigue and loneliness involved in raising a handicapped child in 1975. That was an important year. In August, just after Beckie had turned fifteen, Peg decided to send her to a small residential school in Delaware. For some time Peg had been looking for a place that offered both quality care and a structured training program for children with handicaps as severe as Beckie's. She saw the advantages of settling her in a long-term living situation before necessity dictated the move. She also needed relief.

Peg spoke from experience when she wrote about the ravages—both physical and psychic—of fifteen years of extraordinary demands. In 1975 the effects were noticeable. I was living at home at the time, Peg was working as family and community services director at the local Association for Retarded Citizens, and Beckie was attending a daytime intensive training program. One spring night after working a full day, picking Beckie up at school, feeding, bathing, and putting her to bed, Peg came to see me play the part of Helen Keller's mother in a high school production of *The Miracle Worker*. During intermission I looked out from behind the stage curtain to search for her in the audience. She sat alone in the third row, eyes closed, head dropped forward on her chest, weary, and probably thinking, "If I can

149

just shut my eyes for five minutes . . ." When I got home that night, Peg had left me a note on the dining-room table. "I don't know how you do it, night after night," she wrote. I played the mother of a handicapped child three hours a night for a week. Peg lived that role twenty-four hours a day for fifteen years.

It was with some relief that our family learned of her decision to make a change, to restore to her life some semblance of normality by sending Beckie away to school. It was a difficult decision for her—probably the most difficult she faced as Beckie's parent. It conflicted with a set of values—personal and professional—which she had developed over fifteen years.

When Beckie was born, Peg was strongly advised by every professional she met to put her in an institution. To Peg this was an unacceptable alternative. The state institutions to which retarded people were consigned at that time were dreary places—understaffed and overcrowded. Peg felt strongly that a home environment was important for the full development of any child, for the learning of basic social skills—how to communicate, how to form bonds, how to love. She considered family living so important for children that she had adopted a Korean orphan, my sister Kim, just two years before Beckie was born. So it was difficult for her to contemplate placing her child in an institution.

But what were the alternatives? When Peg was first struggling with the whats and whys of having given birth to a handicapped child, there was almost no communication among parents in comparable situations. She didn't have the slightest idea where to go for services, how to obtain the necessary resources, or even whether she deserved them. There were few educational, recreational, or social services for children with any disability, particularly for those with severe handicaps, and few sources of information about what services were available. Once Peg did uncover the information, she encountered still more obstacles: waiting lists, high tuition fees and no financial aid, and—most frustrating of all—exclusion practices. By the time Beckie was six, she had been rejected from classes for children who were retarded because she couldn't walk, and from classes for children with physical handicaps because she was retarded. At that point Peg was not yet feeling inclined to fight for Beckie's rights—she didn't know she had any. It was another five years before the concept of equal rights entered her consciousness.

Peg met the issue head on. She spent most of the next several years working to change public attitudes—educating legislators; organizing information and referral services; founding parent support groups and workshops; establishing sitter training courses; and urging parents to keep their children in the community, in the neighborhood, with their families. Peg felt that the effective way to change attitudes was to make handicapped children visible to the public. "It helps to like our kids and look as if we do," she wrote. "The important thing is to have them with us—visible as we go about our daily affairs" (Morton, 1983, p. 86). Keeping Beckie at home became part of a larger battle to bring about public awareness and to establish rights for all handicapped children. Now, sending her away seemed a betrayal of that cause.

As a professional, Peg was aware that adjusting to separation from Beckie would not be easy. She had counseled other parents who had placed their children in residential facilities. She could anticipate the ambivalence—the anxiety, regret, and guilt—she was bound to feel. Yet even with this professional perspective, she underestimated the pain of letting Beckie go and the difficulty of adjusting to life after she had gone.

In raising Beckie, Peg was determined to do everything to help her reach her potential. Since she had no access to respite care and few offers of reprieve from family and friends, she had little energy left over for normal life, for other needs. She had no healing time—no time to lounge or to go to a friend's house for lunch, to weed the garden or rearrange the linen closet. More important, she had no time and little energy to cultivate friends and interests outside the world of handicapped children.

Peg may have compensated for the absence of other satisfactions by investing more in her relationship with Beckie. They shared an extraordinarily strong bond—perhaps a mutual dependence. Caring for Beckie demanded a tremendous investment of physical and psychic energy: Peg took satisfaction in meeting those demands. There are few replacements for the intensity of the care giving role, and Peg felt its loss keenly. After Beckie left, she found it difficult to engage in normal activities, to take joy in doing what was supposed to replace her full-time care and concern for Beckie. Friends and family were not able to offer much assistance. Since few people understood Peg's need to keep Beckie home for so long, they couldn't understand her grief over the absence of what appeared to them to be a burden.

The chronic stress of caring for Beckie without relief exhausted Peg; her exhaustion led to isolation; and isolation, perhaps, led her to invest more in her relationship with Beckie. When fatigue finally drove her to place Beckie in residential care, she suffered severely from the separation. If this is a typical pattern, it needs attention. Parents who choose to send their children away to school and the professionals who advise them need to take this separation grief seriously and prepare for it. Friends and family need to find ways to help parents stay involved in mainstream adult life while they are raising their handicapped children, so that adjustment to life-after-placement is not so severe.

When Peg was ill with cancer, friends and relatives responded well. They arrived at the door with meals, flowers, and books, and stayed only a short time, considerate of her need for privacy and sleep. They ran errands, returned library books, picked up prescriptions, drove her to the hospital. Their gestures were imaginative. One relative, having heard that Peg needed certain vitamins to counteract the effects of the chemotherapy, brought health foods—molasses bread, nuts, raisins—loaded with the appropriate nutrients; another brought rich almond tortes and pastries, lovely soaps and bath salts—part of a philosophy that holds that life is full of good rich things to enjoy; one friend suggested that she and Peg take a class in quilt-making—an ambitious project, a lifetime undertaking. Some of these gestures were more appropriate, some less, but they all said, "We care; we want to get you involved with life." This went on for months; and as I loaded the chicken casseroles and quiches into the freezer, I wondered why people found it so easy to approach Peg in her illness and so difficult to reach out to her when she was raising Beckie.

In her essay Peg pointed out that illness brings with it traditions and rituals which help people deal with it. She made a plea for new rituals—for the creation of new traditions that would make it easier for family and friends to give reprieve to parents of handicapped children. She and other parents of her generation suffered for want of these responses when they gave birth to their children, while they were raising them, and when they had to give them up. These parents had to use their energies to fight the battle for basic rights; they had to fight to persuade policy-makers and professionals that their children deserved adequate care and education. As a result, they had little energy left over to teach the general public the proper response to handicapped children.

In the late 1970s Peg encountered a new generation of parents. When she supervised an infant stimulation program for babies with developmental delays, she was surprised and delighted by the heightened demands these young parents made on the teachers, and the teachers, on the parents. As the year progressed, the parents expected more personal involvement from the teachers, and the teachers expected more professional involvement from the parents. If only parents and those surrounding them—family and friends—could establish a similar pattern of give-and-take, in which offers of help and requests for help are expected and freely exchanged, not out of charity, but out of respect.

Unfortunately, the burden of initiating such an exchange probably rests on the young parent. Friends and relatives need to be asked to give time and manpower. They need to be helped to help. This takes energy and patience. If they are intelligent, however, they may realize that no one expects them to get involved in the task of raising a handicapped child, but just to meet the parent on the street without crossing over, to provide an occasional helping hand with normal activities. If they do help, they may, in turn, expect parents to join them as participants in normal adult life; and perhaps this new generation of parents will have the energy to do so.

In the last months of her illness, Peg debated whether to ask one of us to take over her role as Beckie's primary care giver. She was torn between wanting to make sure Beckie had a primary care giver and not wanting to saddle any one of us with the full responsibility. We, in turn, wanted to reassure her without making promises we wouldn't keep. In different ways each of us carried some emotional baggage—some resentment of the amount of time and energy Peg had invested in Beckie's growing up; some anger at

Jennifer Ackerman

being asked to do too much to help, or not enough; some desire to continue Peg's very active role in Beckie's life; and some determination not to make the sacrifices necessary to do so.

We never resolved the issue of replacing Beckie's primary care giver. It was too painful to confront the loss of Peg and to admit that whatever we could give Beckie would be less than Peg had given. Peg did not push for answers; we talked about it less, and ultimately she left the decision to us.

When Peg died, Beckie had several potential care givers—father, stepfather, siblings, and others—but none designated as primary, and none with any real experience in caring for her or sensing her needs. Our family did not gather to discuss the matter of responsibility but instead left conversations to take place as the need arose.

Fortunately, Peg had planned carefully for Beckie's future, and when she fell ill, Beckie's life was in order: she was attending a good school and receiving training and care from people we trusted. Her future was relatively free of financial constraints: Peg and Bill, Beckie's father, had set up a trust fund to cover the cost of her tuition and care and had stipulated that the money would remain in Beckie's name in the event of their deaths.

For the time being, Beckie's financial situation was secure, and the responsibility for her immediate care was in the hands of the school. It remained for someone to fill in for Peg in two areas: as Beckie's mediator with the school and as Beckie's connection to family life. The first should have been relatively easy, but our family was slow to respond. We would have done well to meet with the staff members of Beckie's school to discuss their needs. What sort of interaction did they require? Was it adequate just to check in occasionally? Or did they want us to get involved in decisions concerning Beckie's training and care? Did they prefer to deal with just one of us? Or could we disperse responsibilities among several family members? Did they need relief? If so, how often?

At first we responded to calls from the school in a haphazard fashion. Family visits were sporadic. Six months would pass without anyone's arranging to see Beckie, and then suddenly everyone would show up at the school's Christmas play. Or one of us would mention to a staff member that we thought Beckie should come home for Christmas and then never follow up on the suggestion, leaving the staff to question our commitment.

A recent incident dramatized the necessity for our family to agree to a formal order of responsibility. On a Tuesday Beckie came down with a severe bacterial infection. A germ had entered her system through a skin boil and had caused a build-up of fluid—an enormous infected blister—on her side. The doctor was concerned that the infection might spread to her blood system, in which case she would have to be hospitalized immediately. Marna, the director of the school, tried unsuccessfully to reach various members of our family. She and other staff members spent much of the night draining the infected fluid from Beckie's side and trying to break her high fever with sponge baths and cold compresses. The next day Beckie refused to eat or drink and so ran the added risk of dehydration. It wasn't until that evening that Marna finally reached Beckie's stepmother. What if Beckie's case had required an immediate decision about medical treatment that involved risk or choice? We should have made sure that one family member was always on call with the authority—by proxy from other members of the family—to make a decision in an emergency.

Situations like this will arise. Since Peg died, we have discussed various ways of delegating responsibility for communicating with the school and for making decisions about Beckie's physical well-being. At one point we thought of arranging rotating shifts: each of us would assume complete responsibility for a two-year period. But this turned out to be impossible. Some of Beckie's sisters had settled in distant parts of the country; others were involved in raising their own families and couldn't predict when they would be available to take their turn.

For the present Bill and I have assumed responsibility for Beckie's practical needs. But this is only half the job. What about Beckie's emotional needs, especially her need for a family connection? Peg used to take Beckie home for one weekend each month. These visits were hard for Peg, but she enjoyed the close time with Beckie, and Beckie loved Peg's special attention. She liked the weekend routine: the drive home, when Peg talked and sang and clapped for her; afternoon walks in the wheelchair; mealtimes, when she sat smack in the middle of the kitchen floor to wonder at the traffic of food preparation; dinner in her pajamas; and a long warm bath before bed.

The visits were sometimes disruptive to her training. At home she tended to revert to old patterns of behavior (as we all do). Sometimes she seemed unable to walk without a reassuring hand for support, or to climb steps without a nudge behind the knee. She wet her pants more often and played games with her spoon at meals. When Beckie was living at home, we knew that family members were not her best teachers—the home environment didn't support a structured training program—but we felt that family life taught Beckie social skills meaningful to her total development and gave her a sense of well-being. She learned to communicate, to recognize and love people, to smile and snuggle.

Beckie's visits home must have reinforced this sense of well-being. Soon after Peg died and the visits stopped, Beckie went through a period of depression. Sometimes she refused meals; she withdrew somewhat from the staff and other students at the school and seemed reluctant to participate in her training program. She has since improved, but from time to time she has similar low periods. She may miss those visits. If she does, can we provide a substitute that will satisfy her? Is it the extra attention she needs? The time away from school? Or does she miss Peg?

As an experiment my husband and I brought Beckie home for a weekend last summer. Her stepfather and his new wife had generously offered their house and help for the visit. The weekend was full of surprises. After the long hot ride home, I tried to feed Beckie some juice from a glass. As usual, she bit down hard on the rim of the cup, the glass broke, and I spent a few panicky moments fishing pieces of glass from her mouth.

I'd also forgotten how much weight Beckie had gained at school. It occurred to me as I maneuvered her into the bathroom that she'd be too much to manage in the tub, so instead of giving her the long, lingering bath I know she loves, we showered together. More than once I forgot her toilet schedule. Together we produced several loads of wash. But she seemed to enjoy herself. We hope to bring her home twice a year and to set up regular visits to the school to see her, take her out for ice cream, and talk with the school staff.

There are other unresolved issues. I remember Peg's stories of shuttling Beckie from one expert to another in search of information, only to emerge with the realization that she was Beckie's expert. The teachers, therapists, and miscellaneous professionals had their areas of expertise, but she alone knew the whole story. She was Beckie's primary helper, monitor, coordinator, observer, record-keeper, and decision-maker.

Beckie has lost her expert. Right now she is lucky enough to attend a school where the staff is committed and responsible, where they try to monitor their students' progress with the same care they would their own children's. What will happen, though, if for some reason Beckie has to go elsewhere? Who will be her expert then? Who will be the judge of suggested changes in her treatment or educational placement? Who will know her well enough to speak for her emotional as well as practical needs?

Right now, family members read Beckie's reports, comment on them, pass them along, but do not commit themselves to active involvement in her training. We have no real understanding of her advances and setbacks and can take no joy in anticipating and welcoming new abilities. I remember once, when Beckie was six years old and was just learning to walk, Peg and I took her to the park. Beckie was unsteady on the bricks, but on the cement it was smooth sailing—until a fire truck roared past, sirens blaring. Beckie sat down hard in the middle of the street, stretched out her arms, and flapped with joy. A man in the street turned away in embarrassment, hoping, I suspect, that we would exert some control over this public display. He couldn't know the joy of that first walk to the park without the stroller.

If our family settles for minimal involvement with Beckie, we will lose the joy of knowing her; and on some level she may lose a satisfying human connection. Do we settle for a passing interest? A noncommittal concern? Or do we risk some time and energy to get involved, as much as we can, in the nitty-gritty of her life? These are questions with no answers yet. The search for ways to satisfy Beckie's need for a family connection and to explore our own need to continue that connection is an ongoing process.

REFERENCES

Morton, K.A. (Gorham). Parents, practices, and attitudes: The distance traveled. In R.L. Jones (Ed.), *Reflections on growing up disabled*. Reston, Va.: Council for Exceptional Children, 1983.

QUESTIONS TO CONSIDER

1. Review the questions on p. 147. How accurate were your answers?

2. Why do you think it was so easy for Peg's friends to approach her in her illness and so difficult to reach out to her when she was raising Beckie? What types of grief rituals might help parents of newborn disabled children or parents whose nondisabled children suddenly become handicapped?

3. What are the implications for parents, family, child, or professionals of having one parent as the primary helper, monitor, coordinator, observer, record-keeper, and decision-maker? What is the best way to pass the torch of care for sons and daughters with severe disabilities when parents die?

4. How do you think Beckie's family will manage as mediator with the school and as her connection to family life over the next six years?

Jennifer Ackerman

Janet M. Bennett is the mother of four children. Kathryn, her youngest daughter, has Down's syndrome. In 1978 Janet worked in religious education and media reviewing and then wrote a newsletter for the National Catholic Education Association. Since 1970 she also has been a free-lance writer on educational subjects, with a specialty in mental retardation. She has written about mental retardation in connection with religious education, the church community, families of handicapped persons, films about handicaps, library services, and especially about her daughter Kathryn.

Since the mid 1970s she has been thoroughly immersed in Kathryn's schooling, but with that well in hand in 1983, she is branching out a bit. She is the proprietor of a speciality advertising business and continues to write articles about education. She is not a teacher and has no teaching credentials; many years ago she tried substituting in the schools for a few years and hated it.

Kathryn, now 21, continues to live with Janet and to be active in her community.

Janet and Kathryn Bennett

Company, Halt!

Janet M. Bennett

In the musical *How to Succeed in Business Without Really Trying* the statistician Alexander Twimble describes his philosophy for success in the very conservative company he works for. In the song "The Company Way" he explains how he programs his face to smile automatically at all executives, how he consciously erases from his mind any ideas and suggestions that may try to emerge, while at the same time rubber-stamping any directives coming from the top brass. He maintains an unswerving attitude of admiration and enthusiasm for anything the Company provides, from the menus in the cafeteria to the company stationery and magazine. Twimble sees his survival as irrevocably linked to the Company. Though it may take a good deal of effort, even a deliberate shift in personality, for Twimble it's the only possible way to guarantee his job security.

In my fifteen years as the mother of a retarded daughter, I've found that a major source of distress for parents, and a deterrent to progress for their children, is the very handicap-establishment which supposedly exists to help them. This handicap-establishment is very much like a giant corporation—sluggish, conservative, unimaginative, able to serve individuals only in limited ways. For a number of reasons which I'll try to catalogue here, most parents feel that they have no choice but to play things the company way in dealing with the problem of retardation.

This handicap-establishment has lots of departments, but the two chief ones affecting parents are the local associations for retarded children and public school systems. Both embody all kinds of attitudes, assumptions, and myths which generally go unchallenged in any serious fashion.

Supposed enemies without (a hostile public, recalcitrant legislators, limited funds, and apathetic parent constituency) loom so large that a very real enemy within (the philosophical and operational deficiencies of the organization or school system itself) is seldom considered. I believe that some basic premises underlying the whole enterprise, the entire handicap-establishment, ought to be looked at coldly and critically. Though few parents of retarded children have the time or inclination to explore these matters systematically, I'm certain that most have responded to them in bits and pieces as they've worked through their own experiences with their child. Conversations in grocery check-out lines and on commuter trains bear out the statements which follow.

The Local Association

One reason the handicap-establishment is a problem is precisely that it is established. The institutionalizing of a problem results in a state of affairs not much different from most other organizational activities or business ventures which do not claim help as a rationale, which have no humane or altruistic purpose.

Any bad news or unhappy event does certain similar things. Affected individuals huddle together in shared misery. Outsiders from a small or expanded periphery rally round to support. But sudden immediate emergencies—an accident, a fire, an illness, a death—seem to produce emotions and behaviors which are more efficient, truer, nobler than those which attend a continuing problem of diminishing dramatic impact.

Once the clear fire of basic feelings and instant needs has died down, the practical requirements and pedestrian details of managing a long-run difficulty are less stimulating, less interesting. As time goes on, as mechanisms are developed to deal with the problem on a continuing basis, the familiar everyday dynamics of assertiveness, competition, laziness, defensiveness, insecurity, and the like reappear. After the first heroic efforts surrounding a major disaster like a hurricane or an earthquake, you begin to hear about the organizational conflicts among international rescue or political agencies. Once a family crisis has quieted a bit, the infighting and jockeying for control or escape from duty become evident among relatives.

Parents of retarded children are often dismayed when they first attend a business meeting of the local Association for Retarded Citizens (ARC). In the early days of trying to cope with the new awareness of retardation, parents often need—and need to believe in—a warm and caring fraternity of other parents. Yet frequently they find that parents who serve on the unit's governing broad behave with all the brittle competitiveness of business or politics.

For a year or more I served on one of these executive boards and listened with fascination, amusement, and frustration to the wrangling that characterized most meetings. A fellow board member whispered to me in disgust one evening, "These are all people who get crapped on all day at work, and this organization gives them the chance to crap on somebody else." Though an ARC unit claims to be bent on serving the needs of parents and their children, it is these parents and their children who are, directly or indirectly, the ones who are "crapped on."

Janet M. Bennett

The original idea behind parent organizations was that in union there's strength. The many inadequacies of legislation, education, and public opinion could, it was thought, be overcome by the concerted efforts of a solid front of parents. Support gained along the way from the community and from professional people in the field of mental retardation, medicine, education, or public service (like the Kennedys or Humphreys) would add to the parents' credibility and clout. As hoped-for programs were adopted by schools and government, the parent associations conceivably would be able to phase themselves out of existence.

To accomplish major goals, minor ones are often sidetracked. Major goals must be argued about and modified, often compromised quite drastically, in order to stand a chance of acceptance. What happens ultimately is that large, long-range goals for a lot of parents compete with smaller, short-term goals for single families and a single child. Laws, classes, federal grants all depend on the many, not the one.

Often only moderate gains are made, and only slowly, and seldom are these gains achieved in time to benefit those people who initiated the action. In medieval times men of great faith could undertake to build a cathedral, knowing that it would not be completed until after they, and probably their children, had died. For many people the vision of progress for retarded people is rather like this noble vision of eventual success, but individual parents and individual children cannot afford to sacrifice their personal visions while the universal vision evolves.

The slow process of effecting change modifies people as well as ideas and plans. Those parents who have been active and involved for a long time, who have been instrumental in promoting change, often acquire or claim a semiprofessional status with all the potential power hazards such status implies. As they work through the necessary buffing and polishing of the large issues on local, state, or national committees, and as they endure their own personal buffing through the experiences of their own retarded child, their original feelings, their individualized convictions undergo gradual alteration. In too many cases the long-time parent is indistinguishable from the professional he may once have opposed; he is in greater or lesser measure out of touch with his own instincts and the hot-off-the-experience needs and emotions he felt as a new parent. Indeed, the satisfaction and status such parents derive from these activities are often the very palliatives which modify the impact of having produced a child who is retarded.

The routine joining or belonging to a local association has mixed benefits. The most common reason for joining a local unit is the initial desperate need for reassurance and information. These two needs are met in varying degrees. In a random mix of parents at a meeting, it's likely that there will be one or two individuals with the unique kind of empathy, tact, wit, insight, and intelligence to perform for the other parents that miracle of healing that can come only through personal contact. Further, just the appearance of survivors—people who get their hair frosted, talk of movies they've seen, fret about slipcover material or stubborn carburetors—can have subliminal curative effects. Even the aforementioned administrative squabbling can at times be evidence for a shattered parent that he will someday have more on his mind than this one all-encompassing tragedy.

Information is another matter. When I joined an ARC unit fifteen years ago, I learned all they could tell me about mongolism in about ten minutes. The regular programs or speakers and films only endlessly rearranged these same few basic statements. The unit library was a cluttered mess, with nothing catalogued even under major subject headings.

Most of what I learned in that period came from informal, after-the-meeting conversations with a small group of equally novice mothers. Our own persistent reading, dogged research, and speculation began to piece together a fairly solid picture of the problem. The rest of my learning came from my own volunteer activities with the unit as newsletter editor, column writer, program and publicity chairman, chiefly because in these capacities I had the leverage to command important people who knew things to talk to me and answer my questions.

Several other members also saw information gathering as a necessary activity. They, too, understood information to mean specific details about medical causes and treatment, educational options and approaches, continuous assessment of day-to-day experience and expectations. They independently provided occasional summary reports on particular significant points.

Though the rhetoric of the organization appeared to agree with making information available, in practice most information the organization itself made available had to do with maintaining its own structure (fund-raising, paying dues) or programs (dates and times of meetings, transportation schedules, deadlines for filing forms). I was astonished when, only a month after I had joined the unit, the director called to ask me how to go about institutionalizing a retarded child. (In my original phone call I had said that I had investigated this process on my doctor's advice.) How in the world could a county association not know this? How could I, a newcomer to the problem, know more than those long-involved?

Granted, this was a while ago. Things may have improved. I no longer belong to a parent association; but I have friends who do, and I occasionally read through copies of their associations' newsletters. From my reading and from my friends' comments, very little seems to be different: a little information, a lot of public relations, a few reports, a lot of pictures of civic leaders presenting checks.

Some parents think, as I did, that active participation in the organization is a way of finding out what they need to know, but most parents assist the organization for other reasons. In the mythology of the handicap-establishment, getting involved is the mark of a good parent. The organization is, the newsletter repeatedly reminds you, your organization. A related bit of mythology trades on the image of fraternity. A parent must leap from personal grief and concern to a posture of generalized concern, a passionate commit-

Janet M. Bennett

ment to the interests of all children with handicaps everywhere. A booklet widely distributed in the sixties proposed that turning outward in service to the large community of retarded people represented the approved final stage in the development of a parent. By implication, parents who tarried on the way to this goal were made of poor stuff or were plain selfish, doubtlessly wallowing in their misery.

Such guilt inducing is rampant. "It's always the same few," whine newsletters and nominating committees and unit presidents at meetings. In the white heat of grief and confusion when a new parent approaches a local association, any directives or suggestions can make a lasting imprint. New parents cast about for signals—they want to know how to proceed. Social creatures that they are, they want to know how to behave also. In this strange uncharted territory, they try to do as they're asked, do as the other veteran parents do.

My first phone call to my local unit produced a pleasant-enough response from the office secretary and a promise of some information to be mailed. This material consisted of a short summary of the unit's programs and services and a long questionnaire on which I could indicate areas in which I would be delighted to volunteer. There were numberless areas where I would be useful to the unit; there seemed little they had to offer me. The meetings sounded dull and preoccupied with large and small bureaucratic issues; nothing seemed to have a bearing on Kathryn's development until she could attend a nursery class three years hence. The message was clear: a parent in my circumstances, trying to cope with a trauma of uncertain dimensions, should marshal her forces, muster her energies, and get out and work for the cause.

This message of duty lingers on in parental consciousness. I've watched numberless parents driven by its nagging whisper to constant activity year after year—committees, collections, raffles, dances, bowling parties. Others can't or won't follow this route, but the accusing murmur goes on, a scolding conscience implanted like a pacemaker. The language and methods— urging cooperation, responsibility, and loyalty—are exactly the same as those of the PTA, the YMCA, the Girl Scouts, and churches. But somehow the burden of guilt is heavier because of the prevailing atmosphere of interrelationship, interdependency. A retarded child initiates us into a cosmic fraternity—we're all one, we're all linked together like blood brothers, we're all responsible for everything that happens. God, what a burden! Isn't one burden, dumped on us by fate, quite enough? Must we have the added load of organizational busywork presented as though each of us is a finger in the dike without which all the sad-eyed retarded children in the world will drown?

A retarded child is generally an immediate and continuing drain on body, mind, pocketbook, and time. Too many parents find their already overextended resources further taxed by this sense of obligation to the organization. Some, of course, are affected quite differently; for them the organization provides escape from the realities of a retarded child while giving a consoling sense of doing something worthwhile. For others the committee work and officerships give a new identity and status which would never have been their lot otherwise. For still others, work for an ARC unit is only a more logical choice than the variety of other such activities in which they normally engage anyway out of natural civic enthusiasm.

Regardless of motivation, regardless of whether helping the unit is a pleasure or a trial, should most parents be doing this work at all? Most parents today have more than they can handle under ordinary circumstances. Schools with their lunches, forms, permission slips, conferences, back-to-school nights, homework, projects, concerts, and athletics run an ordinary household ragged through most of the year. Viruses, broken bones, and rashes complicate things in between. And bills and in-laws and jobs keep up a constant current of worry. How can any group dare to make any parent feel guilty about a lack of social responsibility, let alone a parent with a significant extra problem such as retardation?

At the time of Kathryn's birth I also had to manage the school schedules of Amanda, who was in the sixth grade, and Peter, in the second grade; both were timed to overlap and consequently conflict with Martha's kindergarten hours. Between 11:30 and 12:30 each day I had to feed one child, pick up two, drop off one, feed three, drop off two. Kathryn's naps had to fit in whenever they could; breast-feeding was an interesting challenge. I was recovering from a combined Caesarean delivery and hysterectomy and, while trying to manage my own lunches along with the others, unwittingly encouraged attacks from a developing hernia.

If I had had an unretarded baby, I'd never in a million years have thought of volunteering for anything during that period. Now that I had Kathryn, why in the world would I be expected to do anything of the kind? Yet in the face of minimal help from the organization, it was telling me I should help it. And numb from shock and diminished self-confidence, I did my best to comply.

All kinds of groups—churches not the least among them—display this inversion of roles. Instead of being served by the organization, members are required to serve. But it isn't just the unfairness of this that I object to, it's an even more subtly damaging problem. In the process of belonging to and working for an association dedicated to retardation, parents join hands with fate. They cement their own identity as parents of retarded children; they wed themselves to the problem through a myriad of meetings and mailings; they immerse themselves in a society of people like themselves. As I mentioned earlier, there are differences in the immediate and long-range effects of any behavior. While it is probably inevitable, and often helpful, for parents to be caught up in a parent's group in the beginning, such close and constant attachment and identification fairly soon reaches a point of diminishing returns. After that, I believe the process can have a damaging impact on the parents and on the child's future.

Janet M. Bennett

Early on, I decided that I would not be a parent of a retarded child. I would resist the tendency to alter my fundamental identity in response to the twist in the road that had come with retardation. The road might have twisted, but it was still the same I who walked the road. Kathryn was not "a mongoloid," nor was she later on that equally invasive "child with Down's syndrome." She was a child, she was Kathryn, and she had mongolism by whatever name anyone cared to use. An ARC unit or any other kind of group could offer me services or information or moral support or advice, but it would not provide me—or Kathryn—with an identity.

I believe that the very personal disappointment and discouragement and close-to-home practical difficulties of handling a retarded child are quite enough to manage. I think in most cases the change in the parents' perceptions of themselves, of who they are, is both destructive and permanent. Close and continuing relationship to an association devoted to retardation can only give constant reinforcement to this changed perception, can only guarantee that there will be no return to "who I was before." Indeed, in the establishment mythology acceptance is a major goal, and acceptance means taking the fact of retardation into your consciousness and making it part of you.

I recently watched a young woman in a shoe store as her mongoloid daughter marched up and down among the racks, humming, clapping her hands, talking to her image in the mirror. Every bone, muscle, and nerve in the mother's body was concentrated on appearing composed, at ease, unembarrassed. Somehow it seemed that just being the child's mother was not enough, not the major task. What was more important was the role of well-adjusted parent, conveying the message to an ever-observing public that she was managing, she was doing well, and it was not getting her down. Yet the tension in her pose, the studied casualness with which she noted the youngster's activity presented a picture of someone very hard at work in service to a relentless awareness.

Exactly like the nervous mother in church who gradually makes everyone else uneasy about the quite normal and inoffensive wiggling of a small child, this mother's awareness and concentration were almost palpable and certainly contagious. I found myself watching rather nervously to see what might happen, and so did Kathryn, who was sitting beside me. But this mother and her mongoloid daughter, who was almost the same age as Kathryn, were not conscious of us—not because Kathryn was sitting quietly but because the mother's self-consciousness kept her totally absorbed, while at the same time it was being transmitted through the room on extrasensory waves. I took out my notebook and scribbled a reminder to myself: Don't ever cast yourself in the role of well-adjusted parent. It's too much work. It was an interesting reminder, because I had once attempted the same routine.

Under handicap-establishment tutelage a major portion of parents' psychic energy goes to learning the clues to good adjustment. Parents learn to avoid at all cost behavior that will earn a charge of "not facing reality." They strive for constant, unremitting inner awareness of the fact that retardation exists in their household. They've been initiated into a lodge with lifelong membership, and any thought of keeping their distance would be traitorous.

Instead of saying *initiated*, it might be more correct to say *hooked*. Consider the image of beleaguered but dedicated parents toiling selflessly for a cause, their efforts all the more effective because of the poignancy of personal pain. This image is an appealing one for parents who need to see some redemptive value in the disheartening experience of having a retarded child. In the religious traditions we consult in times of tragedy, self-sacrifice has always been represented as noble. But the image of zealous parents is also a useful one for organizations, for willing volunteer parents are the necessary organizational fodder to keep the whole thing going once its started. (The children themselves, whether it's admitted or not, are in the same category.)

The original concept of a parent organization is, of course, barely existent today. Though ARC units began as parent groups, now only a few parents are in any way the moving spirit behind them. Instead these groups defer to the association's executive director (probably a paid professional with generalized social service or fund-raising credentials), the board (usually now consisting of prominent community leaders as well as parents), the programs of the state and national organizations, and the requirements of state and federal legislation. The general membership of parents is instructed in matters concerning them; told what they are expected to do; scolded about contributing, paying dues, volunteering, getting involved. They are also commanded to be grateful for all the organization's programs and to recognize their superior quality, which is undeniable by virtue of the fact that these programs are presented under the organization's sponsorship.

In my own experience with the preschool class in which I dutifully enrolled Kathryn at age 3½, the quality was decidedly not good. But the fact that the class was there at all, that it met state requirements for cleanliness and safety, was furnished with fashionable and approved equipment, and was staffed with dedicated personnel was supposed to be evidence of quality to the consumer. Nonetheless, despite conformity to guidelines, I found the philosophy oppressive and full of clichés, and the routines restrictive; yet it took me eight months to acknowledge the validity of my own instincts sufficiently to take Kathryn out, and several years to overcome my sense of guilt at not having been properly grateful for the fact that the class was offered and that Kathryn had been admitted. After all, aren't parents supposed to take advantage of everything that's offered for retarded children? Wasn't there a waiting list of parents eager and ready to do just that? Who did I think I was, being fussy in a situation like this?

Like labor unions, local associations began in an effort to remedy abuses and to provide needed benefits; but, like unions, they have become dogmatic institutions themselves. In the commitment to the good of a large anonymous constituency, the welfare of individuals is diminished. In the recruitment of parents into the service of the organization, the parents' energies are siphoned away from their primary concern—their own child, their own family. The undercurrent reminding parents to be grateful keeps parent criticism at a low pitch. But, most important, the identity nourished by the association limits the parents' ability to analyze and judge anything except in relation to retardation.

Public School Classes

The other major department of the Company, public school classes, has characteristics equivalent to those of the parent association. This department is even more complex because of the many influences it harbors within itself and because it provides its own mutations for the influences which originate in the local associations. Such complexity means that I can only skim the surface here.

Parent gratitude has always been a part of the public school's picture of the good parent; this image has been used since the beginning of time to ensure good order. Good parents are the ones who do certain things like provide enriching experiences at the library and museum, assure stimulating dinner conversation, and encourage question-answering sessions for their offspring, all aimed at developing a well-mannered, eager, cooperative, and industrious pupil ready for the school's ministrations. Bad parents simultaneously ignore and indulge their children, as they devote themselves to career building or carousing at country clubs. They likewise ignore the school's requirements until such time as the child, predictably, fails his lessons or turns bad. Then, naturally, they blame the school for its shortcomings and shout dramatically, "But he's a good boy—we gave him everything!"

All parents must be grateful for the long hours and dedication of teachers and administrators, whose declared vocation is to work closely with the home in tugging the eager/reluctant, scholar/underachiever, model child/delinquent into the college of his choice or into a good honest job where he can find satisfaction working with his hands. Parents of retarded children must, in addition, be thankful for the even more heroic dedication of inspired teachers, special classes, a mixed bag of specialists (psychologists, social workers, audiologists, speech therapists), and, where it's happening, mainstreaming. What it boils down to is that they're supposed to be, and generally are, grateful that their retarded children are included, allowed in on what regular kids take for granted, even if the process requires that they submit to being "treated to death" by a whole industry of "biocrats" as Ivan Illich, a theorist on medical reform, suggests.

From the moment of diagnosis the handicap-establishment trains parents of retarded children to be so occupied with their problem, always conscious of the specialness of their kids and themselves, that they either haven't time or don't dare to figure out what they really want and whether that's what they're getting. From beginning to end their vision is riveted on and limited to the retardedness of things. The single-mindedness that characterized the beginnings of parent organizations, when it was true that enough was not done for these children, continues uninterrupted even when all kinds of things are being done. But are they the right things?

Whether parents like or dislike their children's special classes, they're held back from voicing criticism by oblique reminders of the early days when there were no classes at all. (Those were the days, remember, when closets and attics across the land presumably harbored a supply of sluggish and slovenly retarded children.) After a long Christmas holiday when the youngster goes back to his class, parents say with relief, "Well, it's better than nothing." Just the term *special class* somehow suggests concession and a veiled threat that if parents get picky, the class will be eliminated. It would obviously be illegal, obviously won't happen; but the nagging primordial fear stays alive among parents just the same.

The advantages of special segregated classes for children of supposedly similar intellectual ability or with physical or psychic idiosyncrasies which permit category grouping have been increasingly challenged by thoughtful individuals in education and other fields. Nonetheless, the wholesale trucking of children to centralized special classes continues. Every day I pass little vans with their odd cargo as they crisscross the countryside, taking this one from here to there and that one from there to here. An hour-long bus trip is not unusual even for children who, by definition, have reduced physical endurance.

The equality of classes, once the children get where they're going, is variable. In any number of recommended reconnaissance tours I've made, such classes have not been impressive. They are either perpetual nursery schools for oversize tots or regular schools chopped up in little pieces and run through a projector at low speed. Innovative techniques promoted by the education industry's obsession with methodology look good to the constituents and the school board and keep the young teachers amused, but little of real value seems to occur.

In one class I visited, about eight young children designated trainable were lined up on chairs to watch that favorite of today's educators, a filmstrip. It was a Disney instructional piece, intended to present the facts about food production and distribution. It careened from a farm and tractors to some kind of warehouse or cannery, then on to a grocery store with shopping carts. The message might have concerned mechanization or transportation, although the narrator, in classic filmstrip drone, occasionally mentioned something about food. All these pictures were rather small scale realistic drawings. They were followed abruptly by illustrations of food groupings, done in a more abstract style on a scale that showed a steak covering approximately the same portion of screen that a barn and silo had required only moments before. The teacher proceeded to point out various food items, which was a good idea since what looked like a modernistic armchair turned out to be roast beef. She lost her bearings a few frames later as she sweetly pointed to some bumpy-looking tan things. "Look at the mushrooms," she purred, having vainly tried to identify what were more likely meant to be Parker House rolls since they were in a collection representing grains. It was a silly filmstrip, badly organized, attempting too much, and in no way suited to a band of youngsters who weren't too dumb to be bored to death with it. When the teacher was not trying to figure out what the filmstrip was about, she was snapping orders to the children to sit up straight, turn around, watch the screen.

Such useless teaching goes on everywhere, not just in special classes, and this is the problem. Things are not well with schools in general today, as a host of education critics keep pointing out. There's too much work with too little significance. Too much time is spent shuffling dittos and filling in workbook pages. These workbooks are a jumbled mess, with incomprehensible instructions and largely useless tasks. Reading lessons concentrate on decoding written material, without acknowledging that a major purpose and incentive for reading is the pleasure of enjoying good writing. Stories offered for the child to practice his reading skills are tasteless and bland with awkward sentence construction. Trickiness masquerades as imagination; the contemporary substitutes for the valuable. Beauty is nonexistent; as critic John Leonard once said about Disney movies, "Cute is beauty, beauty cute."

I agree with the judgment of John Holt, a popular critic of public education, that children are lucky if they get fifteen minutes of real teaching in a school day. From my own observations during twenty years of enduring schools with my children, it's hard not to agree with Holt's advice to keep children out of school altogether, to "let all those escape it who can, any way they can" (Flaste, 1976, p. 35).

A nineteenth century clergyman and social commentator, Sydney Smith, wrote, "Some men through indolence, others through ignorance, and most through necessity, submit to the established education of the times; and seek for their children that species of distinction which happens, at the period in which they live, to be stamped with the approbation of mankind" (Epstein, 1977, p. 88). Exactly my point for parents who have retarded children and those who don't. The former compound the problem—they are so busy insisting that they want in on regular education that they fail to notice that it's hardly worth getting in on. Who would want their children in the hands of people who make claims like this one, which arrived in today's mail: "Student/teacher interactions in nonstructured, informal situations can be optimized to nurture the development of thorough and efficient thinking skills for children"?

Mainstreaming simply means that all kids have an equal shot at mediocre schooling. (Of course, even this is subject to discount since, like so many other educational innovations, what's claimed by public relations announcements is not always fact.) Bringing retarded children into a regular classroom does not necessarily end segregation and discrimination—it may only camouflage it.

A major problem of public education, of course, is that while it's universally available, it's also compulsory and monopolistic. A child has to go, and he usually has to stay where he is put. Retarded children don't exactly have to go in the same sense that other children are legally bound to do so, but they are equally locked into the system once they enter it.

Children of ordinary ability, without limiting handicaps, generally have greater adapting and defending powers in the face of poor teaching. They also have greater opportunity to compensate through their homes or extra-curricular activities. Retarded children's choices are further limited by their very inability to identify or report on an unsatisfactory classroom situation. For all children a change of class, beyond certain minor variations, means money. It means private school or tutoring. It also means time, energy, and conviction.

I took the private school and tutoring route for Kathryn. Regrettably, I didn't have the insight or funds to do it for my other children; the decline of the schools which was obvious during Amanda's first few grades accelerated rapidly during Peter's and Martha's attendance. In any case since that first troublesome preschool experience, I have worked out Kathryn's schooling year by year through a variety of situations, all in the regular classes or regular schools. She has had no special-class placement since the age of 3½.

First she attended a private nursery school and a private kindergarten. Then came a four-year hitch in a remarkable open-classroom situation (ninety children, four teachers) in a public school. Mostly I paid tuition, but midway some administrative shifts meant that what had begun as a free-spirited experiment began to change into a program. This program, in which Kathryn became a pilot child for a federal grant proposal, had mixed benefits. It began the inevitable deterioration of the original vision, but it also permitted my school district to assume tuition payments. Fortunately, even deterioration is subject to bureaucratic influences; the decline proceeded slowly enough to allow Kathryn to enjoy some of the original benefits for a while longer.

This year Kathryn is in a class of eight girls in a small, ungraded Catholic School. In addition, as insurance against the possibility of having no suitable class available at some point, Kathryn is tutored on a rather random schedule by one of the teachers from the original open classroom, who retired after the demise of that fine experiment. With her Kathryn works on short research papers, on some of her regular class assignments, and on expanding her writing ability. They also do needlepoint, recipes, and are about to begin rug hooking. Should we find ourselves temporarily without the kind of school we want, we would expand the tutoring as it seemed necessary.

Janet M. Bennett

In each instance my major purpose was to provide the interaction with nonhandicapped children which does more than any particular instructor can do to teach language and normal behavior patterns. In particular, such contact permits the child to take precedence over the handicap, no matter how loudly the handicapping conditions may clamor for attention.

With money you can do things—even though in our case the money is only barely available, since it's needed at the same time for the older children's college tuitions. But what do you do if there's no money? It would certainly be a start to make low-interest loans available for any educational purpose, not just college expenses. The federally backed higher education loans are not ideal economic arrangements, but they would permit some options for parents who want alternatives.

All bureaucracies demand, "What do you propose?" and if you have no well-thought-out reply, your complaints are dismissed, discredited. I don't agree that the one who identifies a problem must also be the one to provide the solution. I can guess that I have appendicitis, but I doubt that it would be prudent for me to operate. In this instance, however, I do have a few observations which might be helpful.

The preceding pages have spent considerable time in outlining the problems. My recommendations are not nearly so detailed, for they proceed from a fundamental solution, a basic change in outlook, rather than from specific blueprints. This fundamental change—the shedding of the deliberate identification with retardation—permits any needed kind of change to be developed.

What would happen if parents just stopped dwelling on the fact that their children are retarded? Suppose they simply figured out what the children needed, or were ready for, at any given time and convinced the schools—or whoever else had enough money—to provide it. I once wrote an article suggesting public libraries as alternative sources of schooling for retarded children. I still think it's a good idea.

A long time ago I stopped looking at newspaper listings of special programs for retarded children. Now I just notice what Kathryn might like. All kinds of courses are given by community schools, YMCAs, or churches. (I'm not speaking of church programs and religion classes for retarded children; these depend on the same attitudes as the schools.) Since people choose these classes, they are open to anyone who's interested. This holds true whether or not a fee is charged. Grandparents and teen-agers, beginners, or those with some familiarity with the subject—all take the same course. Though there may be beginning, intermediate, or advanced levels, nobody would notice or care if someone took the same level course several times. For most of us and especially for retarded children, taking enough time is more important than special techniques.

Just because there is no headline or sign authorizing the admission of someone who's retarded doesn't mean that retarded people cannot consider these courses. Through the years Kathryn has been enrolled in a variety of such classes, whenever our budget and schedule would permit. She has been the only handicapped child in modern dance, twirling, and tumbling classes, where the ages ranged from four year olds to teen-agers. Currently she is in an exercise class of eight people who are high school students and housewives. The teachers, who are of all ages and backgrounds except special education, have been uniformly interested, unconcerned about problems Kathryn's condition might imply (none have occurred), and casual about skipping over the occasional area where she is not altogether capable. In several instances she was not the least able in the group.

In these classes, the subject is central. The idea is "We're teaching this. Would you like to learn it?" Obviously capability is a factor, but this is always a factor with everyone. I would not register for violin lessons, computer programming, Russian, statistics, or ballet. A battery of tests might tell me I'm smart enough for all those things, but I am not in the least interested in them. Even though they're popular offerings, I know that for all practical purposes I would not be able to learn them. The mental and physical effort would be prohibitive.

Couldn't regular schools present their courses on the same basis? "Here is what we have. Who needs it?" need be the only premise. A corollary to this would be "How can we help you?"

Such a view of education obviously calls for many adjustments of facilities as well as of attitudes. The all-or-none view of scheduling and programming in which flexibility is as strictly defined as are rigid routines would have to go. A retarded youngster who is ready for letters and numbers, though he isn't toilet trained and can't walk, might attend one or more separate sessions in what he needs. A child with the opposite problem, mobility without academic readiness, could have physical exercises and games in the gym. If a child requires rest periods during the day, could there not be a better solution than home instruction or more space available than a cot in the nurse's office? Couldn't a day-training center be included in the space allocations so that physical equipment could be shared by skilled athletes and those who need it for development?

Where would the staff come from? All over the place. There are plenty of former teachers now home with babies who would like part-time work. There's a large group of modern parents who believe in sharing the domestic duties. They, too, would work in well with the free-wheeling kind of scheduling I describe.

Curiously, we like to think that our concentration on the person is the humane way, yet it's exactly this relentless awareness of who, which translates so readily into what kind of, that dehumanizes. Paradoxically, if we look instead at what is needed, we might find that our humaneness automatically becomes more real.

No, it wouldn't be easy. We've gotten used to the shortcut of categories—an N.I. child (neurologically impaired) or the C.P.s (cerebral palsied).

We've also become addicted to programs. It's no surprise to me that the words *program* and *project* begin with pr, the abbreviation for public relations. These programs for the retarded, for the elderly, for the gifted lure us farther and farther from everyone's humanity. I suggest we begin resisting the obsession with such packaging.

In the end both parent associations and schools have one thing to offer. Associations are where parents are. Schools are where children are. Parents need other parents, and children need other children. Except for this, everything is negotiable. Let's stop thinking that everything that happens, everything that will be accomplished must be stamped "For the retarded." Let's stop selling our souls and our children to the company store. Let's stop playing the company way.

REFERENCES

Flaste, R. Embittered reformer advises: Avoid school. *New York Times*, April 16, 1976, p. 35.
Epstein, J. Bring back elitist universities. *New York Times Magazine*, February 6, 1977, pp. 86–88.

QUESTIONS TO CONSIDER

1. What are Janet's values concerning the importance of addressing individual versus collective needs of persons with retardation? From Janet's perspective what are the personal drawbacks to being involved in parent organizations? How could parent organizations change to be more responsive to her needs? How do you predict Janet's values will influence her future priorities?

2. According to Janet's views how does the expectation of parent gratitude interfere with a parent's ability to be an effective educational decision maker? What do you predict will be the nature of Janet's gratitude during Kathryn's later school years?

3. What has been the pattern of Kathryn's schooling? How do you predict that Janet will carry out her philosophy about Kathryn's education?

UPDATE:
A Ten O'Clock Scholar

Janet M. Bennett

At the time I completed the original essay in *Parents Speak Out*, I was really speaking with a forked tongue. Although I concluded my comments then with some suggestions as to what schools might do to improve education both for handicapped and nonhandicapped individuals, I had by then given up all ideas that such suggestions had any chance of success.

I had also given up those pious notions about working within the system which the late sixties had pressed upon reformers. Working within the system is in most instances a brilliant tactic the system uses to squelch agitators, or at least to diffuse their effect. An early example is *Main Street* by Sinclair Lewis, which I've just finished reading. I found it almost unbearable to watch Carol Kennicott's efforts to change the town of Gopher Prairie, Minnesota, by working within the system; she was wretched and nothing changed.

Some time before I finished my earlier essay, I made the decision to take Kathryn out of school entirely. When I said that the schools I had found for her through the years had been pleasant and enjoyable and successful, I meant this in the context of schools in general, which I've never much liked. They were the best schools I could find. But no, they weren't the answer. They weren't what I really wanted.

In each case we had been lucky enough to run into one, two, sometimes even three or four wonderful people—sound, sane, cheerful, quirky humans. And these schools were committed to individualizing, something I consider imperative. But the fatal flaw is that the structure of school itself means that individualizing just can't be done enough. And of course there are the constant bureaucratic time-consumers: milk money, class-picture money, grocery-bag book covers, field trip permission slips, illness excuses, room-mother cupcake baking, lunch packing, mitten and book labeling . . . and ditto sheets, ditto sheets, ditto sheets.

So along about November of 1975, I broached the subject to Kathryn:

"Suppose you don't go to school any more. Suppose you just take courses for awhile and see what you like." Instantly her face lit up, and I knew it was safe to proceed. We began to collect clippings about various course possibilities in a big blue loose-leaf binder, and we talked over our plans as we drove the fourteen-mile run to school each day. But we made no definite decisions. We just wool-gathered all that winter.

I already had a mental outline of what I wanted. At different times in the past I had worried about what I'd do if there were no suitable class for Kathryn. For some time I had arranged for one of her former teachers to tutor her in math and composition one day a week after school, as a kind of insurance. And I had fantasized about a plan to be mobilized in an emergency—involving this teacher and me and using the public library as a school-for-one. We would use their tables, books, AV equipment, and reference staff and materials as our private school system (after all, public libraries were begun as a people's free school), and the rest of the world would be a giant field trip.

Influencing my mental model was my recollection of Plumfield, the country school run by Jo and Professor Baer in Louisa May Alcott's *Little Men*, a book I greatly preferred to *Little Women*. I liked the mix of book learning, kite flying, cooking, small business (Tommy Bangs' egg sales), and practical science and the flexibility and problem-solving approach Jo brought to the whole operation. Each time I thought of this emergency system I liked it better. But instead of needing it suddenly because of a problem, here we are, able to plan such a program at our leisure.

That spring we began a nutritional program for Kathryn with a doctor whose specialty is orthomolecular medicine. Like the education I prefer, orthomolecular medicine is based on an individualized rather than an average-man point of view. It acknowledges that each person's biochemistry is unique; one person will respond to food, stress, medicines, and the environment in a quite different way from that of someone else. We discovered that Kathryn was allergic to wheat and eggs among other things, so we altered her diet and began a regimen of megavitamins tailored to her system. From the beginning Kathryn followed this routine herself, carefully setting out her vitamins—nineteen of them per meal, most with polysyllabic names like niacinamide, 1-tryptophan and pantothenic acid—without error. I must say, I was surprised at her skill.

Our sense of exhilaration began to build as the school year moved to a close. We both felt a tremendous excitement over our new plan, and our involvement with the vitamins and changed diet only added to the feeling that we were entering a new world, where everything would be different and interesting. The summer was free and easy with the wonderful knowledge that this year, the first time in years, it didn't all have to end at Labor Day. I assembled all the ideas and clippings we had accumulated through the winter and began the job of creating our school-for-one.

Initially for most people who attempt home schooling, there's the feel-

Janet M. Bennett

ing that it's necessary to provide a minischool, structured on the same hours per day and days per week as a real school, only carried on at home. In spite of my freewheeling mental image of the where and the what of our school-for-one, in the beginning I, too, felt I should put in about as many hours as a regular school.

As I tried to figure the costs of courses, tutoring, and the like, it was instantly apparent that real school looks like a wonderful bargain—all those hours and for free. (Most people forget that free public education is paid for by taxes, both local and federal.) I couldn't afford anything like such a schedule. Furthermore, I couldn't stand being tied down to that kind of schedule—that's why I had always free-lanced or worked from home. I liked to be able to pop out in the yard whenever I felt like it. And I had always felt guilty about sending Kathryn off to be sealed inside a building for so many hours on lovely sunny, breezy days.

So I quickly revised my plans. I chose a large, mixed group of physical, academic, and artistic subjects that we could afford and that we could manage in a comfortable week's schedule. I presented this list to Kathryn and asked her to rank order her choices. Again I was surprised, this time at her instant acceptance of the process and the ease with which she checked off her preferences in the suitable columns.

The fact that I was surprised at these two things, the vitamin management and her understanding of rank ordering, interested me. It was the beginning of my awareness—an awareness that has persisted—of how much we really don't recognize about our children even when we're constantly scrutinizing and evaluating them. We all stick by the creed that parents know their children best, better than the schools and the experts. But we don't often realize that because our children are in school so much of the time, we parents don't actually know them as well as we might. True, part of the problem lies in our closeness to each other; we often observe automatically, and much of what we see doesn't really register, or it registers according to what we've programmed ourselves to expect rather than what's really happening. But a very significant factor is the amount of time our children spend in school, with school people observing and interpreting according to an institutionalized, often neutralized and mediocritized set of criteria.

What we know of our children is, more than we recognize, seen through a glass darkly, filtered through the haze of a school day and school personnel. A friend told me recently, "I didn't know Joanne could swim that well," as they returned from a vacation trip. Joanne's swimming lessons had been part of a school program, and her mother had only dimly perceived what was taking place. Not the slow but steady improvement, not the enjoyment—or possible distaste—that she might have noticed if she had been permitted to be on hand to watch or participate. Even if the teacher had sent home a note saying Joanne was doing beautifully, would the parents have known what standard she was applying, what that really meant? And might not the lessons have gone more smoothly with the parents as interpreters of the child's learning style?

When Kathryn was learning to swim at the Y, her instructor kept repeating, "Look—and blow; look—and blow." Watching from the balcony, I could see that Kathryn was doing exactly that but was running out of breath very quickly as she paddled down the lane. I asked the instructor if she shouldn't change the order to "Look—breathe—and blow." She said, "No, this is the standard approach. If they do it right, they'll inhale automatically—they'll just have to." Well, Kathryn was a young legalist, and she was not inhaling automatically. She kept looking and blowing until she ran out of breath and started sputtering and struggling. The instructor took this as evidence of a lack of physical endurance rather than what it was, a rigid following of the rules. I took Kathryn aside and suggested that she try to "Look—breathe—and blow," and though she initially protested that she wasn't supposed to do it that way, she did try it and found that she could swim a lot farther without sinking. Multiply this example by hundreds of situations and hundreds of kids, and you can see what I mean by neutralized set of criteria and the need to individualize.

During the school year we're all involved at one time or another in helping with homework and projects. And most of us faithfully attend conferences, PTA meetings, and the like, as well as reading the myriad of bulletins that come home crumpled in pockets or folded in the lunch box. All this, willy-nilly, provides us with the context and backdrop, the information and point of view, against which we perceive and understand our children. And unless we are in on the beginning, middle, and end of the learning process, not just the homework and the conferences, we generally end up deferring to the school's view of what's happening. School pronouncements tend to denounce what they refer to as parent apathy, but even with scrupulous parent cooperation, the fact remains that the ball is in the school's court and the parents generally play the school's game.

Through the years I consciously tried to resist this process. I spent a good deal of my time and thought on Kathryn and her particular needs and requirements. I worked with a kind of informed instinct, plotting and planning to locate schools and tutoring. But even though I was aware of and attempted to steer clear of or compensate for the influence of the schools, I obviously couldn't escape it altogether. Now, at home, focusing entirely on a no-school life, I found that I was in fact noticing more, seeing more about Kathryn, and finding her an even more amazing, multifaceted, and multitalented person than I had known before. I thought I knew her. I thought I had known my other children. Yet this new way of approaching Kathryn's life was showing me a new Kathryn. How I'd love to have had the opportunity to do it earlier. How I'd love to have been brave enough to do it with my other children (Note 1).

That fall we enjoyed a prolonged vacation, relishing the late September and October sunshine. We drove to the shore and played Frisbee on the beach, or splashed about in the still-warm surf, sometimes wild from the track of hurricanes. We played kickball or jogged in our back field. We played cards or read, we painted shutters and took hikes. Though we continued to talk about courses, I wanted to detoxify Kathryn from the effect of school and was willing to take as long as was needed. I wanted to get to know just what she really required—where she was at—and develop a system consistent with our own physiologies and the seasons.

On November 7 of that year, a cloudy, warm day, we took another trip to the shore. Kathryn was tossing the coins into the toll baskets on the Garden State Parkway, and I realized that, in spite of the time spent in school with those cardboard coins that schools like so much, Kathryn didn't really know one denomination from another. Presto! Our first academic project! At home I assembled a jar of real money and began showing Kathryn which coin was which. From then on, our mornings went like this: We got up late and enjoyed a leisurely breakfast (we treasured sleep for months after so many years of early alarms and rushed breakfasts). Then we made beds, loaded the dishwasher, fed the cats, emptied the waste-baskets, and started the wash. Kathryn and I each followed a separate list labeled Things to Do. Then I wrote on a sheet of paper various amounts of money: 15¢, 20¢, 32¢, 9¢. And Kathryn lined the coins up on the paper to match.

From there we went to four cans or packages from my pantry shelves, which I labeled with new prices. Kathryn selected the suitable combinations of coins and placed them atop the items. At first she was quite addicted to working with pennies, but within a month or two she had the process down cold. The whole business took about twenty minutes a day.

In the meantime we slowly embarked on other activities, chosen from our big rank-ordered list. Swimming began with private lessons at the YMCA; Kathryn later moved into the Y's regular after-school classes. She started ballet lessons with a wonderfully skilled and empathic teacher in an adult class at the Garden State Ballet Company in Morristown. The third year there, she was advanced to the intermediate class. One morning a week she went to a former McCall's designer's studio for lessons in needle-point and later embroidery. This class resulted in an exhibition of Kathryn's work at the Montville Township Library.

As I prepared to open a separate checking account to handle the fees for these classes, it suddenly dawned on me that here was another opportu-nity for learning. So Kathryn filled out the application, and I showed her how to write checks and make out deposit slips. She got a great charge out of writing her first check—for a nonacademic item, a Wise potato chip T-shirt saying, Get Wise. A portent, perhaps?

Incidentally, even though we paid fees for most of our courses, it's entirely possible to manage home schooling at minimal cost. There's the library, as I mentioned, or exchange programs with friends and relatives, or other kinds of barter. At one point a stained-glass craftsman agreed to teach

Kathryn in exchange for an occasional loaf of oatmeal bread from me. As it happened, taking on that one additional class would have pushed us into the overscheduled state I work to avoid, so we didn't follow through on the plan. Nonetheless, expense is not a necessity for home schooling.

The second academic effort we took on was typing—and yet another surprise. Kathryn learned the keyboard easily in a week, and with materials I invented as we went along, she became quite proficient and accurate, if a bit slow.

Kathryn has ridden a bike for many years. That first year of home schooling my husband and I bought bikes, too, and the three of us began taking extended bike hikes. One of our favorites, a reasonably strenuous one, is the sixteen-mile, hilly bikeway from Glen Falls to Lake George, New York, and back. Such treks took place whenever we chose, with only our own calendar, not a school's—and no permission slips—to guide us.

In a way our initial schedule double-crossed us. I had expected to present several subjects at a time and to jettison those that didn't work out—meaning those that Kathryn didn't learn well. According to this diagnostic setup, I figured we'd be working our way through a large and changing series of classes within a brief span of time, say a year or so. As it turned out, Kathryn has done well at everything she's tried, so we stuck to our original choices for a couple of years. Here again, I was surprised that I should have been surprised. Why hadn't I known she would do well at these things? Well, because up to now her success had been presented to us by those who taught her as something unusual and surprising. But why did I, who believed in her ability a million percent, also respond as though it was something unusual?

Well, no more. I now know that whatever Kathryn feels like trying she will probably do well with. She may have a slightly longer beginning than some of the others in a class, and she may need a bit longer when something new is introduced. But in no class has there ever been a problem for or with either instructor or classmates. I have repeatedly asked teachers if Kathryn's presence slowed things up for the rest or made their job more difficult, and always the answer has been, "Not at all."

Though each class has been a success, we have, nonetheless, made changes as time went on. But these changes have been for the sake of variety, not because of failure. Kathryn and I consult every few weeks on what we're doing and where we're going. We consider whether to continue the current plan or switch to something else, and Kathryn makes the decisions according to her own feelings at the time. I advise and guide, generally about times and schedules and budget. By the fall of 1982, Kathryn had studied the following: math and money, reading, spelling, composition, telephone work (message-taking, collect calls, answering machines), cooking and nutrition, drawing and painting, typing, sign language, needlepoint and embroidery, ballet, jazz, modern and aerobic dancing, ice-skating, swimming, vegetable gardening, and gymnastics.

Janet M. Bennett

This year her schedule includes math, language, cooking and nutrition, modern dance and gymnastics, acting and singing, and geography. In math she's working on multiplication and verbal problems, as well as managing her checkbook and her monthly bank statement. She and her tutor role-play waitress and customer, with Kathryn figuring the bill and tip. Her language study includes role-playing other situations besides a restaurant, as well as inventing and taping newspaper and TV interviews and weather forecasts. This year Kathryn and I took vast quantities of pictures—of the seasons, our town, and our neighborhood—which we used as jumping-off points for writing sentences and paragraphs. Cooking and nutrition concentrates on making desserts without wheat and developing a repertoire of meals Kathryn can cook for herself. Last year, at Kathryn's request, we also produced a giant picture book listing the nutrients contained in all kinds of foods. I occasionally use it myself as a reference.

Her modern dance and gymnastics is a combination program at the Y. The dance section has a recital in May, complete with sequined leotards and ostrich feathers. Dancing is her real love and we would probably never have realized just how skilled she is if we had not begun the home schooling plan. In gymnastics I watched last week as Kathryn began work on forward and backward rolls on the balance beam and a sole circle dismount on the uneven parallel bars. In acting and singing Kathryn has private lessons with the director of a local acting studio. They do improvisation and beginning voice instruction. She will be taking a summer theater program here (consisting of mime, voice, dance, theater craft, and production) with a group whose ages range from eight to nineteen. Geography is with me. We're making a series of booklets about seventeen countries Kathryn selected. Each booklet covers money, language, architecture, climate, and occupations. We use the library for this course, which I call Country Clichés; we're learning basic information about each country, plus fundamental phrases in each language.

Kathryn also has speech therapy twice a month with a stupendous therapist from Seton Hall University to assist in polishing her use of language, which has been affected by her erratic hearing over the years. And on Friday afternoons she volunteers in the gift shop of Riverside Hospital. She waits on customers, selling things like greeting cards and stuffed animals. Kathryn generally handles the shop alone; she'll receive her 100-hour pin at the volunteers' luncheon in June.

Last spring my husband began teaching her to drive, and it was his turn to be surprised. "She's just a natural," he told me after the first session, though her four-feet-ten-inches requires a pillow as she sits behind the wheel. On Sunday afternoons they go out to an empty mall parking lot, and Kathryn, alone in the car, follows a course my husband sets out with rocks—in and out and around and backward and forward. I can't imagine her tooling around the highways of northern New Jersey and metropolitan New York—but a skill is a skill and good to have in hand.

I mentioned my aversion to overscheduling. All of these pursuits may sound like a lot, but in fact they total only about ten to twelve hours a week. We never start before 10 A.M., we take all day Monday off, and we plan classes to allow for noontime bike rides, sitting outside in the sun, or the long periods that Kathryn spends working on her favorite computer designs or listening to records. I draft all the programs, I outline all the objectives and approaches in frequent written descriptions for the various instructors, and we consult almost daily on what's going on and how it's working. One major point must be reiterated: in none of these classes is there anyone besides Kathryn with an identifiable handicap.

And what about socializing, the big question for those who brave the system and teach their children at home? I've run a small, informal survey over the past year and have found that not one Down's syndrome person, according to the parents, has a single real friend. Sure, they mix and mingle in classes and activity centers and recreation programs and Special Olympics. But the parents have no qualms in admitting that this is not the same at all. Their kids have no friends. Period.

During her school years Kathryn had a number of classmates who came to our house on visits and to her birthday parties. But her close friends have been two: the girl next door, who, sad to say, has moved to Long Island, and a girl we met in a drugstore downtown when a chance conversation revealed that they both knew some sign language and had the same first and middle names. This second Kathryn has been my Kathryn's best friend for five years now. She has problems with some academic subjects, but she's smarter and wiser than most adults I know. She can explain situations and events and emotions to Kathryn in simpler, clearer language than I can produce, and her patience, understanding, and loyalty are nothing short of phenomenal. And because this girl is generally so able, they can go bowling or to movies or the mall by themselves, without me. Kathy is regularly here overnight on weekends; they work out dance routines or watch "Love Boat" and "Fantasy Island." What Kathy draws from Kathryn is warmth, affection, and an easy, relaxed, noncompetitive enjoyment that I suspect is not so readily available among her public school classmates.

As I write, the two of them have gone to the mall to have lunch—Chicken McNuggets, a real departure from the regular nutrition rules—and to poke around the record and earring shops. Last time they did this, they came home convulsed with giggles and retired to Kathryn's room with their packages. In a few minutes they emerged, modeling matching "Grody to the Max" T-shirts lettered in purple and pink. Today was a no-school day for Kathy because of a late-April snowstorm, so we quickly rearranged Kathryn's morning class to make way for the outing.

I wish there were more friends—a whole "Happy Days" gang of them—for Kathryn. She's the kind of kid who should be (probably would have been) spending ski weekends or going to Bermuda on spring break with a bunch of friends, or whatever today's groups are up to. The friend situation is a tough one for handicapped kids, but I don't believe school or no school is the core of the problem. In any case we're grateful to have stumbled onto such a gem as Kathy.

And what comes next? Will we just go on arranging courses forever? No, but there's still lots more to learn and lots more growing for Kathryn to do. What I have in mind is some kind of apprenticeship next, some kind of situation that takes into account Kathryn's abilities, interests, and desires. I don't think all the answers are in on those areas yet. When the time seems ripe, perhaps we'll move toward something on the order of a vocational training program we might design ourselves. In any case Martha, our middle daughter, frequently reminds me that Kathryn is the only one of us not obligated to plunge headlong into the rat race. So, though people often ask me about the future, I try to restrain any future-obsessions I might be tempted to indulge, just as I had to do when Kathryn was an infant. All through the years what was needed for her eventually materialized—not necessarily on time, of course, and not without our share of sleepless nights spent staring at the ceiling, but soon enough.

So that's where we are now. I'm not proposing that all parents take their kids out of school and package a program like ours. But I am saying that for us it's been exhilarating and civilized and elegant and fun—and most of all, individualized. I grew up hearing my father quote Mae West: "I've been rich and I've been poor. Rich is better." Well, to paraphrase, I've done education the conventional way and I've done it my way. My way is better.

NOTES

1. People always ask about legality. Home schooling is legal in New Jersey and many other states. Considerable advice and information on this point and an informative and stimulating newsletter, *Growing Without Schooling*, are available from educator John Holt, 729 Boylston Street, Boston, MA 02116. As for us, our school district always seemed happy to ignore us and hoped we'd do the same for them.

QUESTIONS TO CONSIDER

1. Review the questions on page 173. How accurate were your predictions?

2. What were the catalysts for Janet's decision to provide home schooling? Compare school-based and home education in terms of outcomes for Kathryn and Janet.

3. What are your predictions concerning the nature and quality of Kathryn's vocational training over the next six years? Describe the adult life-style that you believe Kathryn will have.

Dorothy Weld Avis—Tot to most who know her professionally or personally—received her master's degree in social
work when her son, Hunter, was thirteen. Her previous volunteer and staff work with local Associations for Retarded Citizens and a United Cerebral Palsy affiliate in New Jersey
became a career direction for her.

When she first wrote for *Parents Speak Out*, Tot was a social worker in a large residential facility for mentally retarded
people in New York. It was a time when, by court order, there
were the beginnings of deinstitutionalization, interdisciplinary
teams, and changes in the approach to treatment of mentally
retarded individuals.

Tot now has statewide program responsibility for the
Connecticut Department of Mental Retardation at a time when
similar changes are occurring in that state. She now is responsible for carrying out many of the policies about which
she wrote, as a staff person, in 1978.

Dorothy Avis   *Hunter Avis*

Hunter is twenty-four and lives at Camphill Village in
Copake, New York. Despite being diagnosed as autistic, aphasic, and mentally retarded, he is a weaver of raw wool rugs
and of feather-light mohair scarves and is a willing and able
gardener and wood splitter.

Deinstitutionalization Jet Lag

Dorothy W. Avis

"She'll never live to be more than a year old."
"Put him away and forget him."
"They're happier with their own kind."
"Think of the other children."
"Only professionals can give this child the kind of care and training he needs."

Families of mentally retarded or otherwise handicapped children are familiar with these phrases from the not-too-distant past. Institutional placements were based upon these phrases and the philosophies which were behind them. The necessity for lifetime care was a basic assumption. Lives were built upon and around these ideas.

Many parents whose handicapped children were institutionalized with these phrases and assumptions are being asked to accept completely new phrases and concepts. New services and programs are being implemented. Normalization, least restrictive environment, civil rights, residents' rights, parent training, and respite care are but a few.

I favor the new alternatives and philosophies. As a social worker in a large older institution, I am reminded daily of the impact these changes are having on clients, parents, and staff. I view the intent of the new programs and the results very positively.

Discussing the impact and results of the new program is a large order in itself. The impact I want to discuss is the reaction of the many people who are having to change attitudes, rationales, long-held notions, and daily activities because of the changes in policy and philosophy. I see a similarity between the experiences these people are having and jet lag. I call this experience in our field deinstitutionalization jet lag.

A traveler who has zoomed at supersonic speed through several time zones finds himself physically unready for the time zone in which he lands. He is uncomfortable until his body adjusts to the portion of the day in

185

which he finds himself. It takes some time and adjustment. Experienced travelers allow for this. Clients, their families, and many staff members in institutions are having some discomfort as they adjust to the new time zone that changing attitudes toward the mentally retarded require.

Inadequate communication is part of the cause of the discomfort. Families who made the decision for institutional placement long ago have a particular backlog of poor communication which the practices of institutions through the years have engendered. Thus, they have not had the opportunity to incorporate new ideas and to absorb the implications and possibilities. It is these families upon whom I would like to focus attention. I hope to remind professional people of the distance and speed we are asking families of adult, long-institutionalized clients to travel. By looking at the contrasts with which we are dealing, I hope to encourage patience and extra attempts to communicate. Our clients and we need the support of these families.

One elderly couple vividly illustrates the contrast between where their journey began and where they have now found themselves. Their reaction to sudden communication of new expectations includes a number of elements our original phrases and old philosophies embodied. This couple came to see me during a regular visit to see their daughter in the institution. Their daughter is a woman of nearly forty who has Down's syndrome. They had seen a television show on which an enthusiastic proponent of the community movement was a guest. They perceived his message as a promise. The message was that all clients from a given area who resided in the institution would be returned to the homes of their families or to their home area within a year. This plan was given greater color by dramatic stories of institutional abuse.

These parents were considerably upset. They had placed their daughter in the institution as a newborn infant. This decision had been made upon the recommendation of a much-respected physician. The prognosis was that the baby would live less than a year and would not develop beyond the most infantile stage. They were also told that family and friends should be advised that the baby would not be coming home from the hospital and the conclusion would be that the baby had died.

Through forty years they had visited faithfully, had assumed financial responsibility, and had an affectionate relationship with their daughter. They felt they had made the only choice for her and had acted in good faith by the standards of the time.

They tearfully asked if some consideration could be given to their daughter's remaining in the institution, as it had always been her home. They feared that there would not be adequate protection and care for her in any place but the institution. They apologized for being too elderly and ill to assume her direct care. They also found it difficult to imagine how they could cope with explaining their daughter's existence after all of these years if she were placed "down the street."

Dorothy W. Avis

There are obviously many things we could discuss about this reaction, including the couple's mechanisms for coping. They were expressing their reaction to their situation in an individual way. Their reaction was also colored by the only information they had up until that time about what appeared to be a new plan affecting their child and undermining their history of choices. Threatening, to be sure. It was as if they imagined buses pulling up down the street, depositing bewildered retarded people who were going to be living with their own or other families. Based upon the information they had, this was not too far-fetched.

The perspective of those of us closer to the situation would tell us that the range of mentally retarded clients within the institution could not be provided for so simply as a quick description of community residences would indicate. These parents didn't have that perspective. They were considerably less anxious as they heard the explanation of how community placement comes about, how parental participation in the planning is an important ingredient, and how placements are considered on a highly individual basis. The threat turned into an opportunity for this and later discussions which were long overdue for this family that essentially had no one with whom to talk about their daughter.

The new ideas had forced them to reexamine the beginning of their journey with their child and all the years they had felt that they had done the best things for her. The sudden dramatic description of the community movement had compelled them to go through several time zones. "The baby will not live" is quite a distance from "coming home to live" forty years later.

Another family had quite a different reaction. This family had kept a very physically handicapped son at home for fifteen years. He had required nearly constant nursing care and had many serious illnesses and much out-patient therapy while at home. They, in contrast to the first family, hoped the promise would come true soon, so they could see their son more often. They raised many legitimate questions about the details of care that they knew their son needed. They wanted to know how this could be provided in the programs that were described. The promise had said all institutional residents would be provided for. They were ready and interested in details. Their journey had started at a different point, and their expectations as well as their son's needs were entirely different from those of the first family.

Both reactions illustrate how important it is to know who is listening. We professional people need to listen to ourselves and the shorthand in which we sometimes speak. The communication of such an important idea as one which affects so many lives deserves the careful market research which is accorded many much less important ideas. I doubt that many marketing managers would risk threatening their customers. Granted, we won't succeed if we are too timid. But let's channel our enthusiasm and urgency so that we get the most mileage for our clients . . . after we are pretty sure of where we are going.

The contrasts which can help us reflect on what we are experiencing can be illustrated by looking at then and now in terms of institutional practices and policies. It is as if the rules of the game have changed completely. Barriers are crumbling, and a whole new set of relationships is building.

The start of this journey is the admission procedure. In the past this process began with legal papers and often court proceedings. Such things are quite intimidating to many people—regardless of their sophistication. Adding this to the emotionally charged feelings people have about their defective child, as they were called, made for a traumatic event many times.

Old admission papers which the parent was asked to sign asked for a description of "traits of character or tendencies present." The applicant was asked to underline the appropriate words: "obedient, unruly, indolent, industrious, considerate, sensitive, affectionate, cruel, unstable, sexually promiscuous, sexually perverted, inadequate, thievish, untruthful." It is, at best, difficult to make a checklist to describe behavior. The vocabulary reflected the terminology of the day but was faithfully marked for infants and older people as well. Fortunately today the process is considerably more humane.

Several parents have told me that they thought they had surrendered their child to the state when the child was admitted. They had the impression that they were no longer legally responsible for the child and had given up choices and decision making for the child. This impression would have affected the quality and nature of their continuing relationship, thus creating another barrier.

There were reinforcements for the notion that the parent should stay at a distance. The institution admitted clients from a wide geographical area. Thus, transportation presented problems in the days before thruways and private cars. Institutions generally have been outside of town and surrounded by fences. Most of us can recall driving by such places and wondering what went on inside. Surely such a place must contain something fearful because it looked so mysterious and was so far back from the road. A parent shared this kind of impression with me. Her feelings were compounded the day she actually had to drive up that drive and separate from her child at that place. Her feelings have changed over time, but she said there is a flashback each time she approaches the drive.

Practices within institutions seemed to separate parents from their children. Visiting hours were limited, and sometimes visits were supervised. Permissions were required. It is not too hard to interpret that the child needs protection from the parents—or the reverse.

If, in the past, parents requested a home visit for their child, a social worker made a home study—another test of measuring up that parents had to weather. Old records show refusals of requests for visits because of housekeeping standards and other value judgments. Often the reasons given for refusal were that the child needed further training and time for adjustment. I am still not entirely sure what that meant, and in some instances we might wonder what training was being considered. However, if one had accepted the rationale that only professional people could care for the child, then there must be something (beyond a mere parent's understanding) that was going on that shouldn't be interrupted.

As if these elements weren't formidable enough, there was also the process of getting a question answered by mail. In some institutions responses to letters always were signed by the director or superintendent. This person was usually a physician and obviously a very important person since he was responsible for such a lot of people. Some people hesitated to ask or apologized for taking his time when what they wanted was news of their child's progress. When they did ask, responses were often terse and impersonal, lacking in warmth. Letters spontaneously sent from an institution to families indicated serious illness or an accident—or a Christmas appeal, hardly welcoming although understandable within the context of the time and the size of institutions.

Many parents persisted and remained in contact. This took some skills and tenacity. Others dropped out, unable to penetrate the barriers. Some of the latter families have been labeled as disinterested when overwhelmed might have been a more apt description. In our present time zone, we are still pressed by size but are trying to reestablish contact with families of clients. We are asking them, whether they be the tenacious ones or the dropouts, to join us in the present and try to understand where we are now.

A bit of deinstitutionalization jet lag came with letters parents received several years ago when old forms of admission were changed to reflect new types of admission status. A most carefully worded letter explaining the patient's status, voluntary or otherwise, and the accompanying right to ask to leave an institution couldn't bridge the gap, of course. Many parents expressed wonderment and confusion that their now-adult child, duly labeled as in need of lifetime protection and lacking in judgment, was now granted the right to make such important decisions.

Civil rights, voting rights, marriage, the choice of where to live for someone who had been surrendered to a vegetable existence twenty years before? Correct, and correctly so. But it is difficult to grasp this unassisted. Parents who were not permitted to visit on the ward were now invited to visit on the living unit, talk with staff, tour the institution, and serve as volunteers. For some, this still comes as a surprise for they had not asked to visit the ward in so many years and we in our haste may have forgotten to invite them.

The same parents who may have been considered to be a bit of a pest with all their questions are now serving on governing boards or overseeing committees as client advocates. Their suggestions are not only encouraged but are required. This is truly another timing zone. Parents are regularly invited to participate in treatment team meetings for their child. They actively work along with the professional and direct care staff in planning for their child's program, needs, and future. Can these be the same people who were told that only professional knowledge and skill would help their child?

The staff, too, has some of the same problems of jet lag, deinstitutionalization style. Long-time employees remember when talking to a resident was to be confined to instructions. They also recall clients who worked side by side with them or for them for a few cents a week. These were the clients who became idle after a court decision on institutional peonage prevented them from working on campus. A drastic change took place for staff and client; it was long overdue and required a shift of practices and daily roles to be sure. The most difficult shift, I feel, is for families and employees to grasp the different practices and attitudes that a growth- or goal-oriented view of mentally retarded people requires as opposed to the custodial model that was the norm for so long. This calls for retraining and an attitudinal change. Both help in the adjustment to this time zone.

My message is that we who are in intermediary positions between the client's family and the institution should be continually mindful of where this journey began and on what premises it was accepted. We should be readily available and communicative as we are all asked to adjust to where the policies have brought us and the direction in which we are going.

We are apt to get institutionalized in our responses and bury ourselves in the inevitable paperwork that comes with accountability and planning. Let's not forget that there are people in those plans and they don't have an identical viewpoint or opportunity to absorb the directions and philosophies implied. Every one of us has a different capacity for adapting to change and for growing. We must allow for this and the fact that ideas may take a different form when they are implemented into programs. Let's keep an eye on what we think we are doing and what actions we take. Do both add up to achieving the same goal?

Let's not be surprised if some families who learned to cope with the barriers we presented in the past take a while to gain confidence in the new systems and attitudes. They may take a very practical and skeptical attitude toward programs in which we see such a promising future. They may see only today and fear that their relative, who assumes the risk, will be caught in the middle. We have an obligation to earn their confidence.

Most of the families of older residents accepted permanent institutionalization as the only alternative, based upon the best advice available. Let us help them to accept deinstitutionalization and other new concepts on the very best information available at this time, thoroughly and effectively communicated.

How will what we are doing now be viewed in five or ten years? There will be other time zones that we, too, will have to accept. Most travelers adapt in time . . . but must everyone make the trip?

Dorothy W. Avis

QUESTIONS TO CONSIDER

1. According to Tot's perspective, how can parents best be helped to prepare for and recover from deinstitutionalization jet lag? What is the current status of such jet lag? What do you predict the status will be in six years?

2. Adapting to change may be one of the most critical skills for parents with handicapped children. How do you think parents can best be taught to handle constructively the changes that are thrust on them by outside forces? By their own disabled children?

3. What is your response to Tot's final question: "Most travelers adapt in time . . . but must everyone make the trip?" Must everyone make the trip today? Must everyone make the trip in the future? What are the alternatives to change?

UPDATE:
Deinstitutionalization Jet Lag (1985)

Dorothy W. Avis

My earlier essay spoke of basic assumptions and attitudes toward the treatment of mentally retarded or other disabled individuals and described some of the shift we were experiencing then. Where is our deinstitutionalization jet lag now? And what new attitudes and trends are expressed in current policies?

I am now one of the "theys" in a central office—those whom direct service providers regard as out-of-touch with how it really is. Before, I was one of the front-line people for whom policy watching was a favorite indoor sport. Then, my response to a particular new policy was partially based on its timing and its practical application in my own building.

Now that I have participated in policy making, I appreciate much more the complexity of the processes and the number of influences impacting them. Developing policies to fit diverse individuals grouped as the mentally retarded is difficult. Ensuring that these policies achieve humane and constructive results is even more challenging.

My new sensitivity leads me to reexamine interpretations of what is a humane and constructive result. Earlier concepts and provisions for care were considered humane within their historical contexts. In the past, common advice matched practices; e.g., "They're happier with their own kind." Of course, some practices crossed the line and then were considered to be inhumane. New practices represent a pattern of reformed attitudes, societal responses, and policies. The transition involves jet lag, often an expected and sizable amount. That was one of my earlier points. But what are we doing now, and how will it hold up in the future?

Placement and Deinstitutionalization

In my first essay I discussed the beginnings of the deinstitutionalization process and the impact on individuals with whom I shared the experience. Some oversimplified attention-getting techniques provided a considerable jolt to many families and staff members. One of the shifts I described was the rediscovery of parents as partners in making decisions affecting the lives of their institutionalized sons and daughters. There is a happy ending for one of the families cited, the family that had kept the existence of their forty-year-old daughter a secret from relatives and friends. They had visited her regularly for forty years but one day were stunned by the news that she would be home in nothing flat. Summoning their courage, they told their other children about their institutionalized sister, and her siblings became her regular visitors. Subsequently, she was deinstitutionalized, moved to a group home, and is now happily situated in the community. All seem to have overcome the jet lag.

I've had other recent experiences with some of the old phrases. *"She'll never live to be a year old"* is a prognosis still given in some instances. Certainly, there are some accurate estimates of this kind, but such prognostications may also represent a gap between textbook knowledge about relatively rare disorders and the experience of those who live with such children over a longer term. I attended a meeting to discuss a child's possible need for a pediatric nursing facility and/or neonatal nursery. At this meeting were physicians who have attended children in several habilitative nurseries for a number of years. The discussion between them and the neonatologists included children's diagnoses and ages. There was a measure of careful surprise on the part of the specialists when the status of several children was discussed. These children had an original textbook diagnosis of less than a year to live and are teenagers now. They are attending daily special classes outside their residence and have made developmental progress, albeit limited, which far exceeds the textbook prognosis. How can we reach those who write textbooks for physicians of the future? Clearly, interdisciplinary collaboration would be helpful.

"Put him away and forget him" is another example of need and opportunity for interdisciplinary research, cooperation, and discussion. This phrase illustrates the nonperson attitudes that some professionals carry toward some mentally retarded or developmentally disabled persons. "Put away" applies to things, not people. Similarly, the term *placement* also may convey insensitivity and lack of concern for a person as a person. I'm not suggesting we become immobilized by semantics, but discussions and records focus on words and their interpretations. I hope the lexicon of interdisciplinary professionals will continue to improve with regard to meaningful understanding and practical applications.

In my recent experience the need for placing young children out of their own homes to receive training has been reduced by mandated school programs. If outside placement is needed for other reasons, placements are preferably made in a community training home where the education and family-like relationships continue. Even this option is offered only when direct assistance to the whole family has been insufficient. I know of several instances where very medically involved children have been placed either in a training home or habilitative nursery for a few months and the family has rallied and taken the child home again when its strength and support systems were developed.

"Think of the other children" sounds as if it was impossible to include the disabled member without pitting that child against the others. Today we are considering disabled members as a part of the family system. Certainly the presence of a child with tremendous special needs is a challenge to the physical, emotional, and financial resources of any family. For many more mildly disabled children, however, the automatic either-or reaction need not be activated. In the past it often was applied automatically and frequently was the basis for infant placement. A choice was hardly considered. There are now a number of services, including respite services, that can support the family in meeting the needs of all members. These services create the opportunity for choice. Let us hope that the either-or response can be avoided or substantially delayed.

There are still instances (I expect there always will be) where, no matter what kinds of assistance are available, "think of the other children" will constitute a valid reason for placing a handicapped individual away from home. In these cases the need for placement stems from family and community inability to sustain the retarded individual in a home situation, frequently because the needs of other family members are presented as competing with the disabled member's. Since most of these situations concern retarded individuals who are teenagers or adults, many of those families have not had the benefit of comprehensive support programs throughout their lives. Considering the relatively few cases our placement committee has heard, I suspect that there are many families who are making tolerable-to-healthy adaptations to life with a disabled family member. Families do indeed make highly individualized adaptations based upon personal views, perceptions, abilities, strengths, and assumptions.

Let's consider, now, those interrelated concepts that have newer looks about them—least restrictive alternatives, rights and due process, and individualized habilitation plans. These concepts affect not only the choices available but also the environment in which choices are made and the process for expressing the choices.

Least Restrictive Alternative

I was vastly relieved and considerably validated by the American Association on Mental Deficiency publication *The Least Restrictive Alternative: Principles and Practices* (Turnbull, 1981). I had felt all along that the least restrictive alternative was more than a real estate concept. It has much more to do with *how* one lives and what options are available than with geography and size of household.

Least restrictive environment has sometimes been considered synonymous with the idea that all mentally retarded people belong in the community. Most of us, upon reaching adulthood, become wary of *all*, *never,* and such absolutes. Some advocates have made their strongest arguments for all to be in the community and have attached other provisos such as "in groups of six or fewer," a double absolute. How can one advocate for choice and least restriction and then be so absolute in restricting the choice?

The ideal would be an array of choices, locations, sizes, and services, even though it is unlikely that the whole array will ever be available in as timely a way as we would like. In the perfect world persons with mental retardation or other disabilities would be welcome in all communities. All who seek residence would be able to choose from a complete array of choices, cafeteria style. Every option would be available at the time of need. We *are* coming closer to this ideal and that is a positive step.

Rights and Due Process

I recognize the role of litigation and the benefits that have come from its use. I have also had some personal struggles when that process is used for individual gain at the potential expense of others. I have argued against court-ordered placements where the best placement for one individual would require displacing someone else and violating the rights of those who were on a waiting list for that same placement. The lawyer involved said, quite correctly from her standpoint, that she had only to be concerned with her client's needs. I was glad the judge had a larger view and was apparently sensitive to the issues of equity. A few years ago we were pleased to create voluntary admission processes to replace court hearings, which were thought to be an additional and unnecessary ordeal. Now we are entering an era in which this court process is again in effect. We have returned to a process which was labeled regressive, but this time we are there for different reasons—to provide retarded people with due process and protect their rights. Individual views and use of the process are highly personal.

I often receive calls or letters from parents, relatives, agencies, or legislators when they feel all local resources have been exhausted. One morning two calls came in which represented different expectations and adaptations but probably similar levels of pain. They represent also a different mix of the child's and parents' rights and the use of residential resources as a last resort. The first call came from the mother of a man in his thirties. She felt she could not cope with her son's care any longer. Her husband had been killed a few months before while assisting a friend whose store was being robbed. The father's death left the son and mother at home together, locked in a life of isolation. This young man had missed public school education by virtue of an IQ below the educable range and behavior problems that the school district was not prepared or mandated to accommodate more than twenty years ago. He had participated briefly in a local sheltered workshop, but his behavior and inattention had not been acceptable. His behavior remained such that one or the other parent had always to be

Dorothy W. Avis

with him. Family outings were confined to rides in the car, grocery shopping, and doctor's visits. The mother's health and courage were at an end, and she reluctantly requested placement. This mother felt that she had failed.

The second call came from the very angry mother of a twelve-year-old boy. This boy attended an extended-day program provided by his public school: he left home at 7:30 A.M. and returned after supper. Nearly every weekend he had respite care provided by a nearby center. He slept well, and the behaviors his mother described would likely have been considered merely inconvenient by the first mother. The second mother said that their pediatrician had told them how difficult puberty is for mentally retarded children and that they should find residential placement for him before his teen years. Her pain, if one could really weigh it, may have been equal to that of the first mother.

I have discussed such situations and the timing of placement decisions with my colleagues. A truth has emerged, I feel. It is that the end of the rope is the end of the rope, regardless of how long the rope is. It would take a perfect world of ample resources to fulfill all requests at the appropriate time. What then of rights and due process? What should a service delivery system look like? When should choices be made for placement? What should the reasons be? Would a purist for the rights of the twelve year old tell his mother that she should hang in there for another fifteen years or so, like the other mother? Does a child in a family where he is essentially unwelcome benefit more from that environment because it is his home than from one where he may be away from his family but may be accepted positively by those who care for him?

Fern Kupfer (1982) and others in *Before and After Zachariah* speak very frankly to these variations in coping, timing, and humane solutions. Some suggest that stories of heroic parental efforts create an additional burden for parents whose efforts are not heroic or whose approach is different. We may never know what parents truly prefer until all the options are real and available.

Individualized Habilitation Plan

Perhaps this is one absolute that I agree with—given the provisos that the plan be a sensible guide and an individualized plan for activity and leisure which can be implemented and will sustain questioning. Is there life in the IHP? Does it make sense to the client? Did the client participate in designing it? Is it aimed at achieving something that is meaningful to the client? What is it actually designed to do? How likely is that to happen? Will it do any harm? When is enough? How will we know when we've reached that point? I strongly endorse looking at what we are doing and deciding if that is, indeed, leading to the results we want to achieve. I hope we don't get so entranced with making our plans and documenting our efforts that the life of the persons behind such plans is overshadowed.

The expectations of parents have given me pause recently. Having come from the era of being grateful for the nursery class in the church basement, I was surprised when some parents were willing to opt for no class at all unless there was transportation provided. My suggestion about car-pooling and paying a modest fee to cover some expenses was met with angry responses and comments about the right to transportation.

We are coming to a time when what has been available as a given may become less available. The economy will have much influence on the trade-offs, and there may be some reverse jet-lag. Younger parents who have found services in place from the very beginning may have to recreate some of the responses of early parents who scrambled to develop the services. Many parents will find each other in the process, which is the positive part. Parents can do some things for themselves and for each other that no team of professionals can do.

From those who know I am one of these parents, I occasionally get the comment, "You understand because you have been through the same thing." There are basic areas of similar feelings, of course, but the variations on these feelings are numerous and personal. I know how I feel or felt, but I have become much less judgmental about how other parents deal with their lives and their children's lives. Professional trappings may provide greater knowledge and understanding of some kinds of resources, but they do not preclude butterflies in the stomach and a heavy heart from time to time! Sometimes I remind my professional cohorts that it is often wiser and kinder first to assume that parents are doing their best at the moment and then to provide a clear picture of all the options they realistically have.

With respect to jet lag, I believe we are now engaged in an intense process of blending old and new concepts. Sometimes one predominates, sometimes another prevails. Dilemmas frequently arise as we work through the pros and cons to find the right mix of policies and practices. Undoubtedly, additional philosophical, attitudinal, statutory, and methodological changes will be considered in the future, each with its own potential for jet jag.

Granting that the economy and other influences will have considerable impact upon our future plans for people with disabilities, I believe there is an advantageous level of consciousness. I see a likelihood that cuts in services will be resisted and will be more difficult to make as disabled people are no longer hidden. Our priorities may well be modified by the needs of others, no matter how wisely oriented our directions are. I believe further that professionals striving to do their reasonable best to create alternatives for mentally retarded persons within rapidly changing environments will provide opportunities and choices for more meaningful and happier lives—jet lag notwithstanding.

Dorothy W. Avis

REFERENCES

Kupfer, F. *Before and after Zachariah*. New York: Delacorte Press, 1982.
Turnbull, H.R., III (Ed.). *The least restrictive alternative: Principles and practices*. Washington, D.C.: American Association on Mental Deficiency, 1981.

QUESTIONS TO CONSIDER

1. Review the questions on p. 191. How accurate were your predictions?

2. How can policy and practice best be tailored to accommodate Tot's viewpoint that for some parents "the end of the rope is the end of the rope regardless of how long the rope is"? What would you say to a person who thinks he or she is at the end of the rope? What would you do?

3. Describe what Tot means by "reverse jet lag." What are your predictions about future reverse jet lag? What policies (as she describes them) will cause a reaction, and who will be the major reactors?

Frank Warren's autistic son, George, was fifteen years old and living at home when Frank wrote his first essay. Today he is twenty-one, lives in a group home started by the North Carolina Society for Autistic Children, and works in a Durham sheltered workshop.

In 1975 Frank left his profession as a journalist to devote full time to consumer activism, concentrating on the development of services for people with autism. Frank has been executive director of the National Society for Children and Adults with Autism (NSAC), director of the NSAC Information and Referral Service, special projects director for the North Carolina Office for Children, and coordinator for autism with the Federal Programs Information and Referral Project. Currently, he is associate director of Community Services for Autistic Adults and Children (CSAAC), a statewide program providing community homes and jobs for people with autism in Maryland. CSAAC is based in Rockville, a suburb of Washington, DC. Frank helped establish the North Carolina

Frank and Mary Warren   *George Warren*

Society for Autistic Children, the District of Columbia Society for Autistic Citizens, and the Prince George's County (Maryland) Society for Autistic Children. He has been a consumer activist in political action for handicapped people since 1968.

Mary Warren, Frank's daughter, is a contributor to the 1985 update. Mary has a journalism degree from the University of North Carolina at Chapel Hill and is currently a general assignment reporter for a newspaper in South Pines, North Carolina.

A Society That Is Going to Kill Your Children

Frank Warren

To Mary Lou

> Between 95 and 98 percent of all autistic adults are institutionalized. (NSAC Information and Referral Service, 1977)

> Each day that you fail to advocate, each day that you ignore an act of discrimination, each day that you accept another injustice, you accept a society that is going to kill your children. (Dussault, 1977)

It is the custom of the people in the United States to kill autistic children. Yes. Kill them. And it is the custom to ostracize their parents: to treat them as outcasts, as irrational men and women who do not know their own minds, who cannot tell right from wrong. Both parents and children are stripped of their rights as citizens, as if they were convicted felons who have proven that they are harmful and obnoxious to society.

How do the people kill autistic children in this enlightened age? When Sparta thrived, the men took infants who seemed unwhole and left them on the mountainside, where death came swiftly with a single bitter night or with their chance discovery by a hungry wolf or dog. Other cultures, closer to the present day, condoned the smashing of infant skulls against stones or trunks of trees when children were strange, worrisome, or unwanted.

Of course, the people of the United States abhor and reject such straightforward and efficient methods. They shield themselves from the guilt inherent in such outright acts of cruelty. They have constructed elaborate processes—rituals, if you will, in an anthropological sense—to protect their sensibilities from the pain of child killing and from the unpleasantness of inflicting ostracism (and all of the suffering and grief that goes with it) upon fellow citizens whose only crime is the misfortune to have borne and loved an autistic child.

How are these children killed? How are these parents ostracized? What rights are taken away from them? What things are they barred from doing that other citizens freely take for granted? I will take these questions and, by giving examples, citing cases, and sharing my own experiences as the father of one of these beautiful, outcast children, make my case. My beginning statements are not fantasy but absolute chilling truth.

The execution of autistic children takes place in a slow and tedious fashion. It is done with such deftness and subtlety that in most cases the parents, and often those carrying out the death-dealing acts, are unaware that they are killing a child. They think that any number of things—mostly things spoken of in words that carry the connotation of caring, helping, healing—are taking place but certainly not the deliberate ending of a human life. But death comes. And the life is ended. And society is rid of yet another nuisance child.

I feel the sadness now, growing in my chest, for George, my adolescent autistic boy. The process is working slowly toward his end, and the cold eye of an unfeeling society is fixed upon him, and I am only one. What can I do?

To tell you how the killing is carried out so that you will understand it clearly, I must first tell you about the children who are marked. I want you to know who they are, how they came into life, where they live, what their characteristics are, and what kind of people their mothers and fathers are.

They have names like everyone else. They are called George, Tommy, Andrea, Missy, Lorcan, Anthony, Frankie, Wayne, Danny, Wally, Mike, Steve, Sara, and Melinda—for almost any name you pick, there is an autistic child named that.

They came into life just the same as everyone else. They were conceived by men and women, most of whom loved each other, were married and committed to each other; wanted children in their homes to care for, bring up, and educate in the ways of their families and cultures; wanted for them the same things that parents of other children want for their offspring— good lives, success in their endeavors, freedom to come and go in a free society, enough food to eat, clothes to wear, shelter from the cold, comfortable homes, good friends, good services when they are sick, strength to deal with the problems of life, pleasure in living, healthy children.

Autistic children are found throughout the world. They are born into families of all racial, ethnic, and social backgrounds (NSAC, 1977). No groups of people, by whatever criteria of discrimination, are safe from the possibility that some of their children will be autistic.

Part of the reason that these children are killed is that there are so few of them, they are so badly misunderstood, their parents are scattered and have little power to effect social change. Autism occurs in approximately 5 out of every 10,000 births and is four times more common in boys than girls (Note 1). Since autism is so rare and occurs in every level of society, there can be—there is—no concentration of these children or their parents in any place, geographic or social, so that they might easily know each other, organize, come to grips with common problems, and exert political pressure. In a town or county of 10,000 people, you can expect to have no more than 5 who are autistic and, at the most, 10 parents of autistic children. In a city of 100,000 people, you can expect to have no more than 50 who are autistic and, at the most, 100 parents of autistic children. In a state of 5,000,000 people, you can expect to have no more than 2,500 who are autistic and, at the most, 5,000 parents of autistic children. In a nation of 200,000,000 people, you can expect to have no more than 100,000 who are autistic and, at the most, 200,000 parents of autistic children.

The fact is that in towns or counties of 10,000 people it is most common for the leadership—political, social, medical, educational, or otherwise—to be totally unaware of autism or of the 5 autistic people who can statistically be expected to live among them. In cities of 100,000 people it is most common for only a few of the political, social, medical, educational, or other leaders or service providers to know of autism or to provide for autistic people or to know personally even 1 of the 50 citizens who are autistic. In states of 5,000,000 people, or thereabouts, it is most common for most of the leaders to know next to nothing and care even less about autism or the 2,500 autistic citizens who exist scattered about and invisible among the population. In the nation the same pattern exists, and the killing goes on unmercifully, while the leaders respond with the same sympathy to the cries of parents and the agony of condemned children that the ocean gives to drowning men and women spilled into it from a sinking vessel.

Collectively, and in most cases individually, the leaders—local, state, and national—don't care. They can't be bothered. They'd rather spend their time and energy in other ways, they'd rather spend the public money on other things, they don't have time to listen, they won't make the effort to understand, they don't think it is their job, they think it too much trouble to change. In short, they aren't concerned that autistic children are dying, that they, the leaders, are part of the killing process, that parents of autistic children are suffering, and that they, the leaders, are guiding the vast, unthinking machinery that, like a medieval torture rack, is inflicting the suffering. The screams so rarely reach their ears. The tragedy so rarely touches their lives.

What are the characteristics of these condemned children and their parents? The parents have no characteristics different from those of other citizens. They are men and women like everyone else. They are good and bad, successes and failures, rich and poor (by the same ratio as others), intelligent and quick, dense and slow to learn. They work on farms and in cities, they are professional people and laborers, black and white, Protestant, Catholic, Jewish, Islamic. They are no more nor less insane than anyone else.

Perhaps it is not entirely correct to say that these parents have no characteristics that are different from those of other people. It is true that before they become parents of autistic children, they are no different. But afterwards, perhaps they become different.

Parents of autistic children have been known to do things or engage in behavior that obviously sets them apart from the norm. To begin with, they have the unmitigated gall to think that their children should be treated as human beings and not killed by society; that they should be educated according to their educational needs, just as other children are; that they should not be locked up in vast, malignant, concrete warehouses and stifled to death. They feel that they, as parents, should be helped to cope with the problems their children's condition produces; that they, as parents, need some time of their own away from the stress of dealing with autism; that they and their children should be free from the effects of social ostracism, professional ignorance, stupidity, and manipulation; and that they should not be taken advantage of, financially and emotionally, by rich doctors, psychologists, bureaucrats, quack researchers, and others who are padding their pocketbooks while engaging in the same kind of hocus-pocus that has enabled witch doctors, sorcerers, and other charlatans to rip off their fellow human beings since the beginning of time.

I know a beautiful woman who is in her sixties. She is as stable, intelligent, kind, caring, interested and interesting, vital, and loving a woman as I have ever met. She is the mother of an autistic person, a man nearing forty. She and her son have been mistreated, malpracticed upon, legally stolen from, taken advantage of, denied services, denied rights, abused verbally and physically, and generally ignored or treated as fools by a small army of doctors, psychiatrists, bureaucrats, researchers, administrators, and other leaders in the various states in which they've lived. Why? Because her son was autistic. None of it would have happened if her son had been born with the ability to function in the fashion that people call normal. If he had, she would not have suffered in the manner that she has. Her crime was that she did everything she knew how to do to help her son.

When the boy was very young, she noticed that he was not developing as he should and that he was doing peculiar things such as screaming all night long, endlessly wriggling his fingers along the periphery of his vision, making funny little nonsense noises instead of talking, refusing to wear clothes, refusing to be comforted when upset, not looking people in the eye—all those sad and confounding, amusing, bittersweet, and heart-rending little things that autistic children do in those early years. (Remember, parents? You remember. We remember. Doesn't it jolt you into tears to remember? Doesn't it make you laugh and cry inside to look upon those strange and fearful days and see that beautiful child—yours, mine—in diapers, running aimlessly, laughing in the sunshine of that far-off, time-lost day; amused at sounds unheard by us, at thoughts unknown and unknowable; terrified into lost, abandoned wailing at horrors unperceived and unperceivable by us—we who loved so long and painfully and unavailingly.)

So, with rising fear, she took the child to all the places from which help

Frank Warren

is said to come in our society—doctors, psychiatrists who probed with knowing smiles into the deepest personal regions of her life, specialists, treatment centers, hospitals, clinics. This went on and on through years of waiting rooms and corridors, through examinations, diagnostic tests, and lab reports, before a hundred polished desks and a hundred men in white until they both, she and her son, grew old and tired. (Remember, parents? Remember? For she is us and we are her.)

And what did the hundred (give or take a dozen or so) important, knowledgeable people do?

They cleared their throats importantly.

They smoked their cigars and cigarettes casually.

They looked at her over smart bifocals wisely.

They wrote jargon in their secret files so knowledgeably.

They stamped a dozen labels on the child cruelly.

They sent her bills, which she paid and paid and paid religiously.

They sent her away unaided and alone.

They did other things, too.

They held the struggling child down, drugged him and cut out part of his brain; they called it lobotomy, and she paid for it.

They tied him to a table, sent fierce jolts of electricity through the tender, already faulty, already damaged tissue inside his skull; they called it treatment, and she paid for it.

They said he was emotionally disturbed, they said she made him that way, they called her insulting names in a code language they made up to serve their own purposes. They said what they were doing was therapy, and she paid for it.

Finally, when the child had been reduced to a shuffling, drooling, brainless, hopeless creature who could not speak a single intelligible word, could not keep from soiling his pants, could not attend to his simplest human needs, and was given to wild fits of self-destruction in a pathetic effort to rid himself of the burden of life, they took him away, tied him to a chair in a dreary, cold, and stinking ward in a crumbling, overcrowded hospital. They called it care, and she paid for it.

My God, isn't that enough? Oh no, it isn't—not nearly enough. The bond between mother and child is strong. It is flesh caring for flesh, blood reaching out to blood, and does not end when institution doors clang harshly shut. My friend never stopped trying—she is trying now. She never stopped hoping—she is hoping now.

Sometimes when she drove 100 miles to visit her son, the staff at the institution sent her away. She asked them why, and they called her a nuisance. She wrote scores and scores of letters—asking, pleading, demanding, searching, cajoling to improve the conditions of his existence—and they said she interfered.

She saw him sitting, neglected, in his own feces, and they rationalized. "We don't have the staff. . . . We do our best, but there isn't enough money. . . . The legislature won't. . . . The administration won't. . . . The rules won't. . . ."

She learned that he was never taken out to walk in the sunlight. She saw his skin grow pale, his muscles wither from lack of use, his body sagging and old when it should have been young and strong, his broken mind untended, unstimulated, wasted.

Her conversations, condensed from a hundred meetings with administrators, directors, staff people, bureaucrats, service providers over the span of twenty years, went something like this:

"Can you put him in a better ward?"
"No."
"Can you get him out to walk once a day?"
"No."
"He loves to swim. Can he swim sometimes?"
"No."
"Can you build a swimming pool? All the residents could use it. It would be good for them."
"No."
"Can you provide him some education, some training?"
"No."
"The community college is nearby. They will provide trainers if you will identify twelve people. Call it adult education and draft a program for them. Will you take the time?"
"No."
"The institution a mile away has a swimming pool. Can he go there once a week?"
"No."

Once, in the 1960s, she escalated her simple requests into demands, drawing upon the strategy of black action groups. When she was rejected, she went in utter desperation—a lone, weary, aging woman—and lay her body in the street at the hospital, where she caused a flurry of disruption until she was taken away.

Why, you might ask, did she not just take her son home, keep him there, and care for him herself? There are many reasons, not the least of which is that she did that for years until her resources—financial, physical, and emotional—were drained.

Another is that she believed the myths, expounded by professionals, that somewhere in their heads, hidden in their books, behind some closed and secret doors beyond her knowing, was help and hope and care—if only she would trust and lay her burdens in their hands. She did, and they killed her son.

There is no pleasant ending to this story. There cannot be. A living corpse still rocks behind closed doors. A good and loving mother tends her wounds and keeps on trying (Note 2).

The ritualistic killing of autistic children is a fascinating process to

Frank Warren

observe—if you can keep from being fooled by the subtle intricacies of it, or being consumed with rage at the cruelty of it, or being lulled into uncaring by the tedious slowness of it. One must be quite alert to even know that it is happening. Often death itself is the only clue that lets the nonparent know.

"Autistic Boy Found Dead in Mud Near Hospital" was the caption of a newspaper story one day in November. The story read somewhat like this: " 'Death was due to exposure,' according to_____, the deputy state medical examiner, who added that further tests are scheduled to determine how long the boy had been dead.

"Hospital officials noticed that he was missing about four o'clock Wednesday afternoon and, together with state police, searched for him until Friday.

"The governor learned of the missing boy Saturday and ordered several hundred state troopers and National Guard reservists to join the search. They were aided by state police helicopters and citizen band radio operators. . . .

"His body was found about noon Monday in a muddy area one mile east of the hospital grounds. He apparently had fallen into the mud and could not get out, police said."

The paper carried a photograph of a beautiful, thirteen-year-old, dark-eyed boy with bangs that hung low over his forehead and a wistful, far-away look on his soft features. "Footprints found Saturday near the hospital indicated_____may have been alive then, despite the twenty-degree temperatures during the nights he spent outside the hospital."

How could this be called a killing? Wasn't this just an accident? Didn't everybody show concern? Didn't they do all they could? Didn't the governor call out the National Guard? What justification do you have for those harsh and blaming words? Look deeper. There is more.

1. The state in which this occurred had no mandatory education law for the handicapped. They didn't care.

2. Even though the Education for All Handicapped Children Act (Public Law 94–142) was passed in 1975, there was no free, appropriate, public education available for the boy in the community where he lived. They didn't provide.

3. Even though the Congress of the United States passed Section 504 of the Rehabilitation Act of 1973 (the antidiscrimination, civil rights act for the handicapped) this autistic child was closed out of services, closed out of education, closed out of programs provided for others—harshly discriminated against because of his handicap. They broke the law.

4. Even though landmark court cases handed down in 1972 declared that it is unconstitutional to provide education to others while leaving the handicapped unserved (*Mills* v. *Board of Education of the District of Columbia*), autistic children continued to be denied. They ignored the courts.

Here is the final, heartbreaking irony: in a fit of compassion, when death was already at hand, when the process had reached the ragged edge of its conclusion, the government, the governor, the administration of that hospital, of that state, spent something in the neighborhood of $40,000 in five days to find that pitiful body that they had rendered lifeless by their inaction, by their lawlessness, by their refusal to care, by their discrimination, by their denial of rights, by their inhuman stupidity.

You figure it: five days of searching by two hundred people at ten hours a day at a round figure of four dollars an hour. That's not counting the helicopter, the automobiles, the gasoline, the CB radios, the wear and tear, the laundry bills from slogging around in the woods, the telephone calls, the rescue equipment, the secretary's time, the medical examiner's time, the lab reports. Forty thousand dollars! That would have provided one condemned autistic child with five to eight years of individualized education designed to meet his needs, to help him grow, to relieve his parents of the burden of autism for six or seven hours a day, to save them from suffering, to keep him in the safety of his home, to grant him life in our society.

What are the characteristics of these children that people in the United States are getting rid of in this manner? First of all, they have something wrong with their brains. Their brains don't work like other people's brains. It is a physical something. Here, with interspersed comments about my son and other autistic children, is what the National Society for Autistic Children says about autism in its official "Short Definition," adopted in Orlando, Florida, 27 June, 1977:

Autism is a severely incapacitating life-long development disability which typically appears during the first three years of life.

A harried mother, her face drawn with fatigue, large blue circles under her eyes from sleepless nights, her hair unkempt, her clothes disheveled, struggles to keep a beautiful, curly-haired child of eighteen months or so on her lap. The child is moving constantly, crawling, reaching, pulling, never still, fretting, making funny noises, going over her shoulder, leaning backward off her lap, pulling at her dress, going, going. She is in a pediatrician's office and she is speaking. "Doctor, I am afraid something is wrong with George."

The doctor smiles. "He's certainly an active little boy. What seems to be the trouble?"

"He won't sleep. He jumps in his crib all the time, up and down, up and down. He has already torn one crib apart jumping. And he has these tantrums. I don't know what starts them. I can't seem to do anything about them. He screams. I know the neighbors think I am killing him. And it goes on, sometimes all night and all day. He won't let me hold him. And neither my husband nor I can comfort him when he is like that." There are tears in her eyes now, and she tries not to sob. The little boy has pulled the shoulder strap of her dress down. She moves to fix that while the child wriggles away under her arm. She catches him by the leg and pulls him back onto her lap.

"I've examined him carefully, and I can tell you he is a healthy little boy."

"But why does he do this? Why does he scream all night long—sometimes twenty-four hours a day?"

"Twenty-four hours a day?" The doctor lowers his head, smiles slightly, and looks at the woman out of the corners of his eyes.

"Yes. I can't stand it. I am so tired I can hardly move, but I can't sleep. I am afraid if I go to sleep he will get out of the house at night in the dark, and I won't be able to find him in time." She is crying harder now, and her cheeks are wet with tears. Her body is shaking, and she bites her lips.

"Now, now. You are upset. Let me give you something to help you rest. When you have rested, you will feel better. All children have tantrums from time to time. Just ignore them, and they will go away. You've got a very healthy little boy." He writes out a prescription. The boy slips between his mother's knees, hands reaching for the floor. She catches him by the hips and wearily hauls him again into her lap. He seems to be smiling at something invisible in the upper corners of the room.

"Let me know if it helps," the doctor says kindly.

"All right," she says, taking the slip of paper. She struggles to hold the child as she walks toward the door.

In the outer office the receptionist says, "That will be ten dollars."

The symptoms of autism are caused by a physical disorder of the brain and include
    1. Disturbances in the rate of appearance of physical, social, and language skills.

In a small development house on the outskirts of a city of 60,000, a little boy stands on a chair and flicks an electric light switch on and off. "Light, light," he says, laughing. "Light, light, light." His father and mother beam. "Yes, George, that's a light. Good boy! George can turn on the light!" "Light, light," says the child, laughing as if to himself.

Fourteen years have passed. It is another town and another place. A young man, his curly hair turned brown, and a little fuzz beginning to grow upon his upper lip, runs to his father, who is walking toward him along a gravel path. He gives a funny little jump as he runs and laughs.

"Hey, George! Have you been a good boy today?"

The young man comes to his father, throws one arm around his neck while hiding his face with his other arm. He moves his face close to his father's. He takes his arm away and looks into his father's eyes. He has a searching, almost wistful look, and his voice is plaintive, questioning, urgent as he says, "Light. Light." Pause. "Light, light, light?"

His father looks at him quietly and puts his arms about the boy and holds him tight. He looks off into the treetops where the sky is soft blue and flecked with clouds, and he bites his lip until it hurts.

2. Abnormal responses to sensations. Any one or a combination of sight, hearing, touch, pain, balance, smell, taste, and the way a child holds his body are affected.

Pain. It is winter, and a freezing, sleet-filled rain has been falling heavily since dawn. Even inside where the heat is turned high, the cold can be felt coming through the walls and window glass and doors. It is quiet in the house, and a woman looks up from her work in the kitchen suddenly, as if she has been nudged. "Frank, where is George?"

The man is in the back of the house. "What?" he says, raising his voice to be heard.

"Do you see George?"

"No," says the man, "I thought he was with you."

"Oh, my God. He is outside again."

And he is. Standing barefoot on the frozen lawn, the little boy of three is drenched to the skin; the cold rain is running off his clothes and down his neck and along his legs and arms. He is smiling absently as he picks tiny ice-rimmed buds, one at a time, from a camelia bush.

Rubbed down, dry, and warm again, he tries the bolted doors and presses his face against the windows to find his bush and frozen buds.

Balance. It is summer. A neighbor has propped a ladder against the side of his house and is carefully removing pine straw and leaves from the gutters along the edge of his roof. Suddenly there is a yell. "George! Get down from there! Frank! George is on the roof!"

A little boy in training pants trots merrily along the roof line, from one end of the ranch-style house to the other, stands confidently with his toes curled over the far edge, looks down, tosses a stick, watches it fall to the ground, turns, repeats the route, and does the same thing at the other end. The neighbor, with a frozen look of fear upon his face, looks on in horror and amazement.

After coming to the scene, the boy's father looks up and yells, "George! Get down! You come down this minute!" The boy appears not to notice. "I'm getting a switch!" The father picks up a stick from the yard and holds it up. "You come down here right now!"

The boy gives his father a quick glance. He sees the switch and scampers to the ladder. In a moment he is on the ground and running toward his house. "Whew! I thought he was going to fall and break his neck," says the neighbor, relaxing.

"Well. I know that was scary, but I didn't think he would fall. The other day I saw him walking along the top of the fence, just like a tightrope walker, holding out his hands to balance. He walked all the way around the yard and never fell. And once, last year, he climbed on top of his swing set and did the same thing. It's amazing. I guess we'd better move the ladder."

> 3. Speech or language are absent or delayed, while specific thinking capabilities may be present. Immature rhythms of speech, limited understanding of ideas, and the use of words without attaching the usual meaning to them is common.

A child of seven is in a special classroom at a university. He reaches for a button-sized, sugar-coated chocolate on the table in front of him. A man on the other side of the table pulls it away. The child's parents watch from behind a one-way mirror in another room. "Say 'candy,' George. This is candy. Candy. You want the candy. Say 'candy' and you can have it." The man holds the candy near the child's face. The child reaches for it again, and again it is pulled away. "Candy, George. Candy. Say 'candy' and you can have it."

This goes on and on. The boy squirms. He gets up and runs around the room. He is carried back. He reaches again and again. But always the candy is pulled away. At last, after what seems hours, the child looks at the man. "Ca-gn," he says, almost inaudibly.

"Good! Good, George!" The man thrusts the candy into the child's mouth. He touches him and rubs his back. "Good talking! Good saying 'candy!' Good boy! Good boy!"

Behind the glass screen the parents smile and squeeze each other's hands. "He said it! He said it! He can talk! It works!"

> 4. Abnormal ways of relating to people, objects and events. Autistic children do not respond appropriately to adults and other children. Objects and toys are not used as normally intended.

It is Sunday. A hymn is being played softly on the organ. At the front of the church men and women kneel, heads bowed, hands cupped. A priest bends toward them, one at a time, intoning, "This is my body which is given for thee . . ."

From the pews there is a flurry of motion. A small figure in short pants darts into the aisle, his bare legs pumping. "Take and eat this in remembrance that Christ died for thee . . ."

The small figure has reached the kneeling communicants now, and he wriggles in between them, pushing with his hands, ducking his head beneath the altar rail. His father is in hot pursuit. ". . . and live on Him by faith . . ."

The boy is at the altar now. His father is opening the altar rail. An acolyte, a young man who knows the boy, is reaching for him. The boy's feet are scrambling at the front of the altar; one hand is pulling him onto it, his other hand is reaching for the Eucharistic candle. Already he is blowing,

"Whoosh, whoosh," and the candle flickers. The acolyte scoops him up and hands him, struggling, to his father, who quickly ducks out of the sanctuary with the boy in his arms. ". . . and live on Him by faith—and thanksgiving."

Autism occurs by itself or in association with other disorders which affect the function of the brain such as viral infections, metabolic disturbances, and epilepsy. On IQ testing, approximately 60 percent have scores below 50, 20 percent between 50 and 70, and only 20 percent above 70. Most show wide variations of performance on different tests and at different times.

When David was three years old, he screamed for hours, had no language, sometimes tried to hurt himself, scored 50 on an IQ test. It was the same with Clyde.

David's parents found some aberrant professionals who encouraged them to keep him at home, helped them to work with him each day using a specially designed program to improve his behavior, strengthen his abilities, increase his social skills, capitalize on his strengths. Clyde went into an institution "for his own good and to protect his family" and learned to rock and spin and bang his head.

When David was seven, he was in regular kindergarten, playing with other children, learning new things. Tests showed David's IQ at 100. When Clyde was eleven, he was still in an institution, still rocking and spinning—though with much more finesse—and tests showed Clyde's IQ at 40 or below. A leather helmet protected his head.

When David was fourteen, he was in junior high school. In the summer he mowed grass for pocket money and had a part in a summer play. When Clyde was fourteen, he strangled to death on some food when the attendants weren't looking.

It cost the state $144,000 to protect Clyde and his family for nine years. During that time some important doctors made lots of money which they spent and helped the economy.

It cost the state $18,000 to help David and his family for nine years. David is one of the few autistic children who is going to make it. He will earn enough money to pay his taxes, buy the things he needs, and help the economy. Not many important doctors have or will benefit.

Autistic people live (or can, or ought, or deserve to live) a normal life span. Since symptoms change, and some may disappear with age, periodic reevaluations are necessary to respond to changing needs. Special education programs using behavioral methods and designed for specific individuals have proven most helpful.

David got it and lived. Clyde did not, and he died.

Supportive counseling may be helpful for families with autistic members, as it is for families who have members with other severe life-long disabilities.

Frank Warren

A pleasant room sits off a tile corridor at a famous university medical school. In it is a bookcase filled with heavy, hard-backed books, a number of important journals, and a few professional magazines. Impressionist prints, expensively framed, are placed tastefully on the walls. In front of the bookcase stands a polished wooden desk with a glass top decorated with still more books, a calendar, a small file for addresses and phone numbers, a letter opener, and an ash tray which holds the remains of an expensive cigar. In front of the desk and to one side is a table with a lamp, still more magazines, and another ash tray. A comfortable stuffed chair, not overly large, sits next to the table. A woman who is visibly exhausted sits uneasily in the chair, her pocketbook on her lap, looking at a psychiatrist who sits behind the desk asking her questions and writing things unobtrusively on a yellow pad.

"Why were you afraid to keep your appointment yesterday?" he asks in a professional voice. "I wasn't afraid, I was sick." "You felt sick?" "I was sick." "How were you sick?" "I began to get sick on the way up," she says. "Hmmmmm." "When I got here night before last, I was very sick, and I simply could not come in yesterday. My husband came and brought George." "Yes, I know, but I can't help you if you won't come to your appointments." "But I couldn't help it if I became sick. I think it is the flu." The psychiatrist smiles benignly and lights his cigar. He writes something down. "Don't you believe that I was sick?" "Why do you think I don't believe you?"

"You don't act as though you believe me. I was up all night sick at my stomach. My head was killing me. I had a fever. I am still sick today. I would have come if I could have gotten out of bed. Besides, I don't understand what we are doing. Don't you want George here? Don't you want to see him? We have been coming here, driving one hundred miles both ways, for nearly two years. Can't you help George? He just runs around in the halls with one or the other of us following him while you talk to one of us. I don't see how that is helping him. We need to know what is the matter with George. We need to know what to do to help him."

"We want to help him, but we can't unless we talk to you, and when you break your appointments . . ." "But I told you I was sick, and I am sorry that I was, but I couldn't help it." "Mmmm," says the psychiatrist and makes more notes.

Later, on the long drive home, the woman, hot with fever, speaks to her husband. "I don't know why we keep coming up here. Dr.——— doesn't believe anything I say. He keeps trying to make me say things that aren't true. He is not telling us what we can do about George. He doesn't even want to see George. I don't know why we keep coming up here."

Her husband is silent for a while. George is rocking quietly in the back seat. The engine hums. Cars pass. Finally he speaks. "I don't know what else we can do. Those schools for children like George cost $10,000 a year, and that's more than I make—God knows it cost enough to come here. If it's an emotional thing, maybe he can find out how to get him over it. I suppose he is trying to help us. The only other thing is an institution, and we will never do that."

"No," says the wife. "We are never going to do that to George, not ever." And she turns, looks at the little boy, and gently touches his damp curls. "Oh, George," she says softly, "why can't you tell us what's the matter?"

> The severe form of the syndrome may include the most extreme forms of self-injurious, repetitive, highly unusual, and aggressive behaviors. Such behaviors may be persistent and highly resistant to change, often requiring unique management, treatment, or teaching techniques.

It is Saturday, and a man is mowing the grass in the front yard of a small suburban home. A child about four wearing a T-shirt and short pants is walking aimlessly about, wriggling his fingers oddly near his face and making sounds with his mouth that sound like "Pop-wheeew! Pop-wheeew! Pop-wheeew!"

The man and the lawn mower disappear around the corner of the house, following the edge of an expanding corridor of neatly cut grass. In a moment they return, following the widening corridor, and the child is gone. The man stops, looks around, bends down and turns off the lawn mower.

"George!" No answer. "George!" No answer. "George, where are you?" Still no answer. He runs to the house, leans inside the door, and asks his wife, who is sewing in the living room. "Did George come in?" "No." "Well, he is gone." "Frank, he has been trying to sniff gas all day. I bet I pulled him away from the neighbor's garage fourteen times before you came home." "Sniffing gas again! I thought we had all the gas put away where he couldn't get it." "He's learned how to get the lid off David's lawn mower." "Oh."

He turns from the door, already running, and lopes across the lawn, beside a flower bed, through a gate in the fence, across the neighbor's yard, and as he nears the garage he sees the door to the tool shed ajar and two small feet, their soles black from not wearing shoes, sticking out.

"George, get out of there right now." There is no response. Flinging open the door, he finds the child on his knees, his arms wrapped around the mower and his nose and mouth pressed into the open gasoline tank. He is taking deep breaths.

The man takes the child into his arms. The smell of gasoline is strong on the boy's breath, his eyes are glazed, and he is near unconsciousness.

Later, in the night, as the child rocks quietly in a tiny wooden rocking chair which he is scooting with the motions of his body along a darkened hallway near his parents' room, the man and his wife discuss the happenings of the day. "How many times did you put him to bed?" the man asks. "He is up and rocking again."

Frank Warren

"I don't know. Eight or ten times. He will go to sleep when he is ready. You know he rocks all night. Did you lock the doors?"

"Yes."

"What are we going to do about his sniffing gas? He almost knocked himself out today."

"Well, you know what the psychiatrists told us."

"I don't think they know what they are talking about. They don't believe me when I tell them how many times he runs away. And they want us to go get him each time, never lose our temper, take him by the hand, and bring him gently home."

"How many times did you get him back from David's house today?" the man asks.

"I know it must have been every fifteen or twenty minutes. I couldn't get a thing done until you came home. Frank, I can't keep this up."

"I was running after him all afternoon. I think he needs a good switching when he does that. We just can't let him sniff gas."

"You know what they say about switching," replies the wife.

The next day George searches for gasoline all through the morning and into the afternoon. Each time he is brought gently home by his parents, who try to divert his attention. They tickle him and roll with him on the grass. They swing him on his swing set. They play with him in the sand pile. They give him a hose and a bucket of water. Nothing works. Finally his father gives way to his natural instincts. "Damn it," he says to himself, "those people are fools." He cuts a switch with his pocketknife as he watches the little boy trotting away to the neighbor's garage. As the child twists the lid from the lawn mower tank, he catches him.

"No! No! No! No sniffing gas! You will not sniff gas!" He applies the switch hard to the little boy's bare legs as the child flees for home. The next time George heads for the neighbor's garage, he looks back over his shoulder. "No," says his father, reaching for the switch and showing it to the child. The boy stops at the fence. Gas sniffing is over.

In another state, another couple is faced with a horrifying problem. Their son, whom we will call Larry, cuts himself with broken glass in order to smear the bright red blood on the walls of his room. He has done it again and again with determination that confounds his parents. They are using plastic cups, dishes, and glasses, but still the child finds something with a cutting edge, something he can smash and press into the flesh of his hands and arms to get blood. His hands are covered with scars. The walls of his room have been painted again and again to cover the stains. It is a daily, desperate, frustrating effort to keep the child from cutting himself and smearing his blood. When the slashes are deep and require stitches, he pulls them out. He opens the wounds with his fingers and finds the blood again.

What did the professionals offer this couple and their child? Talk. Jargon. Analysis. Tests. Play therapy. Institutionalization. Physical restraint.

Nothing. Some children have been tied to their institutional beds, their hands and arms wrapped tightly against their bodies, their feet and legs bound. Some have remained like that for years. More than a few have died. But these people would not have that. Driven by their care for their son, they searched for a better way. They found it. They had to do it alone, without professional help, against professional advice.

One day the mother read an article in a professional journal about an unusual method of teaching self-destructive children to stop doing violent things to themselves. It was a method used in research, and the results had been dramatic. She showed the article to her doctors. They would have nothing to do with it. So, in desperation, she and her husband made up their minds to undertake the procedure on their own.

She bought a cattle prod at a hardware store. A cattle prod is a heavy instrument, like a short baton or a policeman's billy club. It is filled with batteries. It has a handle on one end, and at the other end are two short, blunt pieces of metal. When the prod is turned on and the two metal nipples are pressed against an object, an electrical circuit is created. It shocks the object. If you press it against your arm, the sensation is immediate and highly unpleasant. The shock will cease immediately upon removal. If you press it where the skin is close to the bone, the pain will linger for a few minutes. It does not burn or bruise, but you do not want it to happen again.

To use a thing like this on a child, for whatever reason, is a desperate, last-ditch measure. In this case, the alternatives were few and grim: The child cuts and cuts himself. Finally he does it and is not found until he has bled to death in his bed. Or he is locked up in an institution and dies there, cut off from life, bound up or drugged senseless or both.

Here is the scene: The child, his mother and father are together in the basement of their home. There is a glass ashtray on the concrete floor. As the parents watch, the child darts to the ashtray, picks it up, and smashes it on the concrete. He quickly sits down beside the broken pieces and begins to press his right hand upon the jagged edges, straightening his arm, leaning his body weight upon it.

His mother turns on the prod. "No!" she says. There is a slight buzzing sound. She touches his forearm with the metal tips.

"Uuuuuh! Uuuuuuuh!" cries the child, and he leaps up, a look of fear and amazement upon his face. He runs about the room, holding his arm. His parents stand back. Presently the child returns to the broken ashtray. He glances at his parents and begins again to cut himself.

"No! No!" shouts his mother. She produces the prod. This time the child sees it and darts away. "Hold him," says his mother. The father seizes the child. There is a struggle. The boy is large and strong. He sees the prod and he is frightened.

"Uuuuuunh! Uuuuuuunh!" he cries in terror.

The mother is trembling now as she comes to him with the prod. She

Frank Warren

knows how it feels. She has tried it on herself. "Hold him," she says quietly. The father and the boy are on the floor. The boy is kicking and fighting to get away, his eyes riveted on the prod.

"UUUUUUUUUU—UUUUUUUUUNH!" he cries.

"UUUUUUU—UUUUUUNH!"

"No! No! Larry. No cutting! No cutting!" she says in a loud voice. There are tears in her eyes. She seizes the boy's forearm and presses the prod against it, holding it there, feeling the electricity passing into her own body. This time the shock is long, and the child screams and screams with pain. When it is done, the boy flees to his room, and the parents stand there looking at each other. The man puts his arms around his wife and holds her as she weeps.

Their program for using the prod is a simple one. Cutting always produces a shock. Otherwise, the prod is kept out of sight. The cutting ceased.

No known factors in the psychological environment of a child have been shown to cause autism.

Do you hear that out there, Bruno Bettleheim (Note 3)? Do you hear? Are we getting through to you? We said, *No known factors in the psychological environment of a child have been shown to cause autism.* Now do you hear? Do you understand?

That means we didn't do it, Bruno. We've known that all along. It means that careful, objective, scientific people have carried out study after study, test after test, interview after interview, and have written paper after paper in journal after journal which show that we, the parents of autistic children, are just ordinary people. Not any crazier than others. Not "refrigerator parents" any more than others. Not cold intellectuals any more than others. Not neurotic or psychopathic or sociopathic or any of those words that have been made up. It means, Dr. Bettleheim, that you, and all those others like you who have been laying this incredible guilt trip on us for over twenty years, you are wrong and ought to be ashamed of yourselves.

"Feral mothers" indeed! You are a feral mother, Bruno. Take that and live with it for a while. It doesn't feel very good, does it? And "parentectomy"? It is my considered professional opinion, after having carefully examined all of the facts, that nothing short of a Bruno-ectomy will improve conditions in this case. And a Freud-ectomy. And a psychiatrist-ectomy. And a jargon-ectomy. And a professional baloney-ectomy.

It is further indicated by the facts in this case that an abject public apology is called for from all that horde of ignorant physicians, smug psychiatrists, know-it-all social workers, inept educators, clap trap therapists—all the people who have assembled wealth and status for themselves by taking advantage of our suffering and the suffering of our innocent children. Don't worry. We won't spit in your eye and tell you to go to hell—a treatment you so richly deserve. Just tell us you are sorry, that you will try to do better. It's not hard. You know you need to do it. We will accept. We will say, "That's all right. It's all over now. It was a bad scene, but we are ready to forget it. Here. Let's shake. Take our hands. We need you. God knows we need you to help us bring some sensitivity into this world for the sake of our children who are absolutely going to be killed if it does not come."

And here is the hard part, friends. We don't really expect you to respond. The system works for you too well—no matter if it grieves us and kills our children. Your professional structure is too strong—no matter if it is built on myths and lies and held together with trickery and mystique. Your status is too self-satisfying. The money, friends, is much too good. And so it goes.

I'm sorry, George. We are all so very sorry.

NOTES

1. Update (1985): These figures have been revised (resulting in numbers three times greater) based on criteria adopted by NSAC in 1979.

2. Update (1985): Miracle of miracles! His mother's epic work paid off! In 1979 this man, no longer young, was placed in a Charlotte, North Carolina, community residence for adults with autism started by the North Carolina Society for Autistic Children. In 1983 I spoke with the director of his program and learned that after a lifetime of institutional abuse this mute and damaged person was gradually learning to use speech. And he goes swimming regularly in a community pool.

3. Bettleheim contends that some parental attitudes, feelings, and child-rearing practices expose a child to such extreme stress that he responds with severe withdrawal, characterized as autism. He recommends that the child be institutionalized so that institutional staff may replace the parents (hence, "parentectomy") and effectively treat the child in a less primitive ("feral," like wild animals, wolves) environment. See the reference list.

REFERENCES

Bettleheim. B. *Love is not enough.* Glencoe, New York: Free Press, 1950.

Bettleheim. B. *The empty fortress: Infantile autism and the birth of the self.* London: Collier-Macmillan, 1967.

Dussault, W. Speech presented at the meeting of the National Society for Autistic Children, Orlando, July 1967.

Mills v. *Board of Education of the District of Columbia,* 348 F. Supp. 866 (D.D.C. 1972).

National Society for Autistic Children, Board of Directors and Professional Advisory Board. *A short definition of autism.* Albany: Authors, 1977.

P.L. 94–142, The Education for All Handicapped Children Act.

P.L. 93–112, as amended by P.L. 93–51, enacting Section 504, Rehabilitation Act of 1973.

QUESTIONS TO CONSIDER

1. Frank describes a system of service delivery that, instead of providing services, will kill his child and others like him. From your present perspective do you believe him? If you were he and had walked in his shoes, would you believe as he does? How is it that, even when some people seek to help George or Frank, they end up hurting them? What can be done, by an individual or a system, that would be only good, not good that becomes harmful?

2. Frank describes desperate parents—parents who are willing to lie down on roadways to call attention to problems, parents who use electric prods on their children. What makes them so desperate—their children? Or the way in which society and its agents respond to them and their children? Or both? Have you ever been so desperate or can you imagine yourself being so desperate? If so, how did you or would you behave? Do you condone or condemn the parents Frank describes? What would you do to help them? Would your help be different from that of the professionals in Frank's essay?

3. Frank concludes with sorrow, and an apology. To whom does he apologize and why? Is he apologizing for a society that kills disabled children by rejecting them and devaluing them to death? Or is he merely forgiving the imperfection of society but not its results? What do you think will happen next with Frank and George?

Call Them Liars Who Would Say "All Is Well"

Frank Warren

It has been seven years since I wrote "A Society That Is Going to Kill Your Children." Many things have changed. Many things are the same.

There has been much enlightenment among professionals whose codes of ethics command them to help other human beings. I like to think that this book has contributed to that enlightenment, and I am glad for the part my essay may have played. But my experience has shown that the darkness is still wide and deep, the thick ignorance is still barely penetrated, and the danger that people with autism and their families face when they approach the helping professions is still real, still cloaked in warm and caring words, and still powered by strong economic forces. Autistic children still face a multitude of barriers to good life. Even today they stand in jeopardy as the process grinds slowly and surreptitiously, avoiding accountability, and results too often in death.

A few months ago the father of a young man with autism described in chilling detail how his son was being deliberately drugged to death in a psychiatric hospital where he had been sent under court order. The father, a physician, had been frustrated at every turn in his years-long effort to save his son. "He is tied to his bed. He is bleeding from his esophagus. The dosage and variety of drugs he is being given is so powerful it is killing him. There is no behavioral program for him. And I can do nothing! Every time I go to a state agency for help, they do nothing. My lawyer can't help me. No one can help me. They are killing my son!"

I do not know the outcome of this story. I do know that every legal avenue was followed by this agonized father. I suspect that his son is dead now and that no one has paid a price for what happened—except the young man and his family. How many others have been ground into oblivion, unknown, unseen, unheard, behind locked doors, watched over by members of the helping professions? How many are dying now, as you read these words?

And the rage—reader, share it. Let it be a part of you, for the sake of these people, for the sake of our common humanity. Let it charge young hearts and minds, impelling them to action. Make change, by God! Make change! Swear that you will! If not you, who? If not now, when? Let your anger swell for this young man! Let hot tears come! Let rage inflame your determination!

If you are a parent, know that you are one with us, bound in a net of pain for as long as our lives go on. They are all our own, our flesh, our blood, our loved ones, our kin; and we must sweep away the corporate injustice and stop the killing process. We must join with every sympathetic force to make this society good for every son and daughter. If not you, who? If not now, when?

Call them liars who would say, "All is better now. We have done good things, and all is well now." If you sit in a place of power, on a board, in an agency, as part of a government or a university, use that power for all it is worth to make change. You will know how. What risk to yourself can compare to the risk that faces disabled people every day of their lives in the status quo?

The Changes

Seven years ago 95 to 98 percent of all adults with autism were institutional-ized (Sullivan, 1977). The regulations of Public Law 94–142, the Education for All Handicapped Children Act, listed autism as a "severe emotional disturbance." Parents seeking education for their autistic children were con-sidered part of the problem rather than the most significant part of the solution. School districts across the nation devalued these children, denied them access, and forced them to participate in intrusive therapy. The Diag-nostic and Statistical Manual of the American Psychiatric Association also listed autism as an emotional distrubance, with no acknowledgement of the physical causes of this neurological disability. The National Institutes of Health had no viable research section that methodically investigated the biological causes of this disability. And no service providers systematically placed people with autism in community-based homes and jobs or trained them to use public transportation. Every significant program for people with autism was in the control of people who doubted the ability of autistic children and adults to be a part of society, to live, work, and play in the community among their nonhandicapped peers, to grow and learn, to de-velop in various pursuits, and to be free citizens. And perhaps as bad, the helping professions still tended to blame parents for the neurological disabil-ity affecting their children.

Even I, seven years ago, was comfortable writing about parents who bought a cattle prod and used it on their autistic son to prevent him from cutting himself with broken glass. I still believe, if the choice is between a shock stick and death at his own hands, the shock stick is preferable.

But I know now that this simple choice never exists. There is always an alternative to the physical pain of such aversive procedures, and I know that every parent, every advocate, and every service provider can find that alternative. I also believe that, under today's conditions, with a growing body of literature on positive behavioral practices, the parent, advocate, or service provider who says he cannot is copping out—or worse.

In short, these sensitive human beings with autism, who feel pain and frustration and who search for fulfillment just as we do, need successful experiences to help them enjoy life rather than suffer pain when they do not behave as we feel they should under conditions that they have difficulty understanding. So how have things changed?

We don't know what percent of adults with autism are institutionalized today. But we do know that the percentage is far less than the 95 to 98 percent in 1977. More importantly, we know that the percentage of those who need institutional care is zero. No person with autism, unless that person is ill, needs to be kept in a hospital. Hospitals are for people who need help to get well. Problems of behavior, communication, or social interaction can best be dealt with in the community, where all the rest of us learn how to behave, communicate, and interact socially. These are not medical problems but are issues best dealt with by persons who understand autism—teachers, counselors, psychologists, and others who are properly trained.

The late Dr. Leo Kanner, professor emeritus at Johns Hopkins University, gave advice which, if followed, will lead to community-based services for autistic people (whom he, in 1943, first identified). To a closed-minded physician he said kindly, "Doctor, remember, the child approaches you. Let him show you. Put aside your preconceptions" (Harris, 1981). Let us say to the service providers, to the agencies, and to the many who doubt, "Look at the men and women with autism. Let them show you. Put aside your preconceptions."

Fortunately, a few programs have recognized the error of past ways and have shown, by simply allowing them to, that people with autism can live in the community, work at jobs among their nonhandicapped peers, earn wages, pay taxes, and enjoy their home community. They do, of course, need specialized services. An example of such a program is Community Services for Autisic Adults and Children (CSAAC), serving the state of Maryland and based in Rockville, a suburb of Washington, D.C. At this writing CSAAC has taken forty-six men and women with autism—all of whom were either institutionalized or living at home with parents—and helped them to be a part of their community. None had ever lived in the community, except with their parents, or had held jobs in nonsheltered environments. Of these forty-six, forty-three are living in townhouses, apartments, and group homes, with no more than four per home. Eight are in school, learning vocational skills. Twenty-six are on jobs in the community, working among their nonhandicapped peers, and twelve of them have learned to travel to their jobs.

In a statement that is reflective of all who are employing CSAAC clients, one employer says, "These workers are not apart from the other workers here. They work, eat, and take time off with everyone. What we are doing is not charity. They earn every penny they get" (Beach, 1984).

Another change came on January 16, 1981, when autism was removed from the category of "severe emotional disturbance" in the regulations of P.L. 94–142, the Education for All Handicapped Children Act. Although this change came six years after the passage of P.L. 94–142 and roughly twenty years after knowledgeable people in the field knew that such categorization was inaccurate, it took a nationwide effort on the part of the National Society for Children and Adults with Autism to persuade rule-makers to budge from their position, which they acknowledged in private was in error. NSAC presented hundreds of letters from parents in every state describing how the severe emotional disturbance categorization was preventing their children from receiving a "free, appropriate public education" and how it was causing many other problems, including intrusive therapy for parents as a condition for education of their children.

In a memo transferring this five-pound documentation of problems faced by parents of autistic children to top officials in the Office of Special Education, Ed Sontag, author of numerous journal articles on education of severely handicapped students and then-acting director of the Division of Assistance to States for the Office of Education, called for the development of a cadre of professionals especially trained to teach students with autism (Warren, 1980). This has been government policy ever since and resulted in the 1981 funding of the NSAC National Personnel Training (NSAC-NPT). At this writing NSAC-NPT has instructed teacher trainers in Massachusetts, Colorado, Louisiana, South Carolina, Kentucky, Washington, Arkansas, California, Maine, Mississippi, New Hampshire, Nebraska, Florida, and Tennessee.

Across the nation school officials are beginning to understand that parents not only are not the cause of their children's autism but also can be the most important factor in their children's ability to cope in spite of this severe disability.

In 1980 the Diagnostic and Statistical Manual of the American Psychiatric Association (DSM III) defined autism in a manner that removed stigma from parents and recognized that the effects of autism are lifelong. This redefining of autism was a result of work done by NSAC and its professional members. The DSM III definition reflects, in all of its salient details, the definition of autism adopted by NSAC in 1977 (Ritvo and Freeman, 1977). The impact of DSM III is pervasive. Although not completely satisfactory, the DSM definition now is vastly more accurate than the previous stigmatizing definition and is being used by professionals across the country to the benefit of people with autism and their families.

Seven years ago we were saying to professionals, "Understand what autism is and what it is not." Now we are saying to the policy makers and service providers, "Understand what people with autism can do!"

In 1982 following a five-year campaign by NSAC, the National Institute of Neurological and Communicative Disorders and Stroke (NINCDS), a part of the National Institutes of Health, made operative a section for research on autism. The results of this event, widely celebrated by NSAC are at this writing just beginning to accumulate. The potential is exciting. A focus for researchers in the biomedical field now exists, and concentrated work on the neurological aspects of autism is under way. The focus of study is shifting from the worn and useless examinations of parental attitudes to neuroscience, where causes and perhaps preventative or curative interventions may be found.

In 1979 The Association for the Severely Handicapped (TASH), with 5,000 members, was the first national disability organization to call not only for the complete end to institutions for persons with disabilities, but also for the complete and lifelong integration of severely handicapped children and adults into society among their peers. NSAC, with 6,000 members, followed in 1980 with a nearly identical declaration and reaffirmed it in 1981 after a bitter year-long fight. In 1982 the Association for Retarded Citizens, with nearly 200,000 members, unanimously approved a resolution stating that all people, regardless of the severity of their disabilities, are entitled to community living. One year later the ARC delegate body passed by a three-to-one vote a resolution calling for the phasing out of all large, multipurpose institutions and cited as a reason its conclusion that such institutions cannot perform habilitative functions. And beginning in 1973 and continuing to date, the American Association on Mental Deficiency—once organized and dominated by the medical directors and superintendents of the nation's institutions for persons with mental retardation—has affirmed the right of all people to live in the community and has adopted legislative goals to secure that right.

These were significant events in the national movement. But still, autistic peole were, and are, largely unserved among their nonhandicapped peers. In the same year that TASH adopted its resolution, CSAAC opened two group homes in Wheaton, Maryland, serving six adults with autism. In 1980 and 1981, when NSAC passed its resolutions, CSAAC opened six more apartments and placed twelve severely handicapped adults with autism in jobs in the community. In 1982, when the ARC passed its resolution, CSAAC expanded its community residential and vocational programs to serve thirty-six clients and in 1983 expanded again to serve forty-six.

The CSAAC vocational program was first to demonstrate that adults with autism can not only live but also can work and earn wages among their nonhandicapped peers—and can be accepted and valued by them. The CSAAC philosophy, first conceived in 1974 by its parent-run board (Dashner, 1982), deserves repeating. Community Services for Autistic Adults and Children believes that all persons with autism have the right to services provided within the least restrictive environment;

that all persons with autism, regardless of their age or degree of handicapping condition, can be served in the community;

that persons with autism can live in single family homes, townhouses or apartments where they have a right to use the telephone, send and receive mail, and receive guests without prior notice;

that persons with autism have a right to work in private industry or government worksites among their non-handicapped peers;

that persons with autism have a right to specialized services which facilitate living and working among non-handicapped peers;

that the least restrictive, positive methods be emphasized in providing instructional and/or behavioral programs for persons with autism to live in the community;

that persons with autism have the right to programs and services available to other members of the community and should not be denied access to these services on the basis of their handicap;

that the principles of normalization should be implemented in all facets of the lives of persons with autism.

Today we hear the words of Gunnar Dybwad saying, "Whether it is a state school, a regional center, a training school, or a developmental center, the typical institution developed in our country over the past 100 years is dead" (1983). And we hear Lou Brown saying, "In the past, we assumed that severely handicapped persons could not perform meaningful work. We were wrong. We then assumed that although they could perform meaningful work, they could only function in sheltered environments. We were wrong again. Now, there are those who offer that they can perform meaningful work in non-sheltered environments, but assume non-handicapped employees and workers do not want them around. Wrong again. In the near future severely handicapped persons will not live in institutions, will not attend segregated schools, and will not be confined to handicapped environments of any kind. As adults, they will live, work and play in a wide variety of environments that contain non-disabled people, and experience the rich variety of stimuli so critical to a decent, humane and productive quality of life" (1984).

The Unchanged

We want to believe those words. Then we can rest. But we know there is no rest yet for those who care, and we can still hear that father's voice saying, "He is tied to his bed. He is bleeding from his esophagus. . . . No one can help me. They are killing my son." So many things are the same.

Something of Human Nature

I will end with a word from my daughter, Mary MacRae Warren, a reporter for the Southern Pines, North Carolina, *Pilot,* who looks into herself and finds what all of us should understand: we all share responsibility for the situations now facing people with disabilities. As parents, siblings, and professionals we have felt the frustration. We have known the love. We can learn from our experience. We can understand the common humanity that binds us to people with disabilities. And we can make change.

Mary's story, written on her brother George's twenty-first birthday, brings keenly to memory the burden he brought to our family and the good ways he changed our lives. I also remember the little girl, so serious, who stayed with him and gave her parents respite. And I remember, too, the anger she felt when George was ridiculed or not accepted by neighbors and friends. She cared then and she cares now. Thank you, Mary.

> I have a short story to tell. It is one of many stories of happiness and sorrow. It is a story of which I am not very proud, and one I have never told my parents. I will tell it now because it is time, and I have learned from my mistakes, as all people can.
>
> George is twenty-one years old today. He is a frequently happy, often troubled young man who has grown up in a society reluctant to accept and care for him even though he cannot fare for himself.
>
> I am very lucky. My crime was easily forgiven by someone who loved me very much, without reservation. George and I were very young. I was his frequent babysitter. As an older sister more interested in ponies and playing outdoors, I felt a great deal of resentment toward George and, of course, toward my persecutors, my mother and father. It was a day like any other day when I had been told to take care of George. They always seemed the same, those days, because I had no choice in the matter, and if I had had one, I would have refused. It was that simple for me. I had better things to do.
>
> We were waiting in the car for our mother to come with the groceries. The recurring memory breaks my heart every time I think of it. He was antagonizing me again. Those unbearable, unreal sounds that haunted and humiliated me. They were the nonsense noises that made the neighborhood children speculate he was from Mars. I could hear their taunts, and rage welled up in me. How could I have a brother like this? He was not right at all. He was a curse. I screamed at him to "Shut up!" He kept on. He wouldn't stop. My suppressed anger exploded. I raised my hand and slapped him again and again across his soft, round baby face. George began to cry, low, mournful whimpers. He never once raised a hand to protect himself. Shaking with fear and anger, [unable to think clearly,] I just looked at him. In that swift instance I felt more shame and revulsion for myself than I have ever felt toward anyone. The rude ugliness of it will never leave me. I hugged him to me, begging for forgiveness. And he gave it to me unconditionally. I shall never forget his sweet, sad face as he accepted my hugs.
>
> In that instance I learned something of human nature and the nature of those who would reject people like George. I had been one of them; sullen,

uncaring, unwilling to care for someone who came into the world with fewer advantages than I myself had. Today, I am a better person for having lived through both the good times and the bad times that our family experienced as a result of my brother's autism. I have a sense of understanding and compassion that I learned from growing up with George. Best of all, I have my brother, who loves me with all the goodness in his heart.

My message is simple. Look into your hearts and into the hearts of all people to see what is real, what makes them real people. For we are all the same. Accept people for what they are and work to make the world a receptive place—not just for those who are perceived as normal.

If not you, who? If not now, when?

REFERENCES

Beach, R. *Community News* (Newsletter of the Community Services for Autistic Adults and Children, Rockville, Maryland), January 1984.

Brown, L. et al. Teaching severely handicapped students to perform meaningful work in nonsheltered vocational environments. In B. Blatt & R. Morris (Eds.), *Perspectives in special education: State of the art.* Glenview, Ill.: Scott Foresman & Co., 1984.

Dashner, E. *History of Maryland Society for Autistic Adults and Children and Community Services for Autistic Adults and Children.* Rockville, Maryland; CSAAC, 1982.

Dybwad, G. A society without institutions. *Community Living* (Publication of Operation Real Rights, Philadelphia), November 1983, pp. 1–3.

Harris, J.C. Plenary memorial address honoring Leo Kanner at the annual meeting of the American Academy of Child Psychiatry, Dallas, Texas. October 1981.

Ritvo, E., & Freeman, B. *The definition of autism.* Washington, D.C.: National Society for Children and Adults with Autism, 1977.

Sullivan, R. *Personal communication.* Washington, D.C.: NSAC Information and Referral Service, 1977.

Warren, F. OSE official suggests need for specially trained teachers. *Advocate* (Newsletter of the National Society for Children and Adults with Autism), Washington, D.C.:, September 1980.

QUESTIONS TO CONSIDER

1. Frank and Mary describe themselves as feeling rage. What enrages them? Would you be enraged, too, if you were they? How do you feel after reading their stories? What action might you and others take to respond to their stories and the feelings they evoke?

2. Frank's first essay seemed to reflect despair—remember his expression of deep sorrow after his story of desperation? His second essay seems to show a different person. What has been the change? What were its causes? What role did Frank himself play in the causes?

3. Frank continues to work in advocacy; Mary has taken up his former profession, journalism. What is each likely to be doing five years from now?

What changes are likely to have occurred in George's life? Will these changes reflect systematic changes in service delivery? What relationship will Frank and Mary's activities have to the changes in George's life, and vice versa? What relationship will your activities have to the changes in the lives of similarly handicapped people?

Part Two

James J. Gallagher is a Kenan professor of education and the director of the Frank Porter Graham Child Development Center at the University of North Carolina at Chapel Hill. Formerly, he served as a deputy assistant secretary for planning, research, and evaluation in the U.S. Office of Education and as associate commissioner of education and chief of the Bureau of Education for the Handicapped.

Gertrude G. (Rani) Gallagher is a graduate of New Haven State Teachers College and has done graduate work at New York University. She also has taught at the Southbury Training School, a regional mental retardation facility in Connecticut.

Sean is now completing a master's degree at Pennsylvania State University in a program of exercise physiology, a choice probably linked to his early life experiences.

James J. Gallagher   *Gertrude G. Gallagher*

Family Adaptation to a Handicapped Child and Assorted Professionals

James J. Gallagher
Gertrude G. Gallagher

Some years ago James Gallagher had occasion to write an article entitled "Rejecting Parents?" (1956). In that article he took professionals to task for reaching a too-easy conclusion that parents tend to reject their handicapped children. Too many professionals seemed to put down parents when, in fact, the parents needed their sympathy and support.

> Needless to say, every parent can be indicted at one time or another if expression of negative values is the only criterion for parental rejection, especially if the observer happens to catch the parent under conditions of stress. When we think of the problems that parents of normal children face and then consider the extra stress which is placed on parents of handicapped children, it is little wonder that the term used loosely could apply to almost any mother or father. What parent could be completely happy or positively oriented to a child who is quadriplegic, or blind, or severely mentally retarded, or, for that matter, completely normal in every respect? (p. 273)

The Problem

In the next year our second son was born, and we were soon to live through some of the problems and issues that were discussed in that article. Our son, unlike his healthy older brother, seemed to have continuing illnesses in infancy and as a toddler. These illnesses were variously called bronchitis, pneumonia, or just plain flu. Although a diagnosis was made early of bronchial asthma, like most parents who have little or no

233

knowledge of such special health problems, we did not realize the full significance of that diagnosis until much later.

The next ten years were a sequence of periodic acute crises appearing against a backdrop of normal development. This, of course, is quite different from the pattern of the severely handicapped child and creates very different parental problems. Our child's intellectual level has not been affected nor his ability to form a reasonable relationship with other youngsters and with family members. His school performance remained good despite his frequent absences, and no one really thought of him as handicapped.

Our son had a hidden disorder, one that could not be seen or appreciated until it went into its acute phase. He must have been hospitalized a hundred times during that twelve-year period, giving us intimate contact with countless emergency rooms, oxygen tents, and interns taking case histories—the same case history over and over again. Our child would progress, in a terrifyingly rapid succession, from wheezing to gasping for breath to absolute helplessness and finally to a coma unless treatment was provided with dispatch and decisiveness.

These attacks often struck with the suddenness of a thunderstorm, coming out of nowhere and suddenly being upon us. One of the chronic parental fears was that this thunderstorm would strike at a time and a place where there would be no shelter, that is, no competent professionals around to help us. The thought of being caught on a highway late at night between towns or in a strange city with no known resources or guide as to where to go is a constant companion of parents of chronically asthmatic children.

One of the ways such a handicap changes the life of the family is that it brings the young family face to face with the prospects of death at a time when most families are filled with enthusiasm and energy. To see one's preschool child in a coma in an oxygen tent struggling for breath is sobering, and the possibility that the child will never reach maturity is one that has to be considered.

The Search for Help

One of the major problems of all parents of handicapped children is finding someone who really knows what this condition is all about and what to do about it. We lived in a university community, but it did not have a medical school. While that community had hard-working and well-meaning pediatricians and other medical specialists, they had rarely seen a case of this severity and really didn't know what to do. We were referred to a specialist in Chicago after local treatments failed, and Sean and his mother made a trip by train for desensitization treatments every few weeks, the first of many futile attempts to apply some kind of rational long-range treatment program.

We were one of the first families to experience the era of cortisone. We were told (after several years of treatments that didn't work, or almost worked, or worked sometimes) that there was a powerful drug that had promise of helping asthmatic children. The trouble was, as the doctors pointed out, it was also powerful enough to have many unfavorable side effects, and it should be taken only when absolutely necessary. We weren't clear at first, and the doctors were rather vague themselves, about what these horrors were. It was clear that a balancing act was required between lowering the dosage and risking an attack of asthma, and increasing the dosage to have him clear of asthmatic attacks but possibly suffering some other side effect. We as parents had to wonder whether in providing for our own security (freedom from attacks), we were harming our child in another way.

Professionals and Parents

Since both of us were trained to work with children ourselves, our relationships with professionals had a special set of qualities and difficulties about them. The anxieties and concerns of parents are such that they often want to credit more expertise and capability to the professionals than is warranted. As parents we would have very much liked to believe in the invincibility and complete mastery of the professionals with whom we came into contact. Our sense of our own limitations and the limitations of our own professions prevented us from doing that. We were particularly uneasy when we ran across a professional who maintained that we had come to the source of all knowledge to straighten out all our problems and all we had to do was leave everything in his hands. Nor did it help, in reading the literature on the subject, to realize that the treatment programs rested upon some extraordinarily inadequate and poorly done research.

Our continuous contact with the medical profession from the late fifties through the early seventies allowed us to see many changes taking place in the delivery of health services, practically all of them for the better for parents. Even in the earlier time periods, we were pleased to find an understanding of how important it was for parents to stay with young children in the hospital. This was most important psychologically, since most young children are terribly uncertain in a strange hospital, surrounded entirely by strangers. The notion that their parents may go and never return, or that they will never see their parents again, is an irrational but not unusual response in the five- or six-year-old youngster. It seemed to us that the growing understanding of child development in the medical profession was reflected in the policies that allowed us to remain in important contact with our son in the hospital.

One of the special problems that we became aware of, only in retrospect, was that our son was an amazingly good patient. He instantly became the favorite in practically any emergency room or hospital where he had to stay. He was typically in good spirits and good humor, stoically bearing his problems and never complaining about any treatment or shot that he received. What we only slowly began to realize was that his model patient behavior stemmed from his fear that he was going to die, hence his complete willingness to bear anything to prevent that.

It is impossible for us to understand the feelings of a child who finds himself suddenly unable to breathe. He can see that those adults who are ordinarily capable, his parents, can do nothing but transport him to where he can get help. Our belated insight into his fears convinced us that any youngster in a similar situation should have extended counseling and discussions with professionals about such terrors, which are almost certain to be there.

One of the disturbing aspects of dealing with professionals is that when one is playing the role of parent, one is automatically stripped of any knowledge or expertise. Even simple parent observations are suspect because of the possibility of bias. Over a period of ten years we both became quite expert in our ability to identify the onset of an attack and to predict the course of that attack. On many occasions we tried, more or less desperately, to share those predictions with physicians with whom we came into contact on an emergency basis. We almost uniformly found our judgments to be discounted.

For example, we became aware of the medical strategy of choosing the least intrusive treatment. If it doesn't work, then the next most intrusive effort or drug is tried until one finds the level of treatment necessary to achieve the desired results. This is fine for the ordinary patient. However, when doctors adopted this routine strategy, we often found our son in the midst of a severe attack before the level or strength of medication could be applied to prevent it. On numerous occasions we tried to point out to the doctor that our son goes into attacks sharply and severely in almost a toboggan-slide style. Unless one could catch him before the toboggan had a chance to gain momentum, he would be in the midst of a severe attack before anything could be done.

Much to our frustration, we watched our son go into such attacks as the doctors ignored our comments and proceeded in a plodding manner to apply slightly stronger and stronger medication as each previous medication failed. All too often we had to observe our youngster in the midst of a severe attack. Fortunately for us, those physicians with whom we became acquainted over an extended period of time formed a relationship of trust with us, which allowed us to work as a team. Then our own observations and years of experience were brought to bear on the situation in a constructive fashion. Nonetheless, it certainly became clear to us how easily the professional ignores parents' feelings or observations or intuitive judgments as to what might be the best course of action.

James J. Gallagher & Gertrude G. Gallagher

Professionals vs. Parents

One of the unfortunate components of the era in which our child was growing up was the predominant theory that parents could be the cause of bronchial asthma, rather than being among its victims. We spent many hours being interviewed and questioned to see if we were, in some fashion, precipitating the attacks of our child through our own anxieties and problems. Since we, in our other roles, were used to interviewing people, the intent of the questioning was transparent in many cases, but that did not make it any less frustrating.

It is obvious that parents are under tension when they have a handi-capped child or a child who is subject to acute illnesses. Our feeling, which remains constant to this day, was to accuse parents of creating the problem, whether the problem is asthma or autism or whatever, is akin to accusing the thunder of causing the storm. Our own tensions were clearly evident, though we tried to be casual upon hearing our child begin to wheeze and thus signal the onset of an attack. Our anxieties probably did contribute somewhat to the intensity of the attack, but that is quite different from being held responsible for the basic condition in the first place.

Such an attitude of "blame the parent," which was not uncommon among the professionals at that time, did create distance in the relationship between parents and professionals and probably caused other unfavorable consequences as well. The parents of asthmatic children can develop an extraordinary sensitivity toward the signs of an attack. We believed that we could hear our son wheezing from a distance of one hundred yards; certainly there was no corner of the house where we could not be aware of his change of breathing pattern in his bedroom. At the same time, our aware-ness that parents were thought to be a contributing factor often made us reluctant to seek immediate medical help on the grounds that we might be overreacting. This sometimes caused us to delay until the condition had gone too far. It definitely caused a certain amount of wariness in our attitude toward professionals. We weighed our statements to them, know-ing that some poorly chosen word might cause them to charge off on this ill-conceived hypothesis.

One serious conflict between us as parents and the professionals came when Sean was in a hospital where the philosophy was clear that parents were a contributing factor to the problem. When the physician in charge suggested at one time that we involve our youngster in an experiment to see if it was his fears and our fears that were essentially causing the seizures, we agreed. The cortisone treatment was replaced with a placebo so that Sean would still believe he was receiving cortisone. We could then see if he could be kept free of seizures by his mere belief that he was receiving the treatment that was supposed to be helping him.

Unfortunately, the result of the experiment was that within twenty-four to forty-eight hours, our five-year-old son was unconscious and in an oxygen tent; he remained unconscious for almost two days. A major confrontation occurred when the physician in charge suggested he might want to continue that experiment. When we refused to allow that to happen, the doctor threatened to remove all support, washing his hands of the entire matter unless we left the treatment program completely in his hands. The terrifying feeling that all medical support would suddenly be removed from our son was one that really caused parental stress and tension!

Instead of accepting the manifest failure of the experiment and concluding that our youngster did need medical treatment to control his seizures, the physician in charge hypothesized that we, knowing that the experiment was going on, in some way communicated that fact to our son and caused the seizure to occur. That same man, without any observable credentials, organized a group therapy session for parents, the effect of which was amateurish and possibly damaging in the sense that it encouraged us to have guilt feelings about the way in which we were behaving or not behaving toward our child. The entire situation had to be resolved by getting a third party, in this case an eminent psychiatrist, to certify that we as parents were not emotionally disturbed and instead were showing signs of stress that were normal given the conditions.

One of the mysterious factors, from a parental standpoint, is why the professionals consistently have difficulty in working cooperatively with one another to the patient's benefit. At one time, since we had become aware of the wide range of factors involved in severe asthma, we tried to bring together the relevant disciplines to create a single treatment program. This meant bringing together a triumvirate of psychiatrist, endocrinologist, and asthma specialist to see if they could agree on a single, comprehensive treatment program. Our attempt to get such people together to talk was only a partial success; it took months before we could get a meeting. It is not encouraging for parents to see that professional roles, status, and internal conflicts so manifestly obstruct the benefits to their child.

Fortunately, this era of seeing parents as the core problem has more or less passed and has been replaced by an understanding that the handicap causes parental stress, not the other way around. As the evolution of families has been more carefully studied, certain identifiable phases can be charted. One of those phases is that of the young family struggling to establish itself. It is a period of identifiable stress during which young careers and young children may both need nurturing.

When one inserts a special problem or handicap into such a situation, then the stress and tensions are magnified. In our case a simple example was whether the father/professor would travel and, in effect, desert the family during a period of crisis, leaving the mother to deal with the problem alone. The issue of whether it was safe to go was one that was constantly with us during the time that the father/professor needed to be out establishing a professional reputation.

The Rest of the Family

There is always the concern that the siblings of the child in question will resent the amount of time and resources the parents invest in the handicapped child. Our knowledge of those dynamics has caused us to be especially concerned about the effect of Sean's illness on his older brother and younger sister and brother. There was no way that we could prevent those feelings of resentment. One can try to create special occasions, vacation trips, or other devices to help ease those feelings, but they will always be there. Perhaps the most useful strategy we used was open discussion with the other youngsters, when they were old enough, about how natural it was to be resentful and then to be mad at themselves for being resentful since they knew why the parents had to spend extra time with the handicapped child.

Separation

Perhaps the most difficult decision that we made as parents was to send our son to the Children's Asthmatic Research Institute and Hospital (CARIH), a special residential asthmatic treatment center, for eighteen months when he was twelve years old. After ten years of failure in attempting to help our son achieve an existence apart from steroid therapy, a physician whom we had come to respect and admire recommended that we seriously consider sending Sean to CARIH in Denver, Colorado. The thought of sending our son away for eighteen months, the minimum time allowed for treatment, meant reorganizing a close-knit family group, and that was not easily considered.

Parents must also worry about rationalizing their own feelings about not wanting to send their child away for treatment, because many times they would feel better and freer if the youngster were away. We came to realize how much a part of our lives he had become and what a gap would be left by his departure. Parents know that sons and daughters will leave home later on but not at twelve! This handicap, like most handicaps, was causing a disjunction in the normal family evolution. The crucial factor in making the decision was the continuing and obvious effect that steroid therapy was having upon our son. His chubby cheeks and retarded physical growth had become too obvious to ignore, and the further possibility that his puberty might be affected caused us to make the decision.

The residential hospital itself had many advantages, both medical and psychological, that seemed to have a positive impact on our son. One was the presence of immediate medical treatment before a seizure became difficult. Sean could, upon the first attack of asthma, go to the hospital and get immediate treatment and then go back to what he was doing. Instead of the long and painful toboggan slide that often occurred at home before we could get him to an emergency room, he was able to determine his own treatment on his own timing.

In addition, the psychological atmosphere of CARIH was one of freedom and independence in which the youngsters controlled much of their own life situation. We were told they were to be as physical and active as they wished to be. If they wished to play football, they could play football. If, as a result of their playing, they had a seizure, they could go and get treatment and then return to the football game. This was a dramatic shift from the inevitable situation in the typical home, school, or neighborhood where the youngster, at the onset of the attack, must stop and find some way to get treatment, which is often delayed to the point that it has to be much more severe and prolonged in order to deal with the problem.

In addition, Sean received psychological counseling at the hospital which allowed him to express some of the related fears that he never could share fully with us. The daily treatment program was designed by the most knowledgeable experts in a rapidly developing field, where treatment sophistication was growing by the year and by the month. The rule that parents could visit only briefly over that eighteen-month stretch and that the child could not go home was their attempt to maintain a treatment program free from the past habits and patterns that had turned out to be nonproductive.

In many respects our experience as parents of a handicapped child was most atypical. One of the most unusual aspects of the story is that it has a happy and satisfying ending for the child and his parents. After his treatment program at CARIH, Sean returned free of steroid therapy and physically mature, having grown a foot taller after being removed from cortisone treatments. He was able to control and limit the occasional bouts of asthma that he still had. One of the proudest moments of our son's life, and of ours as parents, was when Sean was able to participate on a state high school championship soccer team. It signaled for him his ability to master his problem and participate in activities that other youngsters admired and valued.

The Needs of Parents

Our experience has taught us some things that we believe professionals should do to help future parents of youngsters like Sean. First, the professional staff should counsel the parents on the consequences of the handicap—what they can expect to happen to them and to the family as a result of having a handicapped child. Such counseling cannot be done in a one-shot session, since the realization of the adjustments that have to be made comes only gradually with experience. The parents' need to bring the youngster for continued treatment of various types provides the ideal opportunity to make such counseling sessions available.

Some attempt should be made by a professional team dealing with chronic problems to explore support services for the family. The team should examine the human support linkages of the family. Are there relatives or friends who can be helpful? Who can the parents turn to for support and help under conditions of stress and crisis? Professionals should assess the parents' support network and supplement it where necessary with professional services.

Parents also need adequate knowledge of the range of support and treatment facilities available for the particular disorder. It is a rare parent who has even the slightest knowledge of where to go or how to get help for his youngster. Although we were a professional family, used to dealing with the helping professions, many years passed before we fully knew the range of services available to our son on a community, state, and federal level.

Our own academic training made it easier for us to gain access to university hospitals and to help from academic sources that is not available to the ordinary parent. Certainly, some general statement of the scope of treatment facilities available ought to be provided to parents very early so that they can invoke the appropriate options for their situation.

It is in the best interest of both parents and professionals that parents continue to play an active role in the treatment of their youngster and not retreat, leaving the field entirely to professionals. If they do withdraw, the treatment program for the child and family will almost inevitably suffer. We have gradually become aware of the outstanding resources that parents can be in the treatment program, yet most professionals still have a long way to go in fully valuing the parents' observations and sense of appropriate treatment for their child.

Parents, in a desperate effort to be helpful, often do as we did and invest in a wide variety of devices that some physicians might casually suggest. We bought dehumidifiers and humidifiers, placed electrostatic filters on our furnace, got air-conditioned houses and cars before they were popular, and at one time seriously considered replacing all our furniture and rugs with Japanese-type decor to reduce dust collecting in the house. These efforts seem to be part of a parental desire to be useful, to play some important part in the treatment. The unfortunate element is that if these purchases are continued too long, they can add to the financial drain that already threatens the family.

Further, there needs to be continuity of services for the family as the child progresses through various developmental stages. It is highly likely that many parents will have to deal with the problems of their handicapped child for the remainder of their lives. These parents need professional support and input as the child progresses toward adulthood. One of the most difficult times for the handicapped youngster is likely to be adjustment to the unforgiving adolescent society of the secondary school. The child may have special problems of social adjustment and also may experience major concerns over an uncertain adult role. Parents need help in responding positively to these growing pains.

The book *Passages* (Sheehy, 1974) details the progression through some identifiable stages of stress and crisis that an individual faces in the aging process. We need also to be aware of the evolution of the problems of the family with a handicapped child and to create appropriate treatment resources at each step of the way. We should not arbitrarily abandon treatment because some point in time has been reached.

We have tried to avoid the human temptation to say that it all worked out for the best and that it was actually a strengthening and purifying experience. This would be utter nonsense. The strain and tension that was a part of our lives for fifteen years took its toll on us as individuals and as members of a family unit. It was not something that one would wish on other people, and professionals should do their utmost to ameliorate these situations as much as possible. Still, in one sense, there is a modicum of truth in the phrase from the popular song "Without a Hurt, the Heart Is Hollow." We can never meet another family with a handicapped child and not feel a surge of empathy and understanding that would never have been present without our own experiences.

The final words of the article "Rejecting Parents?" still seem appropriate:

> The parents can be, and should be, valuable assistants in the training program of many kinds of exceptional children. A professional person who can understand and accept the reasons for the attitudes of parents, and also understands his or her own emotional reactions to the child and the parents, will be able to provide a richer and more effective training program for the exceptional child. (Gallagher, 1956, p. 294).

REFERENCES

Gallagher, J. Rejecting parents? *Exceptional Children*, 1956, *22*, 273–276, 294.
Sheehy, J. *Passages*, New York: E.P. Dutton, 1974.

QUESTIONS TO CONSIDER

1. It was typical twenty years ago to consider parents the cause of their child's asthma. What was the impact of this blame on Jim and Rani's relationship with Sean and on their relationship with professionals?

2. Describe the characteristics of the professionals whom the Gallaghers found helpful and the characteristics of those with whom the Gallaghers were dissatisfied.

3. From the perspective of Jim and Rani, what are the primary needs of parents with asthmatic children? Suggest a type of professional and a service delivery model (e.g., counseling, printed material) that could be used to respond appropriately to each need.

4. Jim and Rani stated, "One of the ways such a handicap changes the life of the family is that it brings the young family face to face with the prospects of death at a time when most families are filled with enthusiasm and energy." What impact do you think such an early encounter with death might have on family relationships and priorities? In what ways could families be assisted in handling this type of stress?

Philip Roos is the executive director of Mothers Against Drunk Drivers, a position that he assumed in 1983 upon his resignation as executive director of the Association for Retarded Citizens/United States. He is also in the practice of clinical psychology.

Phil has been the associate commissioner for the New York State Department of Mental Hygiene in the Division of Mental Retardation, and was, before that, superintendent of the Austin State School in Austin, Texas, and the director of psychological services in the Texas Department of Mental Health and Mental Retardation. He and his wife, Susan, live in Arlington, Texas and have a twenty-three-year-old retarded daughter, who resides at the Denton State School in Texas.

Philip Roos

Parents of Mentally Retarded Children

Misunderstood and Mistreated

Philip Roos

I was fortunate in having established myself as a professional in the field of mental retardation before I became a parent of a retarded child. I was knowledgeable about mental retardation, as well as mental health, and knew how professionals operated. I could even converse with them in their professional jargons and interpret their cryptic statements. Furthermore, I had achieved some professional status, knew many professionals as colleagues, and had at least some insight into my own reactions to having a retarded child. I should have found it easy to obtain competent professional assistance, and things should have gone as smoothly as humanly possible.

Things did not go smoothly, though. Surprisingly, my wife and I embarked on a long series of catastrophic interactions with professionals that echoed the complaints I had heard so often from other parents. As a result of these experiences, I refined my earlier concept of professional mishandling of parents of retarded children as well as my interpretation of parental reaction to having a retarded child.

Professional Goofs

In a previous marriage, my wife had given birth to a profoundly retarded daughter and had had a series of spontaneous abortions. I solicited opinions from geneticists as to the likelihood of her giving birth to another retarded child. My wife and I were reassured that the danger was negligible. Nonetheless, we selected a pediatrician who seemed particularly sensitive to problems of mental retardation: His wife was a neurologist. I spoke to him prior to the birth of our daughter Val about my wife's history and our concern regarding the new baby. I asked him to be particularly alert to the possibility of mental retardation.

Val's early months were characterized by colic, hyperactivity, inattentiveness, total absence of social response, and sleep disturbances. During the latter part of her first year, she became increasingly hyperactive, would spend hours banging her head against her crib, and failed to reach the typical landmarks in sensorimotor development. As I repeatedly pointed out these indications of developmental anomalies to our pediatrician, he would gaze at my wife and me with obvious disbelief and assure us that the baby was quite normal; we were anxious parents. This and subsequent episodes led me to formulate my concept of professional ignorance: Many professionals simply do not know about mental retardation and have failed to recognize it or have misdiagnosed it and, all too often, give parents misinformation or fallacious advice.

At fourteen months our daughter could not stand alone, did not talk, seemed to understand nothing, and did not seem to recognize my wife and me. Our pediatrician decided the problem stemmed from her feet; we were referred to an orthopedist, who prescribed a complex brace which the child wore at night and part of each day to correct the alignment of her feet. We had embarked on what I labeled "referral ad infinitum" or the hot potato game—the tendency of some professionals to refer hapless parents from specialist to specialist. This tendency may, of course, reflect a genuine search for answers to complex situations; yet I became convinced that it was sometimes less the result of professional ignorance and more the professional's reluctance to confront parents with the reality of their child's retardation. In some cases it seems that professionals are less able to accept retardation in a child than the child's own parents.

Clinging stubbornly to the conclusion that our daughter was probably just fine, our pediatrician next referred us to a neurologist. Since this worthy professional was a consultant to the large state institution for the retarded of which I was the superintendent, I felt confident that he would immediately recognize the obvious signs of severe retardation in our child. Imagine my consternation when, after failing to accomplish even a funduscopic (vision) examination on Val because of her extreme hyperactivity, the learned consultant cast a baleful eye on my wife and me and informed us that the child was quite normal. On the other hand, he continued, her parents were obviously neurotically anxious, and he would prescribe tranquilizers for us. I had suddenly been demoted from the role of professional to that of parent as patient and had experienced the common assumption of many professionals that parents of a problem child are emotionally maladjusted and are prime candidates for counseling, psychotherapy, or tranquilizers. My attempts to point out the many indications of developmental delays and neurological disturbances were categorically dismissed as manifestations of my emotional problems. I was witnessing another captivating professional reaction, the deaf ear syndrome: the tendency on the part of some professionals to believe that parents are complete ignoramuses and therefore to ignore any conclusion they reach regarding their own child. Later I found that suggestions I would make regarding my own child would be totally

Philip Roos

dismissed by some professionals, while these same suggestions that I would make as a professional concerned about other children would be cherished by my colleagues as professional pearls of wisdom. Parenthetically, when I wrote to the neurologist years later to inform him that Val's condition had been clearly diagnosed as severe mental retardation and that she had been institutionalized, he did not reply.

This interchange also illustrated another problem faced by parents—namely, professional omniscience and omnipotence. There is a myth that professionals possess the source of all ultimate knowledge and can make wise decisions affecting other people's destinies. This unfortunate myth has been frequently perpetuated by professionals as well as by parents.

At length our pediatrician reluctantly agreed with me when once again confronted with the overwhelming evidence that Val was mentally retarded. Yet he clung to the possibility that the problem might be less hopeless, perhaps autism or childhood schizophrenia. This attitude of professional hopelessness toward mental retardation as an incurable disease is still rather prevalent among those who operate within a medical model. Unfortunately, it generates self-fulfilling and self-limiting prophecies which impede the development of retarded individuals. Furthermore, parents easily detect such defeatist attitudes and either develop similar expectations or resent those who adopt such a negative approach toward their child.

To clarify his diagnosis of Val, our pediatrician next sent us to a child psychiatrist (also one of my consultants at the state institution) with a strong psychoanalytic orientation. This very conscientious practitioner met the challenge with obvious interest and dedication. He began with the traditional multidisciplinary team evaluation, wherein my wife reiterated one more time her many painful past experiences. We were to go through this traumatic recounting of past agonies many times over, as if each new professional was beginning with a tabula rasa rather than with a thick file in which all the gruesome details were already minutely compiled. I eventually hypothesized that some professionals must suffer either from a compulsion to uncover other people's personal pasts or from a pervasive distrust of their colleagues.

One day the child psychiatrist proudly announced to my wife and me that the evaluation was complete and that he would discuss it with us. I was much gratified to find that he did not try to hide behind the veil of secrecy which, at that time, was so prevalent among professionals. It seemed that many professionals were reluctant to share information with their clients, allegedly because it might be too threatening, too uncomfortable, or in some other way destructive to the client. Our psychiatrist, on the other hand, bravely read parts of the report to us, including our daughter's IQ and the conclusion that Val's problem was unknown, although autism or childhood schizophrenia seemed to be plausible alternatives. Since I was surprised by the relatively high IQ, which seemed markedly incongruent with Val's behavior, I asked for the mental age. As I had feared, the mental age was very low, and it was obvious that the psychologist had made a computational error in calculating the IQ. When I remarked on this to the psychiatrist, who knew I had been a practicing clinical psychologist, he ventured that my own emotional needs might be preventing me from accepting his psychologist's findings and encouraged me to explore this avenue (the parent-as-patient role again). At my insistence, he subsequently asked his psychologist to review his findings and reported back that, indeed, the IQ had been erroneously determined and that rather than falling in the dull normal range, it fell in the area of severe mental retardation. Had I not been a trained psychologist, my wife and I (and the psychiatrist) would have proceeded on the erroneous assumption that Val was really of dull normal intelligence and therefore that her grossly primitive behavior must be the result of some cause other than mental retardation.

Indeed, our child psychiatrist did not accept the diagnosis of severe mental retardation. He undertook weekly joint sessions with Val, my wife, and me to determine the cause of the problem and to counsel with us. In spite of my intimate familiarity with psychotherapy and psychoanalytic theory, I could not help marveling at some of the ingenious and imaginative interpretations and recommendations arising from these weekly sessions.

On one occasion, for example, the psychiatrist accused me of withholding critical information when, in the course of a discussion, I casually mentioned a pet monkey that had been in our home during Val's earliest months. In an attempt to interject a bit of desperately needed humor into the situation, I replied, with tongue in cheek, that I must have repressed my memory of the monkey because of my feelings of guilt for having given the animal away. To my horror the psychiatrist took this as his cue for a lengthy discourse on the dynamics of repression and guilt, which was followed by the imaginative interpretation that Val's problem could stem from intense sibling rivalry with the unfortunate monkey. He insisted we purchase a toy facsimile of the departed beast and place it in her crib, so her reaction to it could be observed. Alas, her reaction was no different from her reaction to anything else placed in the crib—the toy was summarily tossed on the floor without the slightest hint that she recognized it as a symbol from the past.

On another occasion we were startled to hear the psychiatrist describe the use of Chihuahuas in Mexico as foot warmers placed in beds on cold winter nights. My wife and I exchanged anxious glances, fearing for the good doctor's sanity. The relevance of his dramatic account of Mexican foot warmers became evident, however, when he prescribed one Chihuahua in Val's crib every night as a source of unconditional nurture; he generously offered his own dog on a loan basis. Rather than reacting defensively to the doctor's implicit message that his ignorant dog could supply for Val what her parents could not, I asked a practical question—was the dog housebroken? No, it was not. And so it went.

It would be counterproductive to continue with personal examples of

Philip Roos

professional mishandling. Most parents of retarded children can easily top anything which I experienced since, as I stated earlier, I was fortunate in being a professional in the field of mental retardation. I do not mean to imply that all professionals mishandle parents, nor even that those described here did nothing right. On the contrary, they were sometimes helpful and almost always had good intentions. Their mishandling was the result of ignorance and improper training rather than maliciousness or indifference. No doubt things have improved in recent years (my experience occurred in the early 1960s), yet similar reports from parents are still common today, and training in mental retardation is still woefully lacking in the curriculum for many professional degrees, including medicine.

In all fairness, it must be recognized that professionals may also be mishandled by parents. Indeed, a sort of vicious cycle may develop as professional mishandling generates frustration in parents, who retaliate by mishandling professionals. Likewise, parental mishandling of professionals tends to reinforce the professionals' negative stereotypes of parents, which foster the mishandling of parents.

Parental Reactions

When I found that I had become the parent of a retarded child, I was no stranger to the emotional reactions which I experienced. As a matter of fact, I had written and lectured on the subject (Roos, 1963). Although similar emotional reactions and conflicts are probably common to most parents, their handling of the situation varies considerably. While some may be totally overwhelmed by having a retarded child, others cope constructively and grow as a result of their experience. It would be a serious mistake to assume that most parents of retarded children are emotionally disturbed.

In a society such as ours which greatly values intelligence, mental retardation is a formidable handicap. The tendency to equate humanness with intelligence is common (e.g., Fletcher, 1972), and the perception of retarded persons as subhuman organisms is still prevalent (Wolfensberger, 1969). Hence, most parents—though well adjusted—when faced with having a retarded child are likely to experience major psychological stress. The most common patterns which I had identified as the result of clinical experience, understanding of personality dynamics, and work with parents of retarded children include the following (Roos, 1963):

1. *Loss of self-esteem.* Because of our parental tendency to experience our children as extensions of ourselves, a defective child is likely to threaten our self-esteem. We may question our own worth and abandon some of our long-range goals when it becomes obvious that our child will be unable to achieve as we had hoped.

2. *Shame.* While most parents take pride in their children's accomplishments, parents of a retarded child learn to anticipate social rejection, pity,

or ridicule. Their love of their handicapped child is only a partial protection against the feeling of shame generated when their child is pointed out as a deviant or when other children laugh at her. Even after many years of such exposure, I am still not completely immune to the furtive whispers between parents and children which greet my retarded daughter when she ventures onto a playground or into a store with me.

3. *Ambivalence.* The mixed feelings of love and anger typically experienced by parents toward their children are usually greatly intensified toward a retarded child. The greater the frustration generated by the retarded child's irritating behavior and failure to learn, the more likely are the parents to feel anger and resentment. Fantasies of the child's death are not uncommon. Since these feelings are typically accompanied by guilt, some parents may react with overprotection while others tend to reject their child.

4. *Depression.* Most parents are deeply disappointed in having a retarded child and are realistically concerned with his future. To some, mental retardation symbolizes the death of the child and may lead to the type of grief reaction associated with the loss of a loved one. In any case, chronic sorrow can be anticipated as a nonpathological reaction to having a retarded child (Olshansky, 1966).

5. *Self-sacrifice.* Some parents seem to dedicate themselves totally to their retarded child, make great personal sacrifices, and adopt a martyr's approach to life. Sometimes this pattern leads to family disruption, including neglect of other children and marital conflicts.

6. *Defensiveness.* Professionals are familiar with parents who have become hypersensitive to perceived criticism of their retarded child. Often these parents respond with resentment and belligerence. In extreme cases parents may deny that their child is retarded, rationalize her shortcomings, and seek professional opinions to substantiate their own conviction that there is really nothing wrong.

As my wife and I struggled with our feelings regarding Val's mental retardation, we became aware that, although we certainly experienced some of the feelings just described, we were more preoccupied with the reactivation of old conflicts and anxieties. These conflicts and anxieties were not specific to having a retarded child; rather, they seemed inherent in the human condition as experienced by most people and were merely exacerbated by having a retarded child. Yet I have not heard them discussed by either professionals or parents. My wife and I found that professionals seemed strangely disinclined to listen to our concerns, and I still find that these fundamental existential conflicts seem to be completely neglected by professionals in the field of mental retardation. I suspect that many professionals feel uncomfortable discussing such conflicts, probably because they are common to most members of our society and usually lie relatively dormant in most people. Professionals apparently prefer to deal with the traditional parental pathology and effectively avoid recognizing parents' existential conflicts. They may have no simple answers to these conflicts and may become anxious because of the potential reactivation of their own unresolved conflicts.

The most critical conflict areas which are likely to be reactivated by the realization of having a retarded child include the following:

1. *Disillusionment.* As children we are taught to develop totally unrealistic expectations—success, achievement, wealth, love, and status. We expect wise parents, loving and lovable mates, and perfect children. Experience gradually erodes these unrealistic expectations of ourselves and others, leading to a long series of disillusionments in ourselves, in others, and in life in general.

Many of us channel our frustrated yearning for perfection into our children, through whom we hope to realize our thwarted dreams of accomplishment and happiness. Unfortunately, a retarded child is usually an unsuitable vehicle for fulfilling these hopes, so he represents a major disillusionment—often the culmination of a long series of disappointments. If the parents do not have other children, the possibility of their finding fulfillment through their children must be abandoned. Parents may then desperately search for other avenues to self-enhancement, or they may slip into pervasive feelings of hopelessness.

2. *Aloneness.* The need for intimacy seems to be universal, but no one can transcend his individual boundaries and fully share his feelings and perceptions with another. Often the last desperate hope of overcoming aloneness is through our children—products of our bodies, shaped into our image, literal extensions of ourselves. But a retarded child may not be able to fulfill this need because of a limited capacity to communicate and to achieve intimacy. The parents of such a child may feel that they have lost their final chance to achieve intimacy and may become overwhelmed with feelings of aloneness.

3. *Vulnerability.* Most of us begin life with the fantasy that we are all-powerful. As we mature, we learn to recognize our own helplessness and gradually recognize that others, too—including parents, teachers, and heroes—are not omnipotent. Pain, injury, illness, and failure repeatedly confront us with our personal vulnerability, the tenuousness of our control over the world, and, indeed, the fragile nature of life itself. Mental retardation in one's child reactivates these feelings of vulnerability. We are painfully reminded that our most precious possessions, our dearest dreams, can be completely destroyed and that we are totally helpless to do anything about it.

4. *Inequity.* Our nation is founded on the principle of justice for all, and we are taught from earliest childhood that fairness and justice ultimately prevail. Good will triumph, and if our judicial system falters, some greater force will reward heroes and punish villains. When faced with retardation in one's child, a parent may feel overwhelmed with the enormity of the appar-

ent inequity, and the natural reaction is to ask, "Why me?" In trying to answer this question, the parent may conclude either that the punishment is deserved because of grievous sins or that the world is neither fair nor just. The former alternative leads to guilt, remorse, and self-recrimination; the latter threatens basic ethical, moral, and religious beliefs.

5. *Insignificance.* Young children typically imagine that they are important figures occupying a central role in the scheme of things. Maturity brings with it the realization of personal insignificance, yet most of us are raised to yearn for greatness or, at least, meaning. When greatness escapes us, we search for meaning in satisfying social roles, such as those of husband, wife, father, mother. When we are frustrated in achieving a rewarding parental role—as can easily occur with a retarded child—we are vulnerable to feelings of insignificance by being deprived of an important opportunity to achieve meaning.

6. *Past orientation.* Most parents anticipate their children's future with enthusiasm, expecting such happy events as scholastic achievement, success in sports, graduation, marriage, birth of grandchildren, and promising careers. In contrast, parents of a retarded child usually view their child's future with apprehension, anticipating scholastic failure, exclusion from services (educational, social, recreational), inability to work or else menial employment, problems in sexual adjustment, inability to live independently, and a life of loneliness and isolation. Realistically, services tend to become less adequate as the retarded person ages, increasing the parents' frustrations. Hence, while most normal people are future oriented, parents of a retarded child tend to retreat from the future as a source of pain and shift toward past orientation.

7. *Loss of immortality.* The anticipation of our own inevitable death is, for many of us, a major source of existential anxiety. One common approach to coping with this anxiety is to seek symbolic immortality through one's children. Grandparents' legendary delight with their grandchildren illustrates our emphasis on continuation of the family line. When a child is retarded, however, this potential avenue to immortality is threatened, when the child is an only child, this chance for immortality is denied the parents, and they are faced with their finiteness and ultimate loss of identity.

Parents and Professionals Working Together

During recent years parents of retarded children and professionals have been drawing closer together. They often work effectively as members of multidisciplinary teams as well as advocates for retarded persons. Nonetheless, their interactions are still often marred by friction and sometimes overt conflict. The very complexity of working with a retarded individual and the resulting frustrations are likely to generate tensions. The unfortunate fact that mental retardation is still incurable and all too often imposes serious limits on individual development is a constant source of consternation to both professionals and parents. Further difficulties can often stem from destructive stereotypes, from professional mishandling, or from unresolved parental emotional problems.

In addition to these common sources of difficulty, other areas are often unrecognized and can become troublesome. I have found that the following issues need to be clearly recognized and openly discussed if parents and professionals are to avoid working at cross-purposes.

1. *Values.* All too frequently, professionals and parents assume that they hold the same values regarding what is desirable for the retarded individual. Yet their values may be incompatible, leading to conflicts regarding program objectives and long-range goals.

For example, the common assumption by both parents and professionals is that services for the mentally retarded exist to serve the retarded clients. This assumption is not always valid, however, since other beneficiaries can include the retarded person's family (e.g., parental frustrations due to having a retarded child in the home can be reduced), the agency operating the service (e.g., increased budgets and expanded staffs can be justified), the professional in charge of the program (e.g., a favorable reputation can be established), and society (e.g., the number of tax burdens can be decreased). It is now well recognized that the needs of these various individuals are not always identical and that in some instances even the needs of parents and their child may be incompatible.

Even when the beneficiary of a service is clearly the mentally retarded client, there still may be confusion regarding the implicit values on which program objectives are based. Examples of currently popular values, which may at times lead to incompatible objectives, include the following:

Foster maximum individual development so that the client reaches his potential

Provide the client with conditions which are as much as possible like conditions of normal persons

Make each retarded person as happy as possible

Help each client become as economically independent as possible

Help each retarded person to act as much as possible like nonretarded persons

Achieve the greatest possible level of emotional independence for each retarded individual

2. *Objectives and priorities.* Parents and professionals may have different ideas regarding specific program objectives and their relative importance. For example, professionals may focus on academic and abstract achievements whereas parents may be interested in practical objectives that make

the retarded child easier to live with. Professionals may emphasize development of new skills, such as number concepts or color recognition, while
parents may wish to eliminate socially inappropriate behavior, such as
tantrums or screaming. As a result of these different priorities, professionals
may feel a child is making good progress while his parents may feel that
nothing is happening. I recall, for instance, that some years ago my wife
and I were told with pride that Val was beginning to recognize colors.
Rather than reacting with obvious enthusiasm, we expressed dismay that
she had managed to yank all her hair from her head. We suggested that
eliminating this self-destructive behavior should take precedence over color
recognition.

3. *Temporal orientation.* As already noted, parents of retarded children
may feel threatened by what they fear the future holds for them and their
retarded children, so long-range goals may be avoided or rejected by parents.
On the other hand, professionals may structure their programs in terms of
such goals. For example, middle class parents may reject the goal of their
child working in a marginal service job, whereas the child's teacher may
consider this to be a very desirable outcome. On the other hand, parents'
emphasis on current irritations may appear trivial to professionals. To parents who must cope with daily problems of living, however, eliminating
current frustrations may seem much more important than working toward
distant goals, whose value they may seriously question.

4. *Competition.* It may seem ironic that parents and professionals interact competitively, but I am convinced that feelings of competition are often
present, although neither parents nor professionals may be aware of them.
Parents may feel hurt that a stranger is more successful than they are with
their child, and professionals may feel threatened that untrained and unsophisticated parents may succeed where they have failed. As a result, parents and professionals may surreptitiously undermine and downgrade each
other's efforts.

Based on my personal experience as both a parent and a professional,
as well as my observation of many parent-professional interactions, I submit the following suggestion for fostering productive work between parents
and professionals:

Parents should be accepted as full-fledged members of the multidisciplinary
team. They should be considered as colleagues, and their contributions
should be treated with respect.

Parents and professionals should recognize that they may have preconceived notions about each other that may interfere with working together.
Destructive stereotypes and negative expectations should be openly discussed whenever possible.

Professionals should try to accept parents where they are (in their attitude
toward mental retardation) and develop a listening skill that encourages full

disclosure. Most effective counselors, I am convinced, have learned to develop good ears while restraining their tongues. Professionals should resist the temptation to criticize parental attitudes so as not to stifle free expression of feelings or reinforce feelings of guilt and worthlessness. Before parents can develop constructive attitudes toward their handicapped child, they must come to grips with whatever negative feelings may exist.

Professionals should be particularly attuned to the existential anxieties experienced by parents of retarded children, and they must be willing to listen to expression of these anxieties.

Professionals should share with parents all relevant information that is the basis for planning and decision making. Information should be furnished as soon as it becomes available to minimize parents' anxieties resulting from ambiguity and threat of the unknown. Unless there are compelling reasons to withhold specific information, parents should be furnished with the same data, including test findings and written reports, as other team members.

Clear two-way communication is essential to productive parent-professional interaction. Professional jargon should be avoided as much as possible, and technical terms should be simply explained. Parents as well as professionals should indicate whenever they suspect that they are not completely clear on what is being communicated.

In general, professionals should have the prime responsibility for selecting the methods and techniques to be used, and parents—or, when appropriate, the clients themselves—should be ultimately responsible for selecting goals and objectives. Whenever possible, these should be joint decisions involving parents, clients, and professionals. In reaching these decisions, parents and clients must be furnished all relevant information, including a description of available alternatives. If professional members of the team feel that a parental decision is not in the best interest of the retarded client, the matter should be referred to an independent committee charged with review of ethical and legal issues. The establishment, composition, and functions of such committees have been described in detail (e.g., AAMD, 1975; May et al., 1975; *Wyatt* v. *Stickney*, 1972), and they are now commonly assigned to programs and facilities serving retarded clients.

Parents as well as professionals need support and encouragement as they try to cope with the problems and frustrations of helping a retarded individual. Mutual reinforcement, praise, and encouragement can be very useful.

Parents and professionals should guard against competing against each other. They need to be constantly aware of the possibility of competitive rivalries and of the temptation to use each other as scapegoats or to undermine each other's efforts with the retarded client.

Conclusion

In 1950 parents of retarded children founded what is now the Association for Retarded Citizens/U.S., largely as a reaction against professional neglect, rejection, and mishandling. In the ensuing years ARC has grown into a potent force on behalf of retarded persons. Gradually parents and friends of the retarded have been joined by professionals as effective social change agents, participating jointly in major legislative efforts and landmark litigation. Recently, parents and professionals have embarked on cooperative team efforts to educate and habilitate retarded persons. Mutual respect and understanding are growing as the old myths and destructive stereotypes are slowly fading away.

REFERENCES

American Association on Mental Deficiency. *Position papers of the American Association on Mental Deficiency.* Washington, D.C.: Author, 1975.

Fletcher, J. Indicators of humanhood: A tentative profile of man. In *The Hastings Center report* (Vol. 2, No. 5). Hastings-on-Hudson, N.Y.: Hastings Center, 1972.

May, J.G., Risley, T.R., Twardosz, S., Friedman, P., Bijou, S., & Wexler, O. *Guidelines for the use of behavioral procedures in state programs for retarded persons.* Arlington, Tex.: National Association for Retarded Citizens, 1975.

National Association for Retarded Citizens. *Parent/professional Training Project booklet III.* Arlington, Tex.: Author, in press.

Olshansky, S. Parent responses to a mentally defective child. *Mental Retardation,* 1966, *4,* 21–23.

Roos, P. Psychological counseling with parents of retarded children. *Mental Retardation,* 1963, *1,* 345–350.

Roos, P. Changing patterns of residential services. In *National Conference on Residential Care.* Arlington, Tex.: National Association for Retarded Citizens, 1969.

Roos, P. Parent organizations. In J. Wortis (Ed.), *Mental retardation—An annual review* (Vol. 3). New York: Grune and Stratton, 1970.

Roos, P. Parents of mentally retarded persons. *International Journal of Mental Health,* 1977, *6,*(1), 96–119.

Wolfensberger, W. The origin and nature of our institutional models. In R.B. Kugel & W. Wolfensberger (Eds.), *Changing patterns of residential services for the mentally retarded.* Washington, D.C.: The President's Committee on Mental Retardation, 1969.

Wyatt, v. *Stickney,* 344 F. Supp. 373 (M. D. Ala., 1972).

QUESTIONS TO CONSIDER

1. Phil describes various errors that professionals make, yet he ends his story with optimism. Considering your own experience as a professional or with professionals, can you recall making any of those same mistakes or seeing them made? Do you believe Phil's advice to professionals will be helpful in preventing or reducing those mistakes? What other advice would you give, based on your experience?

2. Phil also describes various nonproductive or negative reactions of parents to the fact of their child's retardation or to professionals. Considering your experience as a parent, or with parents, can you recall making any of those mistakes or seeing them made? Will Phil's recommendations be helpful? What other recommendations would you have?

3. Phil has been enormously involved with mental retardation—first as professional, then as a parent, and then as an advocate (with ARC/US). What are the personal and professional experiences that might enable him to contribute in another field of disabilities or in a field unrelated to disabilities? Can people with experiences similar to his contribute something unique to others? What?

PART THREE

George Harris holds a Ph.D. in counseling and has been a psychologist for vocational rehabilitation and public offender counseling programs. He now teaches courses in corrections at Washburn University in Topeka, Kansas, and trains professionals who work with families with handicapped children. He is the author of the book *Broken Ears, Wounded Hearts,* published in 1983 by Gallaudet University Press. It tells his story as the parent of a disabled child. His daughter Jennifer, age 13, is deaf and receives special education at the Kansas School for the Deaf at Olathe, where she lives.

Jennifer and George Harris

Fairy Tales, Beatlemania, and a Handicapped Child

George A. Harris

When she was an infant, I sometimes cradled my daughter Jennifer in my arms and danced with her to music on the radio. Beatles' tunes like "Michelle" were among my favorites, and Jennifer seemed to enjoy holding on and swaying to the beat. She grinned a toothless grin or sometimes went to sleep. Though her birth was premature, I had little reason to suspect that she was deaf or that she would later be diagnosed as retarded, brain damaged, and autistic. I certainly didn't suspect that the doctors would disagree about her, some saying that she had quite normal intelligence and others saying that she had almost normal hearing. Her major heart and orthopedic defects were months and years away from discovery. The truth of her condition and the meaning of it for my life were outside my awareness. I couldn't have suspected those things any more than Jennifer could have heard Paul McCartney sing love songs. Thirteen years later the truth continues to unfold.

I've learned a lot in those thirteen years, and my temptation is to outline my conclusions one, two, three, like the college professor that I am. But these conclusions, these insights, are not so easily communicated as the results of an experiment or the findings of a survey. No, I think one learns best about a handicapped child through experience, or at least by hearing stories about such experiences. I think that professionals in training should be required, for example, to stay with a handicapped child. They need to experience what it is like to go through fitful nights, disturbed by a child who croons at full moons and Donald Duck night lights. They need to feel the power of sleep deprivation to enrage a mind that has been allowed neither to sleep nor to remain fully awake. Parents mainly want professionals to understand such experiences.

Most professionals have not been touched directly by having a handicapped child. I live in Topeka, Kansas, the home of the famous Menninger Foundation, where some of the world's best psychologists and psychiatrists are trained. I met one of the foundation's post-doctoral psychologists once at a party, and we began talking about common professional interests. When I mentioned my deaf daughter, he remarked that having a "deaf and dumb" child must be very difficult. I tried to smile politely, though I thought that it was he who was the "dumb" one. I wanted to suggest that he not automatically associate deafness with dumbness; they do not go together like Laurel and Hardy. One does not cause the other to appear. It is possible he knew this and was only using a colloquial expression. Nevertheless, a feeling of despair enveloped me because the task of educating the uninformed, particularly the uninformed professionals, seemed so huge.

I realize now that he spoke from simple ignorance; he just had never been around deaf persons and didn't realize what he was saying. These days I would probably respond by telling a story about a deaf man I met who graduated from Gallaudet College and now teaches classes in American sign language to awkward-handed hearing folks like me. Though he doesn't hear and his voice lacks inflection, he speaks perfect, grammatical English. Even without spoken language, though, he told a story to our class that anyone could have understood. He pantomimed a cross-country drive with a friend—the monotony of the long stretches of road across Kansas, the excitement of the first sight of the Rocky Mountains, and the fear of negotiating mountain hairpin curves. He told about being in a car wreck and trying to explain the accident to a policeman who, of course, didn't know standard sign language. As he pantomimed his arrival at the Pacific Ocean, I felt the breezes off the ocean and saw the vast expanse of water. When the story was finished, I felt as though I had taken the trip—from the mountains to the prairies. Nowadays, I would tell the uninformed psychologist about this man from Gallaudet.

It's difficult now to make myself recall incidents from Jennifer's history that will illustrate my message. I tried to tell her story as well as I could in *Broken Ears, Wounded Hearts* (Harris, 1983), and now I want to move away from those painful times and go on to other things. However, there are still lessons to be learned from the past. My interpretation of past events has evolved as I've developed personally, and I want to add a few thoughts.

Like any parent of a handicapped child, I've encountered incompetence and insensitivity as well as genius and saint-like understanding in helping professionals. I have been unforgiving of surgeons who charge exorbitant fees and psychiatrists who somehow find a way to blame parents for a child's condition. But I have realized only recently what burning rage I have felt because my daughter is handicapped and how bitterly I have viewed the efforts of any professional who is less than perfect. It is not easy to accept that the world is unjust, that some children are blessed and others burdened. But it's true. Some parents learn to deal with this truth more easily and quickly than others.

Perhaps the feeling of being cursed has been even stronger in my family and has operated unconsciously in me for these many years. In my

professional work, I have increasingly realized the importance of understanding the evolution of a person's family through the generations. Only
recently I learned about and realized the meaning of my own family's
history with firstborn children. My father's oldest sister died of undetermined causes when she was just a young adult. My mother's oldest brother
died in infancy. My aunt's firstborn daughter died in an automobile accident.
My own older sister has had some serious personal stress and lost a kidney
for no known cause. And there is Jennifer, my firstborn—deaf and multiply
handicapped. Coincidence? Probably. But the mind is not entirely rational.
Helping professionals were among the first to get in the way and catch the
brunt of my unrestrained anger. No doubt they deserved considerable criticism for many things, but the intensity of my feeling cursed has been
increased by my own family's history.

Certainly every parent is hurt and inconsolable when a handicapped
child is born. The experience moved me to write a book; others respond in
their own manner, depending on such things as family history and even the
kind and severity of the handicap. As time goes on, I realize that a family's
reaction to the birth of a handicapped child is complex.

There are also superstitious, irrational myths that go beyond the bounds
of any family. In the Grimm's fairy tale "Hans the Hedgehog" (1972) Hans's
father and mother are childless until Hans's father cries out in frustrated
anger that he would like a son even if the child was a hedgehog. So Hans is
born, and he is half-hedgehog. Hans's mother blames the father, saying
that the deformed child is punishment for a wish made in anger. This
ancient notion that parents are to blame for a child's handicap resides in
today's parents as well as professionals. Why else do parents search franti-
cally for the cause of their child's problem, even when knowing the cause
won't help a bit? It is as if parents believe that locating the cause will assign
the blame elsewhere, and something or someone else will be guilty.

Professionals who provide services to families with handicapped children also have their own cultural and psychological heritage. Sometimes
that heritage overlaps their professional behavior. For example, psychologists who point accusing fingers at parents unfortunately translate fairy tales
into psychological theory. Parents of children with autism have been told
that "refrigerator mothers," cold and aloof from their child, are the cause of
the ailment. In fact, the symptoms of autism stem from a brain disorder.
Old myths die hard. Some family therapists claim that every dysfunctional
child is the result of a troubled and stressful marriage. I resist that notion
even though Jennifer's mother and I are now divorced. Our marital problems certainly did not cause Jennifer's deafness, and that very deafness
brought other problems for Jennifer.

Training that endorses parental guilt, even in subtle ways, encourages
and reinforces negative feelings toward parents. Many professionals have a
rather dim attitude toward parents that stems in part from these invalid
beliefs in parents' original sin. Teachers complain that parents don't work

with the children at home; psychologists probe for the marital conflict that causes children stress and prevents them from completing toilet training. One therapist characterized this attitude as the "hate the parent syndrome." Professionals suspect parents and vice versa, and nobody is any better off. Blaming is of little help. As the parent of a handicapped child and as a professional counselor, I can say that I've had the opportunity to be irrational from both sides of the fence. I hope that others can learn from my experience.

When Jennifer was a year old, I could still easily toss her in the air and catch her as she fell back into my arms. She whooped and giggled in her excitement, and she began to shriek in anticipation whenever I picked her up. I was the only one she trusted, and she cried when anyone else tried these acrobatics with her. I was able to do this with Jennifer for several years because she was a skinny kid. Maybe I thought I could do it forever. Or maybe I just didn't think. In any case, one day I tossed her into the air. When she landed, I pulled a muscle and searing pain coursed up my back. I quickly realized that Jennifer wasn't a baby any more—she was a little girl.

One would think that such a lesson would stick with me. But no. I still thought of Jennifer as my little girl even as she began menstruating. Most parents probably see their children as younger than they actually are. (I'm still the baby in my family of origin.) Keeping track of Jennifer's development, however, is difficult because it is so uneven. For example, though she is mature enough to wear bras, she still can't walk to a nearby store by herself, and she is only beginning to prefer movie magazines to Bugs Bunny comic books. She has a boyfriend at school but still plays with imaginary friends who live on the tips of her fingers. The progress of a handicapped child is uneven and out of sync with normal developmental schedules. It's hard to adjust to Jennifer because I never know what to expect.

Understanding Jennifer's mental life and development is all the more difficult because she is deaf. Her use of language is below par for both deaf and hearing children, and when she does communicate concepts, she may be difficult to follow. For example, one day a friend and I were telling Jennifer that we couldn't do something she wanted us to do. Jennifer finger-spelled "C.O." and shrugged her shoulders. I looked at my friend. My friend looked at me. We both looked at Jennifer. "What mean C.O.?" we signed. Jennifer signed "C.O." again, shrugged her shoulders, and walked up the stairs. As far as I know, C.O. is not a standard sign. As nearly as I could figure, Jennifer made it up to mean something like "Oh, well," but she couldn't explain it. When I used it later in conversation with her, she looked confused, as if the sign had no meaning for her. Oh well, C.O.

Jennifer has taught me many things, however, including how to act silly and enjoy it. All children give parents a chance to play again with dolls and electric trains and to play peek-a-boo and hide-and-seek. I have always been a rather serious person, perhaps too introspective for my own good at times. Jennifer cares not a whit about that side of me. But she loves it when

I imitate a chorus-line dancer or John Travolta doing his disco number. She's a great audience and always calls for an encore as she laughs and signs, "Father silly."

One day I decided to teach Jennifer to slow dance. She's nearly tall enough now to be my partner, so I brought her into the dining room and tried to get her to follow my lead. Nothin' doin'. She pulled away in sheer horror at the thought of dancing with her father. I thought that was pretty normal behavior for a thirteen year old, and I thought it was normal for a father to tease his daughter for being shy—as I began to do.

The point of all this is that the behavior of parents with their handicapped child is more normal than not. The basic relationship between parent and handicapped child is formed on the same emotions that exist in any normal family. It's easy to forget that fact when so much attention is focused on the special problems of parenting a handicapped child. What father hasn't tossed his baby into the air and then caught the child as if he were a giant safety net? What father hasn't watched with contradictory feelings of reluctance and pride as his little girl grew into a teenager?

Nonetheless, parents of handicapped children do have some unique problems that I wish teachers and other helping professionals really understood. For example, I believe Jennifer will always need some kind of sheltered living, but I don't know what will be available for her in eight or nine years. Social programs are tenuously supported, as a visit to almost any state institutions would verify. Jennifer needs shelter, but she also needs social interaction; yet I don't know of any sheltered living programs for the deaf that hire competent signers as staff. Perhaps the programs already exist. Or perhaps I'll have to start one. I'm only now beginning to think about this problem.

Some people seem distressed when I talk about this country's social welfare system and my concern about Jennifer's future. Things will work out, they say. And perhaps they will—but not without effort. I think people want to believe in a just and equitable world where good and right triumph. But I believe the future depends on the concern of people who try to make the world better.

One publisher returned *Broken Ears, Wounded Hearts* to me and asked if I could make it a happier story. Reactions to the book have been as varied as responses to an ink blot test. Some people find the book sad; others find it encouraging and helpful. In any event, I don't believe that life is like a dinner-theatre play with three acts and an upbeat finish. I don't believe in glossing over problems because then no one knows what needs changing.

I grew up when "Leave It to Beaver" was a popular TV show, and I remember Ward and June smiling sweetly at Beaver's earnest goodness. But what if Beaver had been a child with cerebral palsy? Life *is* indeed more complicated than a television show. Human misfortune does exist. Can you imagine this version of a "Leave It to Beaver" episode?

Wally: Gee, Beaver, why don't you come out and play ball?

Beaver: I can't, Wally.

Wally: Well, gee, why not, Beav?

Beaver: Golly, Wally, you know my wheelchair won't roll good on the grass.

Wally: Oh, yeah, I forgot.

There is no point in dwelling on misfortune, and we all need light entertainment at times. But we can't ignore the fact that real problems exist and that people sometimes need more help than they can provide themselves. However, I also believe that the ability to face misfortune realistically gives rise ultimately to hope. Solving problems can give us hope, satisfaction, and purpose in life. Few people know this better than parents with problem children.

Some day I will want to become less involved in Jennifer's life than I am now. Parents of normal children look forward to the day when their child-rearing responsibilities will be over; mothers and fathers of handicapped children are no different, even though their children may never achieve self-sufficiency. Some parents may choose to continue day-to-day custodial care of their child, perhaps because the alternatives are unpleasant and inadequate. But if Jennifer is unable to take care of herself and if a decent alternative is available, I will want her to live in some type of sheltered residence.

This clarification of my thinking about my future responsibilities for Jennifer has been relatively recent. I consciously realized only recently that I would not automatically be legally responsible for Jennifer when she is an adult. Of course, many handicaps require that children live away from the family, sometimes from the moment of birth. Other children can be managed and loved better in the home. But a time comes when the child, now an adult, stays at home only because there are no other alternatives. I don't want to abandon Jennifer; neither do I want to give up my right to my own life. Parents of normal children are not legally or financially responsible for them as adults unless they choose to be. Parents of handicapped children have the same legal rights and obligations.

It is difficult to say these things about Jennifer without feeling guilty, but I think many parents extend their responsibility far beyond what is reasonably expected of them. Failure to anticipate this eventual separation of parent and child may, in fact, impede the child's progress toward whatever self-sufficiency is attainable. If parents believe they will always take care of their child, then what does it really matter whether tasks of daily living taught in school are reinforced at home? Many people automatically assume, as I did, that parents of handicapped children have a lifelong legal obligation to provide care for the child. This attitude probably originated years ago when handicapped children lived in their parents' attics and spare bedrooms throughout their adult lives. However, such thinking impedes the

George A. Harris

development of humane sheltered living programs. Our society is only now beginning to accept that handicapped children have a right to an education; it may take some time before it accepts that handicapped adults have the right to live apart from their parents, as independently as their abilities allow. In a normal developmental sequence a child establishes an identity separate from that of the parents, who move on to activities appropriate for their own stages in life. This progression is healthy for all children and all parents.

It startles me to think that in thirteen years of professional training and parenthood, I have never encountered a class discussion or heard advice about the moral and legal aspects of parenting a handicapped adult. It is a mistake to save such discussion until childhood is gone because the parents' vision of the future will have an effect on how they raise and educate their child. Professionals need to examine their attitudes about long-term parental responsibilities and introduce these considerations in a timely way into helping relationships with parents.

It is painful for parents to anticipate the future, especially when there seems to be no respite in sight. But perhaps the future need not appear so bleak. We think children are either normal or handicapped and then conclude that they will either become independent or they will not. At this point the mind refuses to consider the implications further. In fact, however, there are varying degrees of self-sufficiency, and there should be varying types of living arrangements to fit individual capabilities. Jennifer, for example, may not be able to have her own apartment, but she should be able to live in a setting less structured than a total-care institution. There are uncounted ways to live, and our society has only begun to consider the possibilities for handicapped adults. In many if not most cases, handicapped children can lead separate and satisfying lives if opportunities and help are extended.

While I was driving home with Jennifer one recent day, I whistled along with a song on the radio. Jennifer saw me and signed that I was whistling to music. She pointed to the radio, which surprised me because she clearly knew that the radio made music. She seemed to be enjoying my accompaniment even though she couldn't hear a sound. It's hard for me to understand how, but Jennifer has developed an interest in music. She can feel the rhythm, but that doesn't seem to explain why she has become a Beatles fan. In fact, Jennifer has reestablished Beatlemania. We went to a bookstore where she latched onto a picture book about the Beatles' careers and insisted I buy it for her. I know she has never heard Paul McCartney singing "Michelle," and it's a mystery to me why she is so interested in these men. But then, Jennifer has surprised me often. I didn't know a sign to represent the Beatles, so we invented one which literally translates into "bug singers." She carries that book with her everywhere and stares endlessly and lovingly at the cover portrait of the four men. She knows their names, too, and repetitively fingerspells their names for me. Someday, when Jennifer has become a woman and this blossom is fully unfolded, I hope she will humor me by dancing with me to an old Beatles' song, as we used to do when she was just a baby.

REFERENCES

Harris, G.A. *Broken ears, wounded hearts*. Washington, D.C.: Gallaudet College Press, 1983.

Grimm, J.L.K. Hans the Hedgehog. In *The Complete Grimm's fairy tales*. New York: Random House, 1972.

QUESTIONS TO CONSIDER

1. George refers to his "burning rage." What is the greatest cause of his rage? What are other causes of it? What would you do if, as a professional, you were the cause of his rage? Or just the brunt of it? Will George's rage ever pass? Why? Do you blame George for his rage? What is George's opinion about the role of blame?

2. George describes Jennifer as multiply handicapped, yet he expresses his normal feelings about her and his normal behavior with her. Do you think it would be helpful for professionals to focus more on what is normal when working with disabled children and their parents? Why? What would be the advantages and the disadvantages—to George, to Jennifer, and to professionals?

3. George says he wants to extricate himself gradually from Jennifer without harming her. He expresses a "right to my own life." Considering Jennifer's disabilities, how reasonable is it for George to expect a life of his own? Will it occur soon, later, or never? Is there ever an end to parenthood, especially of a disabled child? What services might be necessary to help George achieve his goal? Would those services always be helpful to Jennifer, too?

Curtiss E. Knighton and Willia Knighton both work with the District of Columbia Department of Human Services. They live in Bethesda, Maryland, and have been active at local, state, and national levels in the Association for Retarded Citizens/U.S. Currently both are members of the ARC/US Board of Directors.

Their daughter Denise, who is mentally retarded, is employed at the District of Columbia ARC Training Center and was recently married.

Curtiss E. and Willia Knighton   Denise Knighton

The Colors of the Rainbow

Curtiss E. and Willia Knighton

Paint the Color Pink

"With this ring I thee wed." Standing in our small church, hearing those words spoken by our daughter Denise on a bright June day in 1983, we recall with vivid liveliness memories long buried but never forgotten. They carry us backward in time thirty-three years.

Willia's pregnancy with Denise was a time of loneliness, frustration, and longing for Curtiss, her husband. He had been recalled to military service late in 1950 and was serving in Korea as a first lieutenant. Denise was born June 3, 1951, a full-term baby weighing three pounds eleven ounces. She was an incubator baby for four weeks, until Willia finally was given permission to take her home. She then weighed four pounds twelve ounces. At the time of her birth, there was no talk of difficulty. The doctors said that everything went fine except for Denise's smallness. In retrospect, we can see that she was what is now called a high risk infant. She definitely was in need of early intervention in order to blunt or overcome developmental delay.

"Dear, you are the father of a beautiful baby girl," wrote Willia. Serving in a strange land, torn by conflict, he had eagerly awaited those words. Willia's subsequent letters spoke of Denise's progress and plans for the family "when you come home to us."

During the summer of 1953 Curtiss returned home from Korea, and we began the task of establishing a home and raising our daughter. We had decided Curtiss would remain in the military because he now had 8½ years of service. At the time of our decision, we did not know Denise was a developmentally disabled child. If we had known that, our decision to remain in the service, with its constant change in location and periodic upheaval of home life, might have been different. However, the almost instant medical attention available in the service proved to be an immeasurable benefit during the early years of Denise's life.

After returning from Korea and while awaiting a new assignment, Curtiss decided to make up for lost time with Denise. After she became accustomed to his being in the home, Curtiss constantly played with her, bathed her, and generally cared for her because we felt that Willia should have a break. It was during this period that we felt the first pangs of hurt, a premonition, and then a sure knowledge that something was wrong with Denise. She was hyperactive and constantly on the move; she jabbered with emphasis as if she were talking, but she could speak only four words that could be understood—*mamma, daddy, bye-bye,* and *shit.* Interestingly, she picked up the last word from Willia, who frequently vented her frustration by using this word emphatically. The other three words were painstakingly taught to her. Denise was now over two years old and lacked communicative speech. We fell into the bad habit of anticipating her needs and responding to her jabbering. With difficulty we finally stopped this behavior and began patiently to teach her what to say. She responded, but her best response was still emphatic jabbering.

Our growing feeling that something was wrong with Denise became much stronger during that time. Curtiss soon accepted the fact, but Willia still tried hard to deny that there was anything wrong—"There is nothing wrong with my child!" she said. "Time will take care of everything." Nonetheless, Curtiss sensed that she, too, knew that Denise was not developing normally in certain areas. Like other parents, we found it almost unbearable to have any area of our child's development abnormal. The fact that Curtiss was a psychiatric social worker and marital counselor did not alleviate the very deep emotional feelings associated with having an imperfect child. However, it did force him to face the facts, inform Willia of his feelings and beliefs, and begin to seek help from his military colleagues.

The fact that Curtiss was on the staff of the hospital at Fort Campbell helped tremendously in the plethora of evaluations that followed. Not many parents of a handicapped child find themselves in such a convenient position. The evaluations established that Denise had a profound hearing loss; it was thought a tonsillectomy might help. (Later a tonsillectomy was performed to decrease the chance of infrequent and prolonged infection.) After the neurological examination we were informed of a major problem— Denise had brain damage. Simultaneously, we reached out for each other's hand while the neurologist informed us that the damaged part of the brain affected Denise's hearing and speech. "Your daughter will probably never talk, and it will be impossible for her to do abstract thinking, such as one does in mathematics," said the neurologist. He added that her motor development might also be affected.

In response to our question, "What can we do?" the doctor replied, "First, there is no cure, and very little can be done." He suggested placement in an institution sometime in the future, as our family grew and

Denise became an increasing burden. This was the one recommendation that caused us great consternation. "You can't sacrifice your other children for her." We listened but believed he was nuts. We simply ignored this recommendation; we did not even discuss it! In a state of bewilderment, we waited for the report of the psychologist, a friend who lived next door to us and had often seen Denise in the family setting. We wanted not to panic but to take every recommendation into serious consideration before making a decision regarding our daughter.

The psychologist proffered a diagnosis of aphasia and recommended that his department try to train Denise to speak, using the undamaged part of her brain. He assured us that the training would be very hard and long, with a minimum probability of success. That was perfectly acceptable to us. What was most disillusioning, however, was the information gathered by his department that Denise's birth had not gone smoothly. Her smallness had resulted in the failure of one of her lungs to inflate, interfering with her breathing. Brain damage was the unalterable result.

As parents of a young handicapped child, we were often troubled by the professional system and the medical model that operated within the military system. At times the system hurt us badly, but we were not destroyed then, and we are not now. We resolved that we would invariably fight back. We fared better with the military medical system because we worked from within it and possessed some professional knowledge. However, knowing the difficulties we had, we readily understand how parents working from outside a system can be absolutely devastated by it. Our knowledge of the military system certainly did not eliminate our frustration and dismay with its medical system. In fact, our familiarity may actually have increased our expectations of success, thereby making the pain of our frustration even sharper.

Paint the Color Gray

When Denise was 2½ years old, we were transferred to the Presidio, Letterman General Hospital, San Francisco, California. At the time neither of us realized that we were being transferred to a state that had a very high rating for treatment of mental retardation and other handicapping conditions. The psychology department at Letterman General Hospital continued training Denise twice a week in speech therapy. Willia followed up the training at home. Denise made some improvement, but we began to realize she needed all-day training.

Fortunately, we were in the right place at the right time. The young medical technician who was Denise's instructor at Letterman General Hospital was being discharged from the service. Denise had progressed excellently under his instructions, and we became quite anxious when we heard that he was leaving the service; he was our only hope at that time. However, through his referral and determination Denise was accepted at the San

Francisco School for the Aphasic, a residential school with an excellent reputation for training aphasic children with other handicapping conditions. There Denise studied five days a week, enjoyed the companionship of her peers, and returned home on weekends. She had never stayed away from home before, and we naturally felt great anxiety and fear. Our visits to the school to show Denise where she would be staying reassured us. Our main fear was that, because of her limited speech, she would not understand what we were doing and why. We later learned that she understood more than we gave her credit for.

After several weeks in school Denise slowly began to develop some speech. Her sentences were mixed up (the verb coming first), but the words were there. Don, her teacher, was elated over her progress and felt that five days a week was not enough. "She should be in a continuous learning situation," he said and discussed with us the possibility of Saturday sessions. We readily agreed and soon thereafter began supplemental training sessions that lasted over three years.

During this period Denise began to watch television and constantly made attempts to dance like a ballerina. We became interested in her efforts to dance because we wanted to develop every potential talent she had. In our search for a ballet teacher who would be willing to train an aphasic child, we approached the ballet mistress of the San Francisco Ballet. She was enthusiastic about the challenge of teaching a child with Denise's handicaps. The day came for her initial lesson, and Denise, now six years old, calmly took the mistress's hand and went into the practice room. Our anxiety showed in the questions we asked each other while we awaited their return: Would Denise understand what was being said? Would she respond? How would she mix with the normal children? Would the school keep her? When her lesson was finally concluded, out bounced a smiling teacher and one happy little girl, both looking at very relieved parents.

But our anxieties continued. The following week, after about fifteen minutes alone with Denise, the teacher emerged from the practice room. Willia's heart sank, just as, a few minutes later, it took wings when the teacher informed her that Denise was going into the group practice room. "She has so much natural potential that she should do well." The school did not allow parents into any of the practice rooms. However, after anxiety-filled weeks Willia was told to report to the group practice room. Of course, our first thought was that Denise had failed, and tears came to Willia's eyes as she entered the room. Her tears became exclamations of joy when the teacher announced, "Your daughter is the leader of the group."

Denise continued ballet lessons and her training at the residential facility; she made progress that indicated to us and her teachers that with constant help and pushing, in time Denise could make it. What a different prognosis from the one made seven years before!

In January 1959 the family welcomed the birth of Byron, Denise's brother. We had experienced all of the anxiety and fear that parents of a

Curtiss E. and Willia Knighton

mentally retarded child have when another child is conceived and born. There were fears that Byron himself might be disabled or that we and Denise would have special difficulties accommodating another child in a family so structured around a disabled child. As we later worked with other parents of disabled children, we learned that these were quite natural concerns. Much to our relief, Denise reacted with positive feelings toward her newborn brother and became very enamored of him.

Shortly after Byron's birth we were transferred to Fort Sam Houston, San Antonio, Texas, where Curtiss was to obtain nine months of medical service training and subsequently be transferred to a new duty station. In a discussion of our pending transfer to San Antonio and the problems we would encounter in continuing training for Denise, one of our military friends told us about the Gough School. After our application was forwarded to the school, he interceded for us and Denise was accepted. The Gough School is a school for the deaf that uses methods of teaching similar to those used for Denise and aphasic children at her previous school. During the nine months spent in Texas, the Gough School continued Denise's training and education, and she continued to progress but at a slower rate.

During the eighth month of our stay at Fort Sam Houston, we learned about Curtiss' next assignment: Fort Belvoir, Virginia. Again the question of Denise's continuing education and training loomed. Friends again came to our rescue, referring us to Dr. Monsees, now deceased, who had established a private school specifically for aphasic children, where we enrolled Denise. The tuition was extremely high, and since Curtiss was still a captain, Willia began to explore the possibility of employment. We were determined to keep Denise in this excellent learning environment regardless of the cost. Fortunately, Willia obtained a position with the District of Columbia Department of Public Welfare.

In a school with a very limited enrollment and gifted and dedicated teachers, Denise made enormous progress. She began talking more rapidly, and except for words being transposed in her sentences, she was clearly understandable. Indeed, she soon reached the point where the school could no longer serve her appropriately, and the staff recommended that she attend a public school with a program allowing students to progress at their own levels and abilities. Fortunately, such a school was nearby in Maryland.

Denise was accepted and made the transfer without much difficulty. Here again, in order to decrease the stress associated with the transfer, we visited the school with Denise, saw her classroom, talked to her teacher, and reviewed her history and record with her homeroom teacher. At this school her ability to draw was discovered, and she enrolled in art classes to further develop this talent and give it direction. When her brother was of school age, he was enrolled in the same school, and the open classroom approach was beneficial to him also. At that time our family was living in the District of Columbia, which had no resources for aphasic children. To attend a Maryland school, a nonresident student's parents had to pay tuition. Accordingly, we moved to Bethesda, Maryland.

Paint the Color Yellow

After a year in Maryland, Curtiss was transferred to Frankfurt, Germany, to establish an Army community service program for the Hessian district. We were delighted to learn that in Frankfurt was an organization known as OPINCAR, an affiliate of the National Association for Retarded Children (now ARC/US, on whose board of directors both of us serve). On arrival we immediately joined the association and were informed of the resources available for children with disabilities. Fortunately, there were special education classes, in which we enrolled Denise. These classes were a far cry from the classes in Maryland; however, what she lost academically, she gained in social skills. She worked as a volunteer in the American Youth Activities, which Willia directed, and as an employee at a summer camp for the retarded. Denise also took art lessons from a German painter who spoke excellent English and understood her handicap. We became deeply involved with OPINCAR, and Curtiss served as its president.

It was in Germany that Curtiss made the decision to retire from the Army; he had been offered and accepted the position of assistant executive director of Family and Child Services in Washington, D.C. This decision cut short our stay in Germany; however, the benefits of this overseas assignment were evident immediately upon our return to the States. Denise's language had improved, her socialization skills were developed to a point where she was at ease meeting strangers, and she appeared to be ready for special high school classes. The military system had served the family well. Coincidentally, it had been an integral part of Curtiss's overseas assignment to enhance and increase the Army's capacity to serve its dependent population efficiently and effectively. Our ability to work within the system again proved helpful to Denise and to us, too.

Paint the Color Blue

Upon our return to the United States, we resided in southwest Washington, D.C. We had been told that excellent experimental schools were located nearby. Unfortunately, those schools were nonexistent, and even worse, the public schools in the area had no special classes for disabled children. We made frequent trips to the school in which Denise was placed, explained her condition, and generally made a nuisance of ourselves.

We became committed to the proposition that parents of mentally retarded children cannot let any system treat their children with indifference or ignore them entirely. We wrote letters to the board of education, detailing our frustration in working with a noncaring educational system. Denise herself was completely frustrated. The school's solution to her aphasia and mental retardation was to place her in front of the room so that she could hear—they believed she was only hard of hearing. The fact that her aphasic condition was the primary source of her difficulty in school was never understood. The year passed slowly, and finally we were able to move into our Maryland home.

Eleanor Elkins, former NARC president, had visited Germany during our tour of duty there, and we had become friends. Both Eleanor and OPINCAR members had advised us to join the D.C. ARC when we returned to the U.S. The association was struggling to stay afloat and needed help. Curtiss did join the association soon after the family's return, and Willia became involved at a later date. We devoted all of our spare time to the association, helping to fight the D.C. school system on behalf of children with disabilities.

Paint the Color Green

Once back in Maryland, Denise enrolled in the Charles Woodward High School. The program allowed students with disabilities to participate in the classroom with regular students and take special classes according to their needs. Denise's artistic ability was recognized, and she was constantly called upon to assist with materials needed by her classroom or the school. We were the proudest parents in the world when, at age twenty, Denise graduated from high school.

During the summer after her graduation, Denise spent three months at North Chicago University undergoing a series of tests to determine what she was most suited to do as an adult. Most of the students being evaluated there used sign language extensively as their means of communication. Denise purchased a sign language book and proceeded to teach herself. Subsequently, she has taken courses in sign language at Gallaudet College for the Deaf and is quite proficient.

"What kind of work can we get for her?" was a constant question we asked each other. We decided her work must include opportunities to use her artistic abilities. After much consideration we approached the D.C. ARC executive director about hiring Denise as a teacher-aide in the ARC Training Center. Again, friends responded, and Denise was employed to instruct mentally retarded children and adults in handicrafts and art. There she met a young man who was a counselor at the center and later married him.

On July 24, 1982, the marriage of Audrienne Denise Knighton and Lenard West took place at St. Augustine's Episcopal Church in Washington, D.C. Denise continues to work at the D.C. ARC Training Center; her husband is a counselor in the Washington, D.C., school system and is enrolled in the University of D.C. School of Nursing. Denise and her husband are making plans for her to attend art classes at Gallaudet College for the Deaf.

In reviewing our years of struggle to educate and train Denise to her present level of ability, we believe that parents of disabled children should keep several guidelines in mind:

1. Develop every area of potential skill that your child indicates. Know your child and don't undersell his or her ability.
2. Have patience and endurance—it is a very long and sometimes bitter battle to help a child develop.
3. Learn the system in order to deal effectively with it.
4. Push hard to require any system that you encounter to accept responsibility for your child.
5. Plan for your child, bearing in mind the system's limitations.

Life with Denise has been a many-colored rainbow—with hues both bright and subtle. But just as there must be a storm to precede the rainbow, so there must be sunlight to display its colors. Our life together has been all of this—stormy and sunny, brilliant and subtle. Our futures may well bring new shades and new intensities.

QUESTIONS TO CONSIDER

1. Curtiss and Willia describe how the system helped them and how they struggled against it. What system are they describing? What help did it give? What problems did it cause? If you were part of the system, what would you have done for them and Denise?
2. What role did a parent support group, the ARC, play in the lives of Curtiss and Willia and Denise? Will it always have a role to play in their lives? If so, what kind of role will it be?
3. We do not know much about Denise or her husband, Lenard. What kind of people do you think they are—what traits do they have, and what is the character of each? How did Denise come to be the woman she is— what influence did her parents have on her? What will the future hold for Denise and Lenard? In what way will Curtiss and Willia be part of their future?

Curtiss E. and Willia Knighton

Lowell Weicker, Jr., is a third-term senator from Connecticut whose Senate responsibilities include chairmanship of the Subcommittee on the Handicapped and the Appropriations Subcommittee on Labor, Health and Human Services, and Education. Prior to his election to the Senate in 1970, he served in the U.S. House of Representatives and in the Connecticut state legislature.

Sonny Weicker, born six years ago, has Down's syndrome. He is a student in the Fairfax County, Virginia, public school system.

Lowell and Sonny Weicker

Sonny and Public Policy

Lowell Weicker, Jr.

Not long ago there was a party at our house, complete with cake, clowns, and happy faces. The occasion was Sonny Weicker's birthday. Six years before, when Sonny was born with Down's syndrome, there were—at least momentarily—more tears than smiles, more apprehension than hope. "You have several options," said Father Baumiller, head of genetics at George-town Hospital. "To leave the baby now, to think about it and then leave the baby, or to take the baby home."

But there really were no options, just one obvious course of action: to keep, love, and do our best by Sonny as we had by six older children. The challenge certainly would be greater—but so were the potential rewards. Hundreds of letters of reinforcement poured in from parents, all conveying the same message: Have patience and love, they said, and you will be repaid, in kind, 100-fold. We had the chance to make a difference in Sonny Weicker's future such as we could not make for any of the rest of our family.

In recent decades we in the Congress were presented with a similar set of options regarding America's thirty-six million handicapped citizens: to pretend they didn't exist and push them onto the sidelines of life, to further delay taking any action on their part, or to embrace their struggle for inde-pendence as our own. But here, too, if we were to be honest with ourselves, there was really only one correct course of action. We had an opportunity to make a difference in the futures of America's disabled citizens, and we had to make the most of it.

I have long taken inspiration from the words of James Russell Lowell in the hymn "Once to Every Man and Nation": "Then it is the brave man chooses/While the coward stands aside/'Til the multitude make virtue/Of the faith he had denied." Experience has taught me that, generally speaking, the harder a decision is to make, the more urgent it is that it be made. This has certainly held true for me as a parent and a legislator.

I was elected to the House of Representatives in 1968 and to the Senate in 1970. My tenure in the Congress has coincided with the passage of nearly all of the landmark legislation securing the rights of disabled citizens, from the Architectural Barriers Act in 1968 to the Social Security Disability Amendments in 1980. I supported these initiatives, but the primary role I was to play was not in their passage, but in their protection against those who sought to undermine them. My commitment to advancing and securing the civil rights of America's neglected minority has been a long one, but Sonny's birth and my fatherhood gave me renewed energy and greater credibility with my colleagues and disabled people alike. I was fortunate to be able to turn my life's circumstances to the benefit of my own child and others like him. For him and me, the timing of his birth coincided almost perfectly with recent major political events.

In 1981 Ronald Reagan took up residence in the White House, supply-side economists overran the Council on Economic Advisers, and the new cabinet pledged allegiance to a budget that savaged social spending while issuing the Pentagon a blank check. The scenario of the Office of Management and Budget had Congress making a cameo appearance in the role of rubber stamp. On Capitol Hill more than a few of my colleagues were prepared to play along. After all, the president had won big in the general election and was still on his political honeymoon. And he wasn't called the Great Communicator for nothing.

The imagery employed by the president implied an enlightened federal policy toward disabled people. He spoke about self-reliance, about expecting more of ourselves and less from our government. As the new chairman of the Subcommittee on the Handicapped, I found this music to my ears. After all, most of the programs authorized and overseen by the Subcommittee aim at getting handicapped people out of dependent and demeaning life-styles and into meaningful existences, off welfare rolls, and onto payrolls.

I, too, was a great believer in private initiative. Private initiative had built my son's school—Resurrection Children's School in suburban Virginia, a preschool for children ages two to five with and without handicaps. In one resource center Resurrection combines a preschool with a parent education program and an outpatient occupational therapy service. Founded by a parent who could not find what she wanted for her own child, Resurrection is a living testament to what private initiative and parental involvement can do for handicapped children; but it is also a living testament to the need for federal funds to get projects of this kind off the ground. From 1972 to 1978 this preschool was funded as a national demonstration model by what was then the U.S. Office of Education. For the implementation of its innovative programs, the center has received grants from such organizations as the Katharine Pollard Maddux Memorial Mental Health Foundation, the Washington Forrest Foundation, the Northern Virginia Association for Retarded Children, the Service League of Northern Virginia, and a number of private donors. Resurrection School is truly a public/private partnership that, for our

Lowell Weicker, Jr.

child and many others, has served as a bridge to the mainstream of life. Here, during the critically important years between two and five, Sonny made great strides in his language, cognitive, social, motor, and self-help skills. And his nonhandicapped classmates learned at an early age to understand, respect, and relate to a handicapped peer. So as the father of a two year old who was already reaping the benefits of early education and mainstreaming, I wanted to believe that even the most conservative members of the new administration would oppose turning back the clock on helping handicapped Americans help themselves.

In February 1981 events proved otherwise. The administration weighed in with a proposal to cut funding for handicapped programs by 25 percent and to provide block grants to the states or repeal the laws themselves. According to its way of thinking, $200 billion was not money enough for the Defense Department, and $2 billion was too much for the handicapped. The so-called Program for Economic Recovery called for forty-five categorical grants administered by the Department of Education to be collapsed into two programs—one block grant to the states and the other to local educational agencies. Estimating that 13 percent of the federal funds in these forty-five programs slated for consolidation went toward administrative overhead, the Office of Management and Budget argued that the 25 percent budget shortfall in handicapped services would be covered by savings due to increased efficiency.

The administration was on the verge of inciting civil war in the education community, turning agency against agency, program against program, constituency against constituency, all competing for shrinking dollars. The block grant to the local educational agency was to be divided up among several groups of students with special educational needs—the economically disadvantaged, the physically or mentally handicapped, children with limited English-speaking abilities, children in school districts undergoing racial desegregation, and illiterate adults. Likewise, the proposed block grant to the states would have lumped direct educational services for the handicapped, neglected, and delinquent children with a variety of support services to classrooms, libraries, and state educational agencies.

One question that deeply troubled me was this: What happens if, in the hue and cry that will attend these block grants, some voices are undeservedly heard more clearly than others? Would that mean that only those programs would be funded? Would we see, as we did in the early sixties, some school districts again using federal funds to build lavish gymnasiums while their handicapped students were shunted to the side? Would the quality of a handicapped child's education differ dramatically and drastically from county to county and from state to state? The hearings that had led up to passage of the Education for All Handicapped Children Act in 1975 (P.L. 94–142) concluded that less than half of America's disabled youngsters were receiving what could be called a quality education and that about a million were shut out of the public education system entirely. Were we to return to those bad old days? It seemed likely if the policies and practices of the new administration were to come to fruition. If the Reagan administration had gotten its way in 1981, 4.1 million disabled children would very possibly no longer be receiving the "free, appropriate public education" mandated by Public Law 94–142.

One of those children might be my Sonny. Of course I thought about him! But I also thought about his disabled and nondisabled classmates at Resurrection School, and I concluded, very quickly and without reservation, that all of them would bear the brunt of unwise policy. Every one of them—disabled and nondisabled alike—stood to lose. In the long run we all would be shortchanged. I stiffened my resolve to fight. It was as though the Lowell hymn were meant for me, and I made my choice, though I, too, was a Republican.

The administration did not get its way. Why? Because the disabled people in this country and their advocates repudiated a long-held cliché that they were not a political constituency, or at least not a coherent one. It was assumed that in the rough and tumble world of politics they would not hold their own as a voting block or as advocates for their cause. But that assumption was blown to smithereens in the budget and policy deliberations of 1981, 1982, and again in 1983. In fact, I would be hard-pressed to name another group within the human service spectrum that has not only survived the policies of this administration but has also defeated them as consistently and as convincingly as the disabled community has. Indeed, it has set an example for others, who were believed to be better organized.

In 1981, for instance, the special education budget ended up with a $70 million increase, rather than the 25 percent cut the administration proposed. The story was much the same for the rehabilitation and developmental disabilities programs; proposed consolidations were defeated and categorical funding was maintained. The Architectural Barriers Board was not abolished as the administration had hoped, and Section 504 of the Rehabilitation Act of 1973, the linchpin of civil rights for the handicapped, was kept intact. Vice-President Bush wrote me afterwards that the Task Force on Regulatory Relief had benefited from "the personal views and experience of those most directly affected by [the 504] regulations" in reaching its decision not to seek changes in them.

In 1982 the administration, which promised to come back again and again to achieve the budget cuts and policy shifts it wanted, proved true to its word by recommending a 30 percent recision in special education state grant funds for the 1982–83 school year. It also sought to consolidate ten special-purpose programs into a single fund—among these were the deaf-blind centers, programs for the severely handicapped, early childhood education, and special education personnel development. Fully expecting this new offensive, my subcommittee staff mobilized and secured the signatures of fifty-nine senators on a letter to the president urging full funding of special education and opposing any change that would weaken the law. A majority of the members of the Senate Labor and Human Resources Committee also were lined up in support of full funding. In an important but tangential way, Sonny was making his mark on the Congress. It is an irony of great dimension that a child's disability was a powerful force for good!

Once again, with its budget cuts and block grants more or less beaten back, the administration tried to accomplish some of the same goals through deregulation, this time of special education. Among other things the administration sought to eliminate the requirement that parents be given a copy of their child's individualized education plan (IEP). Again, a proposed policy hit home. I was well acquainted with Sonny's IEP and the importance of this document in evaluating his level of educational performance, setting goals for him, outlining specific services for helping him reach those goals, and establishing the extent of his participation in regular classes and the duration of his need for special education. As parents, Camille and I could not imagine an IEP without parental participation; parents are by law equal partners in decisions affecting their children. Enough parents and other advocates spoke out on the issue that the administration decided not to rewrite the regulations.

In 1983 I took on the chairmanship of the Appropriations Subcommittee on Labor, Health and Human Services, and Education. That put me in charge of appropriations for handicapped programs as well as authorizations. The main witness at one of the subcommittee's first hearings was the new secretary of health and human services, Margaret Heckler. When the subcommittee's questioning reached the subject of disabilities, Mrs. Heckler volunteered that the administration had demonstrated its support for handicapped children by promulgating the Baby Doe ruling, which prohibits discrimination in medical treatment of newborn infants with handicaps. I pointed out what seemed to me an inconsistency between Baby Doe and the administration's efforts to undermine almost every federal program designed to aid handicapped children and adults. What if, after making the decision to keep Sonny, my wife and I could not find the professional care and instruction necessary for him to reach his full potential in life? And what if our inability to help him had been caused by federal policy? I wondered how many millions of other people would suffer along with Sonny.

At the same time the administration was bragging about Baby Doe regulations, it was pushing a 30 percent cut in the Developmental Disabilities Program, a program on which 3.9 million Americans depend to ensure that a complete range of services is available to them throughout their lives. The president, taking his cue from a 1982 Heritage Foundation report, began blaming the declining quality of our public schools on court orders requiring the schools to take the lead in correcting "long-standing injustices in our society: racial segregation, sex discrimination [and] lack of opportunity for the handicapped. Giving our students the quality teaching they need and deserved," said the president, "took a back seat to other objectives." What about the quality teaching needed—and deserved—by students who are disabled, disadvantaged, and discriminated against? They are our students, too. Those of us for whom they are also our children must speak out against this type of distortion. Doing so may not make us popular with presidents or principals—or some of them at least. But I long ago gave up on getting dinner invitations to the White House. For me, my principles and my Sonny are more palatable than presidential purees.

We can all take inspiration from the story NAACP leader Roger Wilkins tells of a time in 1965 when he sat in on a high-level discussion of the Voting Rights Bill. During that meeting, Wilkins recalls, Vice-President Humphrey suggested that the civil rights movement in Selma, Alabama, was influenced by Communists. As Wilkins tells it, Humphrey was one of his greatest political heroes and he didn't want to cross him. But a clear thought cut across his fear: There was no reason for him to be in that room of power except to say, for poor black people who couldn't be there, the things they would say for themselves if they had access to power. When it came Wilkins's turn to speak, he told Humphrey that if he visited Selma he would know that the people there lived such hard lives that no Communist was needed to motivate them to rebel.

To say for our children what they would say if they had access to power—that is our responsibility as parents. We have an obligation to repair and strengthen the bridges Congress has built to bring disabled Americans into the mainstream of life. Those who would bomb those bridges must be stopped by astute political organizing and grassroots action at the local and national level. As the Children's Defense Fund has noted, there is so much more to fight for and with than bureaucrats with numbers that don't add up. "We have the lives of millions of children who need our help if they are to grow up healthy, educated, uncrippled, and with a family." The Weicker family knows that, all so well. So do many other families, each with its own Sonny.

Every new attack on the foundation Congress has laid for the fulfillment and independence of each and every disabled person must be fended off, and new building blocks must be added to the foundation. One such building block is the Education of the Handicapped Amendments Act of 1983. In addition to extending the life of the discretionary programs under the act for three years, this legislation expands the range of children served both in terms of age and type of disability. Provisions are made for earlier interventions, beginning at birth, under the preschool and early childhood programs while post-secondary programs are broadened to include all disabilities. The options that Camille and I were given when Sonny was born were in the front of my memory as I worked to secure this new law.

The EHA legislation of 1983 also establishes a new demonstration activity dealing with the critical transition from school to employment and emphasizes the need to train parents to participate in their children's special education. It strengthens federal data collection and evaluation responsibilities and improves provisions for reporting to Congress. It increased overall

Lowell Weicker, Jr.

authorizations to account for inflation both for special education and for special institutions such as Gallaudet College and the National Technical Institute for the Deaf.

Clearly a foundation is there in terms of our public policy and the resources we are willing to commit to carrying it out. A similar foundation has been laid for Sonny's future—one he can build on year by year. From Resurrection School he has moved on to a normal elementary school. There his IEP calls for him to take special education classes, but he will be mainstreamed in physical education and lunch and will be closely monitored for mainstreaming in other subjects.

I firmly believe that Sonny is going to be able to lead an independent life. Obviously, he will need help in watching over his financial affairs, but I fully expect him to finish school, take up some form of useful employment, and live independently. That is a far cry from the old stereotype of the Down's syndrome child still operative in so many people's minds—a fat child sitting in a corner with his tongue lolling out of his mouth. Thanks to people who love him and a government that has been helped to care, that stereotype has no relevance for Sonny's present life and even less for his future. That is how it should be for Sonny and for all disabled people. As it is true of the Weickers, so it is of families in every nook and cranny of this nation: We can make virtues out of faiths that others would deny.

QUESTIONS TO CONSIDER

1. Lowell describes his family's ultimate response to Sonny's birth as a very positive one: They could make a difference in his future such as they could not make for the rest of the family. Was this solely because of his position as senator? Or was there more to it than that? What else was at work? What about a man's faith, principles, or character—what difference do they make, if any, in raising a disabled child?

2. As a senator, Lowell quickly realized how Sonny's future could be affected by political events. Granted, he had a special perspective, but politics aside, does he give any indication that Sonny's life will always be in some jeopardy? If so, what is the nature of that threat? How can professionals respond to it? How can they respond to parents who feel threatened or believe their children are constantly in the path of danger?